A Lifetime of Love

Training and Caring for Your Dog

Hope Chambers

Print ISBN: 979-8-9882503-8-8

Digital eBook ISBN: 979-8-9882503-7-1

Table of Contents

Book 1:

That's One Smart Puppy

The Ultimate Care Guide to Raising a Happy, Healthy, and Obedient Puppy

Introduction

The kids are screaming with excitement as we head to the car. After six months of begging, I finally gave in, and for her 14th birthday, my daughter Kelsey is getting the puppy of her dreams. Of course, she had no idea what puppy she wanted. At first, it was an Australian sheepdog, then it was a chihuahua, and then an Alaskan Malamute. After explaining to her that there are dogs out there that have been abandoned and some that have never had a home, to begin with, it was settled. The local shelter was where she would find her best friend.

When we arrived, we were introduced to Mama Daisy. A beautiful black and white Shih Tzu that had been abandoned. Thankfully, a local superhero had found her and brought her to the shelter, where she would be cared for and loved until her forever home was found. Surprise, surprise, Mama Daisy delivered three beautiful puppies just two days after she arrived. While she had secured a forever home with one of the employees, it was time for her babies to find theirs.

As we entered the room with the puppies, Kelsey dropped to her knees, and a little black ball of fluff ran straight into her arms. It was clear that the bond created at that moment would last a lifetime. She announced that his name was Sam, and we all agreed it suited him. We drove back home, where a new kennel, soft bed, puppy food, and tons of toys awaited our bundle of joy. The joy on their faces was enough to make me think that this was the best decision I had ever made.

Then reality hit, and as we walked in that door, little Sam turned into a terror! I would walk around the corner of the hallway, and there was Sam running with a toilet paper stream following behind. "Sam! STOP." He would glance at me for a second before running down the stairs, through the kitchen, and to the living room. The stream of paper gets longer by the second. Of course, Kelsey was off at school, and this had now become my clean-up.

Sam is a cutie for sure, his hair grew long, and Kelsey brushed him every day. She would even put a tiny little pony on top of his head to keep the hair out of his eyes. Yet, that sweet demeanor only seemed to last while she was around, and the moment she left the room, Sam would leave a puddle on the floor! Ugh!

Leaving my new leather pumps on the floor was my first mistake. Sam was teething and developed a taste for shoes of any type. Not just shoes, though, wooden chair legs did just as well, how on earth do I hide those?

The frustration set in, and I started second-guessing my decision. What have I gotten myself into? Kelsey goes to school every day and is off with her friends, playing soccer or band practice the rest of the time. Just as I finished the thought, Kelsey walked through the front door, dropping her book bag and getting down on her knees. She yelled out for Sam, and sure enough, that little fluff ball sprints down the hall and runs toward her, wiggling that little butt the entire way. That settles it. Sam can stay, but I need to step up and focus on getting this puppy trained if he wants to live through my wrath!

Puppies are a big responsibility, bigger than most people think. They don't come preprogrammed, and everything they learn, they learn from you. If you are struggling with a similar situation, whether the puppy was for you or for your child, don't worry, I have your back.

I have been studying, caring for, and training dogs for the last thirty years, and while some have brought me to the brink of madness, they have always brought me back with their unconditional love. Each of these pups has taught me valuable lessons, and every up and down brought me a little closer to understanding what they truly need.

Come along with me to learn the steps we took to turn Sam into a smart, obedient puppy.

Chapter 1:

So, You Want a Puppy...

Are You Sure You're Ready?

Dogs are spectacular, and they are just so cute, especially when they're puppies. Yet so many people seem to forget that dogs grow up, and they continue to grow up for an average of 15 years! Adopting a puppy is easy enough to do, but caring for that puppy for all those years can become difficult, especially for people who work long hours or enjoy traveling.

Before committing your time, money, and energy to a dog, you need to ensure that you are adopting them for the right reasons, not just because they are cute! So, what is your reason?

Worker Dogs

Dogs have been bred for a multitude of reasons over the years, and knowing how lazy humans can be, the first breeds we engineered were designed to do our work for us. Whether you are looking for a farm dog to help care for your livestock, a guard dog to protect your family, or a hound dog to accompany you on hunting trips, I can guarantee there is a breed for you.

These dogs have been bred for their strong instincts, but if you are looking at adopting a worker pup, you are going to have to buy a lot more books! They require rigorous training and a strict routine in order to succeed in the jobs assigned to them.

It is important to remember that just because your dog is a worker, you don't get to treat them like an employee. There is no clocking out after a hard day. They don't even get to take leave for a vacation in Hawaii. They are part of your family and need to be treated as such. Loads of snuggles, a comfortable home, and one-on-one play time are needed to maintain a strong, healthy relationship between the two of you.

Family Dogs

Got kids? Get Labradors! Just kidding, there are tons and tons of breeds with sweet, relaxed natures that are perfect for the family, no matter how young your kids may be. There is nothing more special than growing up with a loving dog, and the bond between a child and their dog is unbreakable. However, kids go to school, they go to camp, and they have sleepovers. This means that you are ultimately going to be reasonable for the care of their pup, so it's important to ensure that your relationship is just as strong.

If you are looking at adopting a puppy for your children, make sure to do research on the different breeds. While all dogs are ultimately family-friendly, depending on how you raise them, of course, there are some breeds that may not tolerate tiny tots that don't understand why they shouldn't pull ears. The last thing you want is for your dog to be harmed because your children aren't fully trained. Okay, you don't want an injured child, either.

Companions

If you are looking for somebody to comfort you, adventure with you, and spend every waking moment with you, then a dog is definitely the right choice. Companion dogs are a little more specialized than family dogs. The bond you create and the love they have for you is a selfish one, and it can be difficult for either of you to allow a third party in. There is no set breed that makes a good companion, only how you decide to train and bond with them.

Replacement Dogs

Losing a loved one or a pet can leave a terrible hole in our hearts, and regardless of what people say, adopting a new dog to fill this void is not necessarily a bad thing. Our dogs are often our life rafts when we are drowning in sorrow, and the joy they are capable of bringing back into our lives is irreplaceable. However, dogs, especially puppies, are hard work.

They make plenty of mistakes, which can be frustrating on the best of days. They are also very capable of understanding and mimicking your emotional state. If you are in a bad headspace, your dog may be too. It's important to ensure that you are in a safe emotional space to care for them, teach them and deal with their mistakes responsibly.

The Cons

Let's quickly run through the cons, although for some of you, these may count as pros too. I promise I am not trying to put you off on adopting a puppy, but you need to know what you are in for when you invite that little ball of chaos into your life.

How Far Does Your Wallet Stretch?

Money, money, money! Dogs are not cheap. You are going to need to budget appropriately to ensure that you provide them with the best care and life that you can. Dog food expenses are usually the first thing that comes to mind, especially when you find out that cheap no-brand dog food at the grocery store is not quite enough. But this is, in fact, one of the cheaper parts of owning a pooch.

Yearly veterinarian check-ups, vaccinations, parasite medications, and regular grooming can take quite a chunk out of your salary. Let's not forget that unexpected illness and injury can also wrack up quite a veterinarian bill. This is one of those in sickness or in health situations, and if you aren't prepared to provide your dog with medical care, regardless of cost, then you may need to rethink your decision.

Medical care and food are the bare minimum needed to keep your dog alive, but being alive is not enough. You are going to need toys, bedding, walking equipment, and all the other little knick-knacks that are sure to accumulate in your closet. These are not once—off expenses, especially for chewers that go through toys like candy. Be prepared to purchase replacements every couple of months!

Say Goodbye to Spare Time

This is a bit of a pro and a con, depending on your personality and lifestyle. If you like to sleep in late, get used to being an early bird. If you enjoy lounging in front of the TV. Get used to cutting your Netflix time short, it's walking time. Dogs, just like people, require attention, and while you have been at work, they have been alone and bored.

You need to understand that you are as much their companion as they are yours and treat them as such. Most dogs aren't too needy, and simply giving them a snuggle while you read your book is exciting for them.

Patience Is a Virtue

Have you ever met a person that tests your patience almost to your breaking point? You know the ones I am referring to. You find yourself gritting your teeth, counting to ten, and, occasionally, diving behind a trash can to hide when you see them in public. This is how your dog is going to make you feel.

When you stand in that puddle of pee or find your favorite shoes chewed to pieces in the living room, you may find you have actually developed a stress-related eye twitch. Thankfully, these occasions are few and far between, and the many good days are enough to cancel the feeling out, but it's important to prepare for them and find the best coping mechanism to deal with them when they happen.

The Undoubtable Pros

Hopefully, you haven't decided to throw this book in the trash and skip out on the idea of owning a dog altogether because there are some absolutely fantastic pros that will definitely outweigh the cons, over and over again.

Never Be Alone Again

This may feel a bit weird at first, having a little creature stalk your every move. Get used to zero privacy bathroom time! However, after a while, you won't actually know what to do with yourself when your pup isn't around. Dogs have a remarkable ability to provide us with unconditional love, even after we have been a bit mean to them. All that goofy goodness releases some breathtaking chemicals and hormones in our brains that greatly reduce anxiety and stress. Just the thought of arriving home to your dog can spark a reaction.

This companionship is not only unique to us. Dogs love company, and when you're not around, they can get quite lonely. If you already own a dog, it's a good idea to adopt another.

Babysitters

You probably shouldn't leave your kids at home with your dog alone, but dogs are surprisingly good teachers, and they don't even know it. Children learn a great deal of responsibility from owning a dog, and research has indicated that they actually develop cognitive, emotional, motor, and social skills quicker than children that don't own dogs.

Safety

Whether you have a giant breed or a tiny tot, dogs provide us with invaluable security. They are quick to alert you to strange sounds at night and are loyal enough to protect us to their last breath. Some breeds (with a little extra training) are even used to detect medical conditions such as seizures and can alert you before it happens.

Getting Out Of Your Comfort Zone

Exercise! We have all heard it enough times. Regular exercise keeps you mentally, emotionally, and physically healthy, but just how many of us actually get off the couch and do it? Puppies require regular walks, playtime, and sunshine and when they don't get it, you will suffer the consequences. And by consequences, I mean a destroyed house!

Getting out will not just benefit your health, it is also a great way to meet new people and make some friends. There are not many people who can resist stopping to pet a cute dog.

Science Says So

The researchers have spoken, and we must listen. There are some remarkable studies that have been done on just how beneficial owning a dog can actually be. Other than ensuring we exercise and regularly lifting our spirits, dogs can actually reduce health issues. It's been found that pet owners, especially seniors, had a 50% reduction in health problems. If that's not enough, it has also been found that people who have suffered from major surgeries or illnesses recover much quicker if they own a pet (Carr et al., 2019). Talk about a reason to live!

Your Lifestyle Matters

If you have gotten this far, your mind is clearly made up, you are getting a dog! Now you need to decide which kind of dog will best suit you. Read through this section carefully. Even if you already have a breed in mind, they might not actually work with your lifestyle. It's best to compromise before you invite a dog into your life that you can't actually care for.

Housing

This should not really require an explanation, but shelters all around the world have proven me wrong. Around 18% of the pets currently in shelters have been surrendered because of their owners' housing situation (Weiss et al., 2015). This may not seem like a lot, but let's do the math. The ASPCA estimates that around 6.3 million pets are surrendered each year in the United States alone (ASPCA, 2022). That means that 1.13 million pets have been dropped off at shelters because of housing issues. Be smarter, and be better.

If you are not in a secure housing situation or if you have plans to move to another country, don't adopt a dog. If you live in an apartment, regardless of how many walks you think you can have a day, do not adopt a big dog. If you live on a large property, you're in luck, you can have your pick of the litter!

Fitness Levels

We have already spoken about how your new pup is going to transform you from a couch potato to an Olympic gold medalist. However, if you know that you won't be able to stick to a constant exercise routine, it's best to choose a couch potato breed. Siberian huskies are gorgeous and are often on the top of most adoption lists, but not many owners can actually handle them. They require at least an hour and a half of exercise a day, and most of that should be focused on running.

In comparison, an adorable droopy-eyed basset hound needs around two 20-minute walks a day and a calm play session. See what I am getting at? Don't overestimate your abilities.

Fur Alert!

Dogs have fur, dogs shed their fur, and you vacuum it up. It seems pretty simple and easy enough to handle, but some dogs have *a lot* of fur. I mean a lot. Even with regular grooming sessions, you will need to regularly brush them and vacuum your house daily. If you are a bit of a neat freak or somebody that suffers from allergies, this may not work in your favor. In that case, it's probably best to avoid the urge to adopt a Burmese Mountain Dog and opt for a short-haired terrier instead.

Do You Want a Worker?

The idea of a working dog is great, but it requires a lot of commitment and a strict routine to actually train them for their jobs. If you are looking at adopting a dog for security reasons, pick your breed wisely and find a professional training facility that can assist you in training them correctly.

Dogs that work medical jobs, such as leading the blind or detecting different medical conditions should be adopted from approved breeding and training facilities only. Do not risk your or your family's lives by thinking you are capable of training them to that degree.

Herders and hunting dogs, on the other hand, are surprisingly easy to train as their natural instincts kick in almost immediately. This can sometimes become an issue if you do adopt a herding breed but don't give them a job to do. If your border collie becomes bored enough, don't be surprised if you find them herding up the neighborhood kids.

Adopt or Shop?

In a perfect world, we wouldn't even have shelters. All the dogs would already be in a warm, loving home. Sadly, it's not a perfect world, and shelters have had to open as a consequence of humanity's lack of responsibility. There are plenty of misconceptions about shelters, and people often think that the dogs there are scruffy, ill-looking beasts, and the others have been thrown away for being aggressive or naughty.

There may be one or two Lady and the Tramp-looking characters there (not that looks make dogs any less deserving of love), but the vast majority are beautiful, healthy, and loving. They just need a second chance at life.

Simply put, if you have the choice, adopt!

Rescue Dog Considerations

Rescuing an adult dog from a shelter is not for the faint-hearted, and you can never be quite sure what you will get. Especially ones that have had to deal with years of trauma. Luckily, puppies are much, much easier. While many of them may have been subjected to some kind of trauma, they are still in their developmental stages, and it does not take much more than a loving home to build their confidence.

Always ask the shelter if they can provide you with a background for your pup. It's not always possible, but they will at least be able to provide you with a medical certificate. This kind of history may not seem important now, but if anything had to go wrong, medically or behaviorally, with your dog in the future, these records will help you and your veterinarian to figure out the cause.

Mixed Breeds

There is nothing that I love more than a mixed-breed dog! My oldest dog is a gorgeous brindle mix, and whenever somebody asks me what he is, I simply say, "A bit of sugar, spice, and everything nice." However, there are always pros and cons to everything.

Mixed breeds are like a box of chocolates, you never know what you will get! This could be taken as a pro or a con. They have diverse personalities and skill sets, which can be very exciting for the adventurous owner and a little disappointing for those who have high expectations. Just because they look like they have a bit of Labrador in them does not mean that they will act like one.

One of the biggest pros is that they are less likely to suffer from genetic disorders due to their colorful gene pool. The chances of behavioral issues and general medical issues are also lower as no inbreeding has taken place.

Pure Breeds

What you see is (almost) always what you get. Whether you're adopting them for their skills, beauty, or personalities, by keeping the gene pool "clean," dogs will retain their classic breed traits.

Unfortunately, there is always a con. Purebreds can suffer from genetic disorders and, in some cases, behavioral issues due to inbreeding. Most of these disorders are breed-specific, and while they can be avoided through correct breeding, it's important to be aware of them! If you intend to shop for a purebred, you will need to choose your breeder wisely and ensure that they can provide you with a full genetic and medical history for your pup.

Dog Breeds

Dogs can essentially be split up into seven categories based on what they were bred to do. Learning a bit more about each of these groups and the unique breeds will hopefully help you to find which dog will suit you best.

The Hard Workers

The working group contains some of the oldest dog breeds in history. These pups were bred for hard labor in even harder conditions. So, it is of no surprise that they are incredibly strong and generally large. Alaskan malamutes and Siberian huskies are the original sled pullers, but St. Bernards, Bernese mountain dogs, and even rottweilers all played a role in pulling carts. Other members of the working group, such as Great Danes, boxers, and Dobermans, are a little less stocky and a bit more agile and have mainly been used as farm and family protection.

Despite some of their looks (looking at you, boxers), they are all highly intelligent, which makes them easy to train but harder to keep busy. These dogs need constant mental and physical stimulation to keep them happy. Thanks to their protective and loyal natures, they all make great companions and can readily fit into any family.

The Herders

Herding dogs work just as hard, if not more, than their working group counterparts. As the name suggests, they were bred to herd and move sheep and cattle. This requires a great deal of intelligence, energy, and agility. Some breeds include border collies, German shepherds, and English sheepdogs. While they make great family pets, they generally prefer to pledge their loyalty to a single owner, and once you have been chosen, there is no escaping.

Herding breeds are arguably the most intelligent breeds in the dog kingdom. This is why many of them are still used as working dogs today, with the German shepherd dominating the police force and search and rescue teams.

The only downside to owning a herder is their never-ending energy. Seriously, have you ever seen a tired border collie? This can become problematic, especially if they don't have a job to focus their energy on. One of the best ways to relieve this pent-up energy is by getting your pup involved in agility training.

The Sporters

The sporting group was bred to be the ultimate hunting assistants. While they don't necessarily hunt themselves, they are experts at locating and retrieving game. Ever wonder why Labradors love water? It's because they were bred too.

Retrievers and Brittanys were used to retrieve waterfowl from lakes and ponds during a hunt. They don't mind getting soaked because they have specialized water-resistant fur. While they are skinny-dipping, the pointers, spaniels, and setters are on the move and doing what they do best, pointing out hidden wildlife.

These dogs form strong bonds with their companions, so much so that you will start to wonder if they can actually read your mind. Their soft natures and fun-loving personalities make them good family pets, and they are particularly fond of children. These are outdoor dogs, and cooping them up in a house all day usually doesn't end well. If you decide to adopt one, make sure that you have the space and yard for them.

The Sniffers

Oh, the hounds! Hounds are incredibly diverse in their looks, abilities, and personalities. On one hand, you have the sight hounds, which are built for speed. They are lightweight, agile dogs that can run at the speed of light to catch anything that moves. On the other hand, you have scent hounds, which are short, stocky dogs that can't seem to keep their noses off the ground. They may not be able to catch the target, but they can track it for miles.

The most notable sight hounds include greyhounds, whippets, and Irish wolfhounds. These dogs have an exceptionally high prey drive and are loaded with energy. It's important to train your dog in recall from an early age, especially if you intend to take them for regular walks and hikes. Greyhounds can run up to 45 m/h (Greyhound W. 2020), and you really don't want to be on the other side of that leash when they catch sight of a rabbit.

Our drooping-eyed, short-legged scent hounds are just as special but less likely to take you for a run when you least expect it. Basset hounds, bloodhounds, and Beagles are the most popular breeds. If you have one of these, you can expect long, slow walks. Not because they are lazy but because they are taking in an incredible amount of information through their noses.

All hounds make good companions, but some are a little more child-friendly than others. If you are looking for a family dog, opt for a calmer basset over a prey-driven greyhound.

The Lapdogs

This group contains the teacups, toys, and mini breeds. While they have been bred for a variety of reasons, they currently hold two critical roles in society. Being attentive companions and looking fabulous while doing it.

They make up for their tiny size with their explosive, sometimes stubborn personalities. They are incredibly loyal and will put up a strong fight to protect their owner until the bitter end. The most famous toy breeds include Chihuahuas, pugs, shih tzus, and Pomeranians. Their size and outgoing personalities make it easy for them to fit into any lifestyle, making them popular options for owners that live in apartments and seniors that are unable to handle larger breeds.

While toy breeds make great family dogs, their small size does make them vulnerable to heavy-handed children and larger dogs that like to play rough. Don't let their small size fool you into thinking they are low-maintenance dogs. They still require regular grooming and a good exercise routine. The only difference is that their little legs don't need to walk too far to get their steps in.

The Protectors

The terrier group are the ultimate protectors. They are hardy dogs, with the first short-legged terriers being bred to dig up rodent holes and protect homesteads from rat invasion. Long-legged terriers were later used for hunting small game.

Sadly, some terriers were bred purely for entertainment. Staffordshire bull terriers, pit bull terriers, and Spanish bull terriers were all originally bred for bull baiting and blood sport after the English bulldog was found to be too slow. Thankfully, we have moved past this dreadful part of history, and instead of shunning these breeds, we have welcomed them with open arms. Staffy's are now one of the top choices for family and child-friendly dogs! It is quite spectacular what a bit of love can do.

The smaller terriers, such as Jack Russels and Boston terriers, double as the perfect lap dogs. A warm blanket and continuous cuddles are all they need to keep them happy. All terriers are high-energy and incredibly playful. Sometimes, too playful, and their stubborn nature can come out if playtime is ended early. They are companion-driven and prefer to stick by their owners' side. Fiercely loyal and alert, these pooches will do what it takes to protect their family.

Everything In Between

Last, but certainly not least, we have the non-sporter group. This diverse group consists of all the dogs, too unique to fit into any specific category. They were bred for a variety of reasons, but most of those jobs have become redundant, and many are now used for dog shows.

Believe it or not, the royal and ever-so-cheeky poodle was once used to retrieve birds from the water. The high-energy and ever-playful dalmatian was once used to pull carts and hunt, while others, such as the aloof yet loyal chow chows, were used for anything and everything. Some held higher positions, with the Pikaneese receiving the title of royal sentinel. That explains the attitude! A few of these breeds are still used for work, but most have retired and become loving companions and simply enjoy the comforts of home life.

It's very difficult to go into the temperaments and skill sets of this group as it consists of so many breeds. It's best to research each one separately if you intend to adopt.

Chapter 2:

Preparing For Chaos

This title may be misleading and a little exaggerated (or is it?) but it's always best to prepare for the worst and be pleasantly surprised! Before you bring your puppy home, you will need to make some modifications to accommodate them. Try to think of it as bringing home a two-year-old child. You wouldn't give them free access to your pool, right? Well, I hope not, at least.

Your puppy is in a vital developmental stage, both mentally and physically, and they generally learn by watching their moms and through trial and error. Trial and error become a bit problematic when they want to know what would happen if they chew a bottle of bleach. It's important to create a safe environment for them to survive and thrive. Your puppy's perceived death wish is not the only thing you need to prepare for. If you don't have children and haven't owned a puppy before, you have to get ready for your life to turn upside down.

You can try to keep your house the way it is, but it's inevitable that you will end up having toys scattered from one end to another.

Creating a Puppy Play Zone

In order to keep your house in some sort of order, you should figure out where you can make a puppy play zone. The size of this area and how you fence it off are going to depend on your puppy. When indoors, your living room is usually your best bet, and if you have a yard and a porch, I suggest you create one there as well.

There are a couple of ways to fence off these areas. Crates will be used as a resting area for your pup. However, you can purchase add-ons to these crates, which are open on the top and can be extended to the size you want, much like a fence. You can also purchase actual puppy playpens. These are typically made from a fabric mesh, but you can purchase metal ones as well.

You can use these as long-term playpens for small dog breeds, and they are especially important if you give your small puppy unsupervised time in the yard.

For larger dogs, I recommend using baby gates to confine them to a room of your choosing. I truly love baby gates and still use them today. They are a great way to still have visual contact with your dog, but they keep certain rooms in your house free of fur and mud. My living room has a door that leads to an enclosed porch and the yard. I use a baby gate that closes access off to the rest of the house. During the day, my puppies have access to the living room, porch, and, when supervised (as puppies), the yard.

Obviously, everyone's house is set up in different ways, so you will need to figure out what works best for you. If you are happy with your entire house as a playpen, that's fine too! Once you have set up your space, you will need to clear it of all things dangerous and then load it up with all things fun. Which means toys, toys, toys! So many toys! Chew toys, squeaky toys, balls, puzzles, and stuffed toys. We will run through the different types of toys and what each one is used for. However, for now, just remember that dogs are all different, which means that they love different types of toys. I suggest that you buy one of each kind for your puppy to start with so that you can figure out which ones they enjoy the most.

Feeding Areas

I prefer for my dogs to eat their meals in a different room, and I usually choose the kitchen or dining room. I like to do this because I find that it lessens the chances of them food guarding and begging, and it allows us both to stick to a routine.

Dogs should not have free access to food all day, especially puppies that don't know when to stop! Set meals allow you to monitor their daily intake of food, and if you have a multi-pet household, it stops one dog from being a glutton while the others starve. It is much more hygienic to do this, as it stops flies and ants from invading your home. Your dog should have access to water, regardless of where they are. Have a bowl of water outside, in their play area, and in their feeding area. Dogs are resourceful, and if they don't have a water bowl outside, don't be shocked to find them in the bird bath.

Resting Areas

Resting areas are typically set up in their play areas, but I prefer three. A dog house outside, a crate in my living room, and a bed in my bedroom. My dogs quickly learn that once they get into the bedroom, the lights go off, and it's time for bed.

Dog Beds

When choosing a bed, do yourself a favor and pick one of the more expensive options. The foam in the cheaper ones breaks up quickly, and your dog ends up sleeping on the hard floor. A good quality bed will last years, and you won't need to replace it repeatedly.

Puppies grow like beanstalks, so make sure you buy one that will fit their adult size. When they are smaller, you can wrap a couple of blankets around the sides to make the bed smaller and cozier. Speaking of blankets, these are more important than you might think. Puppies aren't quite capable of regulating their body temperature properly, which means that they can get cold real quick. A good fluffy blanket will remedy this, and if you live in a cold area or one that has regular snowfall, I suggest that you buy a heated pad. These come in a variety of sizes, and you can slip them under your dog's bed. It's easy to set the temperature, and your dog will enjoy a very comfortable sleep.

Crates and Dog Houses

If your dog will be spending time outdoors while you are at work, you will need to put up a kennel with a dog house or have a fenced yard with a dog house. The most common dog houses are wooden, but if they are poorly made, they don't last long. The wood often rots, and it is very difficult to clean them. Plastic dog houses are much more hygienic and are light enough to be moved around. Make sure to keep the house undercover and out of direct sunlight so that your dog doesn't end up like beef jerky!

Crates are not for everyone, and that is understandable. It can take a bit of time to get your dog used to them. However, if you are keen on crate training, it's best to set one up before your puppy arrives and start training them immediately.

Warning! Puppy Dangers!

Alright, let's get into puppy dangers. Puppies are a bit stupid… Well, let's say they are still learning. Although some dogs never seem to stop "learning." You will need to take matters into your hands and remove any dangerous items from their reach.

Household Cleaners

Yes, they will actually attempt this. I have found my puppy with its head in my laundry detergent powder and another casually chewing on my bath soap. Thankfully, neither occasion ended badly, regardless of the panicked emergency vet visit and a massive bill. It's not just solid cleaners that you need to watch out for. Any liquid cleaners that spill can become a very deadly juice to a puppy that tries to lap it up.

Rodent and ant poisons are specially designed to be tasty enough to attract their prey. This smell will likely lure your dog in as well. There is no way to know the survival rate of a dog that has eaten poison, regardless of how quickly you get them to the vet. If you regularly use these poisons, it is best to ditch them and deal with your problem in a more natural way.

Chewables

Smart dogs won't chew foreign objects. Reasonable dogs will chew something up and leave it in bits. Yet, there are also those dogs that are stupid enough—sorry, "learning"—to chew something up and swallow those bits. Any sharp plastic pieces can actually cut through your dog's gastrointestinal tract, leading to numerous health issues and stomach ulcers. Soft pieces of fluff or fabrics can cause a buildup and blockage in the intestines, which in some cases require surgery to remove. I have been there and done that when my dog decided to eat the lining of a tennis ball. You really don't want to have to deal with it!

The problem is, you won't know that your dog is this kind of chewer until you catch them in the act. If you find something that has been chewed up, make sure that you can actually see the pieces on the floor. If you don't, monitor your pet carefully, and if you see any signs of discomfort, take them to the vet immediately. Chewing and swallowing inedible items is not only bad for the stomach, but it can also be straight-up dangerous. Puppies may chew on live wires or even batteries. Try to keep items like this out of their reach.

Escape Artists

Toy dogs are the usual suspects here. They can't seem to help but squeeze through those little gaps. It gets to the point that they are honestly just showing off to irritate you. This is one of the main reasons why you should use an outdoor playpen for unsupervised small dogs. You will also need to walk around and secure your fence. Making sure to block up any sneaky holes at the bottom.

That being said, larger dogs are not innocent either. Every now and then, one of the giant breeds figures out that they can actually scale that baby gate or fence pretty easily. This usually comes down to having manners and proper training but can occur if your dog suffers from separation anxiety. We will cover how to solve these issues a little later in the book.

Danger Zones

You may think that all dogs can swim, and while most can, your stockier breeds are much less adept. Especially if they have never been in a pool before. Puppies are full of energy but don't really have the stamina needed to paddle to the stairs if they fall in the deep end. Some don't have the height to stand on those stairs and jump out. If you have a pool, it's a good idea to put a pool cover on it when not in use. Swimming lessons are also important and can be a lifesaver in some situations.

Have you seen how uncoordinated puppies are? Some literally fall when they are just trying to walk straight. They also seem to have no spacial awareness and will likely not even realize the stairs are there until it's too late! Baby gates work well to keep your dog from going up or down the stairs, and for the first week or so, depending on their age, you should be carrying them up and down. Once they get a little older, walk up and down with them and be ready to catch them if they tumble. Trial and error.

Puppies like to believe that they are Christopher Columbus reincarnated but lack the common sense and skill set to survive in the dangerous world. If your front door leads directly to the road, do not leave it open! Even if you think that your puppy is safely confined to their play area, do not leave it open! When you are outside on walks, your puppy should always be on a leash, but don't think they won't walk off the sidewalk into the road if you are not watching. They will learn, but it can take a bit of time.

Not Even the Garden is Safe Anymore

We already know that puppies are chewers and will taste test anything that they come across. So, it's no surprise that once they are out in the garden, they will take a bite of the first juicy green they spot. In most cases, this is harmless, and once they realize it doesn't taste that great, they won't try it again.

Don't forget about pesticides and poisons. If you regularly spray your garden with pesticides or your grass with weed killer, you can poison your dog. Ditch these products and find a healthier way to deal with the problem.

These are just a few of the plants that are poisonous to dogs. If you have these in your yard, I suggest that you pull them out or keep them out of your pup's reach.

Absolute No, No's	Toxic but Not Deadly in Small Doses	Not Toxic but Certainly Not Good
Aconitum (Wolfsbane)	Belladonna	Asparagus Fern
Daffodils	Hydrangeas	Lilies
Delphinium (Larkspur)	Ivy	Hyacinths
Foxglove	Laburnum	Lupine
Hemlock	Lily of the Valley	Sweet Pea
Oleander	Rhubarb	Tulips
Rhododendrons	Geraniums	Umbrella Plants
Wisteria	Peace Lilies	Poinsettias
Yew Trees	Philodendrons	Mint
Aloe Vera	Morning Glory	Parsley

It is completely normal for dogs to occasionally chew on grass, as it aids in digestion. This is not something you need to be concerned about, but it's a great idea to purchase and plant specialized pet grass, which is safe for them to chew and a lot more tasty than regular grass.

Prepping Your Family

Make sure your family is on board with you adopting a dog. You may be the one doing all the work, but if your spouse doesn't want a puppy, they are bound to get annoyed when the puppy does something wrong. Your puppy can feel the tension, so don't subject them to it.

Parenting Style

Once everyone is on board, you are going to need to pick your parenting style, and all of you will need to stick to it. There are essentially three to choose from. Authoritative, Authoritarian, and Permissive. Permissive parenting means you let your dog do what it wants and when it wants. This is not really a good style to start off with, as puppies aren't excellent at thinking for themselves just yet and can get into plenty of harmful situations. Authoritarian parenting is very strict and demanding on a dog. It involves punishment for negative behaviors and very little reward for good ones. If you want a dog that obeys your every command but is absolutely petrified of you, then this is the style to pick. Just kidding, please don't pick this one.

Authoritative parents are more in tune with their dogs and can judge the best approach for each situation. This type of parenting involves nipping bad behaviors in the bud by reinforcing the good ones. Dogs that grow up in this kind of household are found to be much more balanced in general.

Then there is the bad cop, good cop parenting style. When you are the good one who lets the dog sleep on the couch, and your spouse is the horrible one for shouting at them to get off. This has never worked, won't work, and will never work. This creates a fragile relationship with one owner and a manipulative one with the other. Never mind the confusion your dog is going through. They never quite learn what is good or bad, they just learn how to not get caught.

Training Your Kids

Yep, I am serious! You need to train your children before you can train your dog. First things first, your kids need to stick to the parenting style and training that you use for your dog. If you don't want your dog to have human foods, ensure that your kids aren't sneaking them scraps under the table. While this seems harmless, dogs learn quickly, and don't be surprised when they start snatching food straight out of your child's mouth.

Secondly, you have to teach your children how to correctly handle and play with a dog. It's pretty simple for us, but kids have the attention span of a puppy and should be reminded often. Pulling a dog's tail or ears, barking or screaming in their face, and sticking your fingers in their eyes, or worse places will likely end up with somebody being nipped.

This happens way too often, and dogs are readily rehomed for it. Even though, let's be honest, it wasn't their fault for reacting appropriately to something painful. If you notice that your puppy avoids your children at all costs, then they have likely hurt them accidentally. You need to address this immediately and help mend their relationship to keep them both happy.

Chapter 3:

Too Late To Turn Back Now

The day is finally here, your puppy is on his way. The excitement is unbelievable, and everyone has caught the happy giggles. You walk him through the door, and you can't help but want to kiss and hug him. Except, your kids do too, and now your spouse is at it, and your mother drove from out of state to meet the little one. Suddenly, your pup is being passed around like a volleyball!

This is not really the first impression you want to make, and it's not the best way to introduce a scared little pup to a scary new space. As hard as it is for those around you, you are going to need to keep your puppy to yourself, at least for the first few hours. Introduce them to each room quietly and calmly before bringing the family in.

Once the introductions are over and your puppy is comfortable, you will need to begin your very first training routine. This includes basic household etiquette. Basically, the two of you are going to work really hard at protecting your carpets from pee.

Listen to Your Puppy!

Dogs are superb at communicating how they feel through body language. Unfortunately, we aren't good at actually reading this body language and making the right decisions based on it. It's important to understand what your puppy wants and how they feel, especially in social situations. Dogs have different thresholds, the same way that we do. This could be a pain, patience, emotional or fear-based threshold. When they reach it, their main priority will be to protect themselves.

Puppies are new to this world and have spent most of their time with their mom and littermates, learning dog socialization. They are still trying to figure out this human interaction thing, and too much "love" can overwhelm them, causing them to react negatively toward us or become scared to engage with us.

Keeping your puppy below this threshold, and giving them an opportunity to relax and recuperate when they start to reach it, is the safest way to introduce them.

Basic Body Language

We will talk about body language in more depth in the chapters to come, but for now, let's discuss the basics. A happy puppy is one that runs toward you in clear excitement. Their tongues are out and lolling about, and their tails are wagging so hard it looks like they are doing a terrible hula dance. Playful puppies will typically bounce as they walk and readily jump up onto your lap or lick you if they get the chance.

When to Stop

It's time to stop if your puppy is trying to get away from you. If they are trying to push out of your arms or keep jumping off your lap to walk to the next room, they have had enough. They may cower and try to make themselves as small as possible. If you don't listen and keep attempting to force your love on them, they will growl or attempt to nip you. This can really put a damper on the situation, but at the end of the day, you caused it. This nipping is not naughty or aggressive.

Remember, puppies haven't learned human manners yet, and this is a perfectly acceptable behavior in the dog world.

Time to Meet the Family

It's best to introduce your puppy to their new home first. Place them in a calm, quiet room and show them their beds, toys, and water bowls. It's doubtful that they are going to take any interest in these things at first. They are probably ignoring you, much to your dismay, and running around sniffing their new environment. Give them the opportunity to do this, and don't be upset when they pass out in their beds immediately after. This has been a big day and that little dog can only take so much excitement.

Once they are comfortable and know where the good places to hide are, you can start bringing your family in to meet them! This is not the right time for cuddles, and it's best if everyone sits on the floor calmly and speaks softly. If you want to give your puppy some extra motivation, introduce some treats. If your puppy approaches somebody, give them permission to stroke and speak to them and if the puppy reacts excitedly, they can go in for a hug.

Again, it's likely that your pup is going to pass out after this interaction and if somebody wants to take the opportunity to snuggle them while they sleep, go for it. As long as he is still happy and doesn't try to run away, you are all good.

Is This a Crate or a Prison?

Using a crate is a debatable subject and while some people swear by it, others will flat out refuse to even play with the idea. The thing is, a crate is an incredibly helpful training tool as long as you learn to use it correctly. Confining your puppy to their crate when you are tired of dealing with them is not okay. If you treat the crate as a prison, you can be sure that this little inmate will do everything in their power to avoid serving their sentence.

Choose Your Crate

First off, pick your material. The most common crates are made from metal mesh. These seem uncomfortable, but if you buy the right size, they are often the best ones to use. They provide ventilation and sunlight, and your dog won't feel as claustrophobic. You can also buy plastic or wooden crates. Plastic and wooden ones are sealed, and you will need to ensure that they are big enough and provide enough ventilation. Plastic is definitely best for an indoor situation, as it is much easier to clean if your puppy has a potty accident. Trying to get the pee smell out of the wood in your living room will drive you to madness.

Puppies and seniors seem to prefer enclosed crates, as this quiet, dark space gives them a sense of security and a moment to get away from the world. This, however, is going to depend on your dog's personality, and while I highly recommend these for seniors, it can be pricey to buy your puppy two different crates. If you want to provide them with a bit of privacy, save your money and throw a few heavy blankets over your mesh cage to mimic the feeling.

Another money-saving tip is to buy a crate that is going to fit your dog when they are fully grown. This will also work in your favor during training as a larger crate allows your puppy more room to play, and they will be more likely to use it. Adjustable crates are also a great option but can become costly.

Once you have the crate set up, make it cozy! A thick mattress or blanket should be used to line the bottom, and throw in a couple of toys to keep your dog busy.

Crate Training

Crate training is easy enough if you are capable of self-control. Don't be surprised if your puppy cries or moans during the first few tries. Hold in the urge to rush to their rescue. They are master manipulators and will learn that a few tears will get them the freedom and attention that they want.

Step One: Comfort First

Lure your puppy into the crate with toys. Once they are in, give them plenty of treats and get them excited about being in the crate by using vocal rewards such as "Good boy/girl!" Don't close the door just yet, and if they come out, it's no biggie, you have all the time in the world.

At this age, they are still a bit insecure and much prefer being as close to their protector as possible. It can take some time for them to feel comfortable being alone. This is when covering your crate, at least two of the sides work well.

Step Two: Keep Calm, This is Just a Drill

It's time to work on closing the door. Sit calmly next to the crate and let them settle in with one of their toys. As hard as it's going to be, try not to pay any attention to them at this point. Read a book or play a game on your phone if you have to. If you concentrate too hard on the situation, they will know that something is up and anticipate a change.

Close the door about halfway and wait. They are probably going to give you the evil eye and push the door open again. If that happens, wait for them to relax and try again. If they sit calmly for a minute or so without pushing the door. Reward them! It's best to do this through the side of the crate, as rewarding them at the door may motivate them to walk out.

Step Three: Braving The Door

Closing the door. You're going to repeat the steps above, but take a deep breath, protective parents, this time, you will close the door completely. The sound of the latch will alert them immediately, and they may start crying and trying to push their way out. Sit next to the crate, but do not pay any attention to them. The moment they stop crying or move away from the door, treat them!

Remember, you are trying to reward them for being calm and relaxed in the crate. If you panic and open up the door or treat them too early, you are teaching them that freaking out is the right behavior.

Don't confine your puppy for too long. Give them a couple of minutes and open the door again. Keep repeating this throughout the day until they feel comfortable with the door closed.

Step Four: Evacuation

This is the scariest step for us. It's time to leave the room. It's best to do this when they can sit in the crate calmly for at least ten minutes. Use the steps above as usual, but this time you are going to leave the room. If they cry, you will need to ignore them until they calm down. Once calm, enter the room again, treat them, and open the crate door. Short sessions are best, and you can slowly increase their time in the crate when you are sure they are comfortable.

Oops, I Did it Again

Housebreaking your puppy should be your first priority. Potty mistakes are definitely the most infuriating part of puppy ownership. Even if they don't annoy you now, they will later when their bladders are much bigger. Don't forget: Your puppy is not behaving badly when they use your carpet as a toilet. How on earth are they supposed to know that they should be going outside? If anything, they think they have made the best decision by using the carpet because their pee won't spread to their bed or the rest of the house.

If your dog doesn't know that they have done something wrong, how can you punish them? The idea that rubbing your dog's nose in their pee will stop them from going inside is a myth. Your puppy isn't able to make that association! The only thing they learn from this punishment is that pottying at anytime, anywhere, is bad.

When they need to go potty, they are going to sneak as far away from you as possible to avoid the consequences. So don't be shocked when you find stinky presents in hidden places.

Making a Potty Area

First thing is first, puppies have tiny bladders. At this age, they will need to pee every 1–2 hours. Yep, that's 12–24 pees a day. That means that no matter how many times you take them for walks or let them outside, they will probably end up peeing in the house. If you aren't prepared to wake up in the middle of the night, then a potty area is even more of a priority. Choose one spot in your house to avoid confusion and extra clean-ups. The best place for this is in their play area.

Potty Pads

These are large absorbent pads that you can lay on the floor. Most puppies will readily take to using them for their business. For larger puppies, I suggest laying down a few or putting some newspaper underneath to avoid any leaks.

Whenever you catch your pup using one, reward them with a treat so that they understand that what they have done is good. Once they use the training pads regularly, you should stop rewarding them for it, as it can interfere with your outdoor training. Stopping the treats won't discourage them from using the pads, but it will encourage them to potty outside, as they will soon learn that that experience is more rewarding.

You won't need to use these pads forever. They are simply an outlet for your puppy when they are unable to hold it in any longer. As your dog gets older, they will be able to control their bladders better and notify you when they need to go outside.

If your pup misses the target or ends up pottying somewhere else in the house, just let it go. Clean it up, and move on! If you continue to reward them for using their training pads, they will get the point, and the mistakes will stop.

Training

Potty training is really, really easy. All you need is a bag of treats, an outdoor area, and a ton of enthusiasm. The first step will be creating a routine. It's easy to avoid mistakes if you give them enough time outside to do their business. The first potty break should be the moment you wake up. The second, after breakfast, and then every 1–2 hours until bedtime.

This is not possible for everyone, which is why the potty pads end up so important. As they get older, you will be able to extend the time between the breaks. Once your pup has full bladder control, they need to go outdoors at least four times a day. Anything over six hours will guarantee a mistake or a bladder infection.

Dogs learn best through positive reinforcement and association. If you go wild with excitement and reward them when they potty outside, they will learn this a good behavior.

I like to use a cue word for training, and before we go outside, I say, "Let's go potty!" The moment they finish their business, I make a massive deal out of it and give them several treats. This way, they can make the association between the word, the act, my happiness, and the reward.

The rewards are temporary and are only used to reinforce the good behavior until it is fully ingrained in their minds. Once they are fully potty-trained, you can stop the treats and just use vocal rewards.

Chapter 4:

Healthy Puppy, Happy Puppy

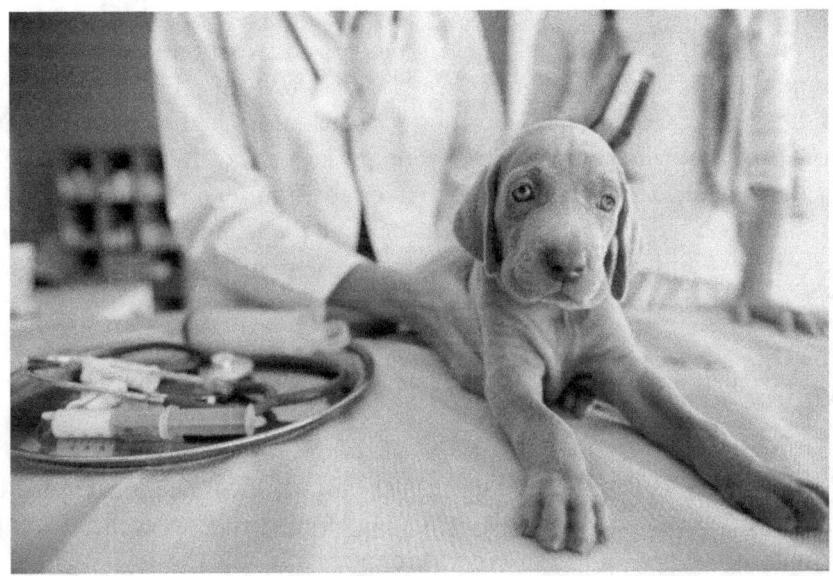

The best way to cure your puppy of an illness is by making sure that they never catch it in the first place. This is done through a healthy diet, regular exercise, a comfortable, healthy environment, and through the use of medical advancements and vaccinations. All those nasty little bugs and diseases that our puppies used to pick up are now preventable.

If you haven't had a pet before, it can be daunting to find the right veterinarian. The best way to do it, in my experience, is by talking to other people who have dogs. They will be able to recommend the vets that they use and help you to avoid ones that they have bad experiences with.

Don't be afraid to change to a new veterinarian if you believe they are better suited for you and your dog. It's critical that you find a place and a person that your dog can feel comfortable and secure with. Remember, this is the person who is going to regularly use a rectal thermometer on your pooch. You best be sure that they like them!

Where Do I Start?

Pet insurance is a relatively new concept, and to non-pet owners, it sounds like a waste of money. For the first few months, it may seem so, but oh my word, when your dog gets sick, it is an absolute lifesaver! You can generally purchase different packages, much like our health insurance. Accidental plans, which cover any injuries, are as cheap as $4 a month, while some of the more expensive plans include vaccinations, dewormers, and grooming. Regardless of the plan you choose, I assure you, you won't regret it.

Microchipping and Identification

All dogs should be fitted with a collar and an identification tag. This may not seem so important, but if your dog were to go missing, you would regret not doing it. Your identification tag should consist of your dog's name and your mobile number. You don't need to put more information than that, other than perhaps a second number if you aren't great at keeping your phone on.

I highly recommend that you microchip your dog as well. These harmless, super tiny microchips are injected under your dog's skin. Each chip has a unique code, and local vets and shelters will have a scanner that they can use to ID your dog. The code is attached to your name, phone number, and email address, and they will be able to contact you if they find your pup.

Understanding Genetics

While unlikely in mixed-breed dogs, genetic disorders are sadly becoming more common in purebreds. Different breeds are susceptible to different disorders, so if you have a purebred dog with no background history, you will need to discuss the possibilities with your veterinarian. They will be able to assess your dog, identify any concerning symptoms, and inform you of any disorders that your breed may be prone to. If they do find something abnormal, they will conduct blood tests to detect any abnormal genes and give you an appropriate treatment plan that could prevent or stall the disorder.

Hip Dysplasia is one of the most common genetic disorders. It mainly affects larger breeds such as Labradors, German shepherds, and Great Danes. Hip Dysplasia occurs when puppies grow too quickly, and their weight places strain on their underdeveloped skeleton. This causes the hip joints to deform, which can become extremely painful. Surgery is the only way to fix this once it occurs.

Other disorders include Brachycephalic syndrome, which is a respiratory deformity that mainly impacts flat-faced breeds, and chondrodysplasia, which impacts long, short breeds such as bassets and dachshunds.

Medical Records

The first thing your veterinarian is going to ask you for is a medical history or breeder history. After this, your vet will ask you a couple of follow-up questions, such as: What do you feed them? How often do you exercise them, and what kind of environment do you live in?

You will need to be transparent, so don't try to hide anything. Veterinarians deal with all kinds of people each day, and some are too embarrassed to admit when they have made a mistake. Most people aren't as good at lying as they may think, and your vet will be able to see the truth when they examine your pup. If they don't, remember that you are compromising your dog's health and well-being. There is no shame in making an error, and each check-up should be treated as a learning experience for you.

You should keep all of your dog's medical records, vaccinations, and breeder certificates in a file. That way, if you do change veterinarians or if you have an emergency, you will be able to give them all the information they require.

The First Visit Is The Scariest

So, what actually happens after all the questions are completed?

First off, it's weighing time. That is, if you can actually get your dog onto their scale. Dogs act like scales are minefields, but then again, don't we all? Your puppies' weight is significant as it will impact their growth. These weights will be documented and referred to during the next check-up. This will provide an accurate growth chart and show you if your puppy is gaining or losing weight too quickly. If they are on the thin side, you may need to increase or change your food. However, if they are on the chunkier side, you may need to up your exercise time.

Your puppy will then be poked, prodded, and felt up and down to check for any abnormalities, dermatitis symptoms, and for fleas that may be using your pup as a bounce house. Eyes, ears, and mouth will be checked for any injuries, signs of illness, malnutrition, and dehydration.

The chances of anything being wrong with your puppy at this point are very low, so don't worry too much. Fecal floats are usually done routinely during check-ups. For this, your veterinarian will take a fecal sample using a pipette. This is just an all-around fun, family-friendly activity for both the pet and the owner. Sarcasm aside, it is essential, and once the sample is checked under a microscope, your vet will be able to identify any worms or eggs and treat your pup accordingly.

Important Pricks and Jabs

Once your dog has been treated or given a clean bill of health, it's vaccination time. These are less fun, and it's at this point that your dog may decide their vet is their new archenemy. Nevertheless, these vaccinations are incredibly important and can mean the difference between life and death in puppies.

What are They For?

Vaccinations are split into two categories. Mandatory and optional. Mandatory vaccinations may vary from state to state, and optional vaccinations are recommended based on your lifestyle.

Mandatory Vaccinations

DHPP, often referred to as 5 in 1—This cocktail protects your dog against distemper, parvovirus, parainfluenza, and 2 types of hepatitis.

Rabies—As the name suggests, the rabies vaccine is used to protect your dog against the rabies virus. Rabies is always fatal unless your dog is vaccinated or receives immediate treatment after they have come into contact with another rabid animal.

Common Optional Vaccinations

Lyme – If you and your pup enjoy hiking and if you live in an area that has a high Lyme disease rate, your veterinarian will likely recommend this vaccination.

Bordetella – The Bordetella vaccination is a must-have for puppies but is less common as your dog ages. This vaccination protects against kennel cough and is typically a non-negotiable vaccination for puppy schools, daycares, and boarding facilities.

Leptospirosis - This vaccination protects your dog against Leptospirosis bacteria, which is spread through urine and feces. While it isn't mandatory, your vet will recommend it if your dog is in frequent contact with wildlife and other dogs.

How Often Does My Dog Need To Endure This?

Your pup will receive four sets of vaccinations in the first year. The first is only given once your dog is fully weaned and 6–8 weeks old. Thereafter, they will be vaccinated at 10–12 weeks, 14–16 weeks, and 1 year of age. This is to build up enough immunity to effectively fight the potential illnesses. Once these vaccinations are complete, they will need to receive booster shots to maintain that immunity. These boosters are given every 1–2 years, depending on your lifestyle and your veterinarian's suggestion.

Getting Your Puppy Used to the Vet

Nobody likes going to the doctor, and we at least understand what they are telling us and doing to us. Imagine being a dog that suddenly lands up in a strange place with strange people that seem to smile at them yet proceed to violate them with thermometers!

To get them comfortable going to the vet, you should get them comfortable with getting in the car first. If they only get into the car to go to the vet, they will do the math and realize that a car ride is a one-way ticket to Injectionville. Take your puppy for regular car rides and get them used to stopping at random enjoyable places like a family or friend's house or a dog park.

When you get to the veterinarian's office, keep rewarding them for any good behavior. If they walk through the door nicely, treat. If they sit well in the waiting room, treat!

The moment you walk into the consulting room, your veterinarian will do the same thing to create a happy association with your dog. Reassuring your dog and rewarding them through procedures is vital, and it's important to leave on a happy note so that they are not scared to go back. I am a big sucker, and after every vet visit, my dog walks out with a new toy.

When Should I Panic?

Every little sneeze or stumble can send you into a panic when you get your first puppy. I remember staying up and watching my little one breathe. Counting how many seconds between each breath and spiraling into dismay if it varied too much. It was a little crazy, but that's love for you!

The good news is while your puppy's immune system isn't quite up to scratch just yet, it is actually pretty easy to keep them alive.

Creepy Crawlies

Ugh, these are gross. If your pup spends a lot of time outdoors or has frequent contact with other dogs, it is likely that they are going to pick up some parasites.

Worms

Worms are usually picked up from contaminated soil, rotten foods, and feces; as we all know, and if you don't, get prepared! Dogs love eating cat poop and in fact, rolling in any poop that didn't come from another dog. It is absolutely disgusting and often makes us question why on earth we decided to adopt such foul beasts. Yet, we still bathe them off while holding our noses and trying not to throw up.

This kind of behavior makes it easy for the nasty little worms to infect them. The most common worms include hookworm, roundworm, heartworm, tapeworm, and whipworm. The first sign of a worm invasion is an increase in appetite and scooting. Scooting is when your pup places their butt on the floor and drags themselves along it to cure the itch. Carpets seem to be the favorite scooting arena, with the white ones being first prize. If left untreated, your pup will start to lose weight and develop diarrhea, and you may find blood or worms in their poop.

Thankfully, this is easily treatable and preventable. Doggy dewormers are a must, and it's recommended that they are given every three months to prevent infection.

Ticks, Fleas, and Mites

Fleas are extremely itchy and irritating, and you will find your dog scratching themselves uncontrollably. You may even see the fleas jumping off your dog's skin. These are not really life-threatening, but that doesn't mean that you shouldn't treat your dog for them immediately. They can infest your house, and if your dog continuously scratches, they can create wounds.

Honestly, there's not much that can freak me out as much as a disgusting fat tick. These sneaky little bugs that burrow into your dog's skin. These are a little more difficult to see, especially in long-haired dogs, but regular brushing and strokes will help you to check for them. If you find a tick, you will need to pull it off and pop it (eww!) immediately. One or two ticks are generally not a problem but depending on where you live, some ticks carry Lyme disease. You will need to monitor your dog carefully for any symptoms and check yourself for any ticks.

If you notice that your dog is constantly itchy, yet there are no signs of fleas, they probably have mites. These are microscopic and, if left untreated, can cause mange, which is highly infectious and contagious to other animals. If you take your dog for hikes or regular walks through forests and tall grass, it's best to medicate them throughout the year.

Chewable parasite medications are available, and these will kill off any ticks, fleas, and mites and prevent them from attaching to your dog. These last one to three months, depending on the brand you purchase. Some of them contain a dewormer, making it easy to treat your dog for everything all in one go.

Kennel Cough and Sniffles

Bordetella, or kennel cough, is a nasty and incredibly contagious virus. It's called kennel cough because it is one of the most commonly spread viruses in boarding and rescue facilities. The most common symptom is a cough or hack. It becomes more severe when your dog exercises. In healthy adult dogs, this cough is usually nothing more than an irritation that goes away with a few days of rest.

However, in young or senior dogs that are immunocompromised, it can cause some serious damage to the heart and lungs. If your puppy is coughing while resting, you will need to isolate them from any other pets in the household. It's best to take them to the vet for treatment, as you don't want to risk it turning into pneumonia.

Belly Aches

Be prepared to deal with quite a few stomach issues. Puppies aren't the smartest when it comes to eating weird things, and it can take them a while to figure out what is good and what is bad.

Diarrhea

Diarrhea is usually caused by eating food that doesn't quite agree with their stomach, but it could also indicate that your pup has worms and, in severe cases, parvovirus. Parvovirus is deadly, and it is mandatory to vaccinate your dog against it. It is highly contagious and spreads quickly. If you notice worms, blood, or slime in their poo, it's time to panic.

Vomiting

Vomiting is often due to overeating or, again, eating things they shouldn't. My pup once threw up the pieces of an entire Tupperware lid. Why would he eat that? I have no clue, but he is a dog, and that's what dogs do! It's best to check if there are any foreign objects or blood in the vomit and contact your vet if you are worried they have eaten something toxic.

Constipation

It is a bit more difficult to find the cause of constipation. Overeating can cause it, as their little bodies aren't able to process huge amounts of food in one go or even in one day. Blockages from eating weird objects are also a possibility. If you suspect this, you need to get emergency assistance, as it could become life-threatening. The other possibility is that your puppy is simply holding it in too long. You need to give them regular potty breaks and keep up the exercise.

For all stomach upsets, it's best to stop feeding them for 12 to 24 hours. Give them electrolytes and probiotics, which will help keep them hydrated and restore the healthy bacteria in their stomach. The rule of thumb is if it happens once or twice, you don't need to worry. However, if it continues over 24 hours, it is time to panic!

Puppies Sure Do Love Mud

Oh boy; they do indeed. I am yet to see a puppy that can resist rolling in sand, mud, or worse. This is not only fun for them, but it is also a way for them to groom themselves and scratch that itch they can't reach. It's just unfortunate for us, as we aren't too keen on muddy paws on the clean floor or a wet, dirty body sleeping on the couch.

What You Need

First things first. You will need to get equipped. Nail clippers are the most common and easiest tool to use for nail grooming. However, nail grinders are a good choice for large dogs with extremely thick nails.

Buy a good sensitive skin, natural shampoo. Regardless of whether your puppy suffers from a condition or not. They will inevitably drink the water they are bathing in and lick themselves dry. You really don't want them to be ingesting chemicals!

A good brush, depending on your dog's hair type, and I suggest you get a water brush as well to use during bath time. If you have a breed that is going to need regular haircuts, you can look into buying pet clippers. These are expensive, though, and you may want to stick with the groomers for now.

A doggy toothbrush and natural dog toothpaste are a must. This may not seem important now, but you will regret not doing it when your dog enters their senior years and has to get a number of their teeth extracted.

Scrub a Dub Dub

Give your dog a good brushing before you get to the bath. This will untangle any knots, remove the excess fur and loosen up any dirt on their skin or hair. Using lukewarm water, fill your bathtub or dish tub up to around your dog's knees. You want them to be able to comfortably sit down and not feel the need to swim.

Lather them up with a natural puppy shampoo and use your water brush to really get under their fur. Make sure that you wash their bellies and armpits well. Once you're done, rinse them off thoroughly. Empty the dirty water and rinse your dog's legs off again to make sure there is no shampoo lingering. Don't wash their faces unless you are using a tear-free puppy shampoo, and even then, be careful. You want to avoid getting water or shampoo in their ears, eyes, mouth, and nose. Once the bath is done, dry them off. It's best to get your dog used to a hair dryer early, especially if they will be going to the groomers, where it will be used regularly. Put it on the lowest setting and on the lowest heat so that it is not too overpowering. Again, avoid their faces.

Whether you use a towel or a hair dryer, it's good to ensure that their bellies and armpits are completely dry. This is where your puppy stores its heat, and if that area is wet and cold, you are putting them at risk. Their bodies should be dry enough that when they do give a little shake, no water sprays you.

Let's See That Pretty Face

Once their bath is complete, use a damp, warm cotton cloth or similar and wipe their faces clean. You will need to do this a few times to ensure that you actually get all the dirt off. You can gently clean their eyes with a cotton pad if that is easier. For their ears, dab a cotton pad into baby oil and gently clean around the underside of the ear. You don't want to go too deep, and you don't want any oil going into the ear canal, as this can cause infection.

A good bath and face cleaning should be done around twice a month. If you have a pigsty puppy, then move it up to weekly. Bathing is not natural for them, and their skin secretes special oils which keep their fur waterproof. Bathing them too often can damage the skin and reduce the oil production, leading to dermatitis. This is another reason why buying a natural shampoo is best, as there are no harsh chemicals to damage their skin and glands.

Lastly, it's time to brush their teeth. Be gentle, and don't force your pup into it. You want this to be a fun experience, and you should reward them during each step. First, just place the toothbrush near their mouths. If they aren't worried, reward them. Then you can put it into their mouths. Reward them if they are good. You can then brush the front teeth and work your way to the back. Go in gentle, circular motions and make each session as short as possible. You probably won't be able to get in and brush their teeth completely on the first try, and that's cool. You have time. I like to brush my dog's teeth every second day for just a few minutes at a time.

Mani-Pedi

This is likely the hardest grooming step to get your dog used to. Ever try to hold down an Irish wolfhound for a nail clipping? That's not the kind of nightmare you want to deal with later in life!

Hold your puppy still in a sitting position. Lift their front paw up and backward so that it is comfortable, then reward them when they sit still. Put the clippers over the nail and reward them when they are calm.

Next, clip the nail. This is when your pooch is going to get a fright. That noise is quite intense and unexpected. Give them a break and a ton of treats, and then repeat the steps above.

It's unlikely that you will need to clip your dog's nails when they are a puppy. Running on hard surfaces and asphalt will file the nails down naturally. Even so, it's best to practice getting your puppy in that position and the sound of the clippers, even if you don't actually cut a nail. You will need to get them into a standing position to work on the hind nails. However, if you are just practicing, work on getting the position for the front paws perfected first.

A full grooming session may be a bit too much for a young puppy to sit through. Try to split up the steps throughout the month.

Chapter 5:

Relationships Are Built on Treats

Is puppy-specific food really worth it? Yes, yes, it is. Dogs, just like people, have specific dietary requirements that need to be met as they go through each life stage. Think of it this way, feeding a baby a cheeseburger is probably not the best way to facilitate healthy growth. Luckily, some brilliant people out there have made our jobs easy and formulated specialized diets that keep our dogs healthy during each of these stages.

For the first year or two, your puppy is growing. Rapidly! They also expend a huge amount of energy, which means they require some pretty vital nutrients and proteins to facilitate this. Once they are fully grown, they will need to be fed a diet that can maintain their bodies' health while still providing them with enough energy for moderate exercise.

Once they hit their senior years, they are unlikely to be less active, and a lot of the ingredients in puppy and adult food can lead to some serious weight gain. Senior dogs will develop a number of age-related medical conditions, and a senior diet will contain vitamins and minerals that will ease these aches and pains.

Let's Get Chewing

As daunting as the dog food aisle may be; you only need to risk it once or, to be fair, once for each life stage. For the first year or two of your dog's life, you will need high-quality puppy food. Thereafter, you can move on to an adult diet and swap to a senior one when your dog hits seven years. I, personally, like to use the same brand throughout my pup's life because why fix something that isn't broken? Constantly swapping brands will mess with your dog's digestive system, and you can expect some nasty results.

Vital Ingredients

Let's not jump down the rabbit hole of dog nutrition. This is a complicated science that is best left up to the professionals. All we need to know is the most important ingredients to look for.

Protein content and amino acids are arguably the most important ingredients to look for when choosing food. According to Dr. Ochoa, puppies require a 22-32% protein content. To put this in perspective, adult dog food has an average of 18% (Lauren, 2022). This, along with a higher amount of calcium and phosphorus, is required to build and support healthy bones and muscles.

While adult and senior foods try to stick to a lower fat and carbohydrate content, puppy food should be loaded with it. This is because puppies expend an abnormal amount of energy. I swear, they can actually walk up walls when they get excited enough. Dr. Williams and Dr. Downing found that a diet with 10-20% fat content and 20%

or more carbohydrate content is recommended to meet your puppy's needs (Williams & Downing, n.d.).

Size and Breed Matters

The majority of dog food brands will sell their kibble in three different sizes, small, medium, or large, to better suit your breed. If you have a mini breed, it's probably best not to give them kibble the size of their paws, as these can damage their teeth.

If you have a highly specialized breed, you should purchase breed-specific food. These are specially formulated for your dog and contain minerals, vitamins, and ingredients that are best suited to the breed.

Most breed-specific foods cater to small and mini dogs such as Pomeranians, pugs, and Yorkshire terriers. However, you can now purchase food designed for Labradors, Great Danes, and German shepherds, which specifically supports bone growth and joint health.

If you are unsure what to buy your pup, ask your vet or your breeder. They will be able to recommend some good ones.

Kibbles and Cans

Dry food is the most popular option for pet owners. It is easy to store, doesn't go bad quickly, and it's a breeze to measure out and feed in the morning. They contain all the protein, minerals, and fat that your pup needs to grow and remain healthy. Dry food is also great for your dog's teeth, and each time your pup chews, the rough pieces will dislodge any plaque that may have built up. However, this food can become a bit boring, and it is always nice to switch things up a little.

Canned food is definitely tastier, and if given the chance, your dog will choose it every time. The soft chunks and gravies are fantastic for easy eating and digestion, making it a great option for dogs recovering from illness or injury. If you intend to feed your dog canned food, you will need to brush their teeth more regularly to keep them clean.

While canned foods can be just as healthy as dry foods, it's important to do your research before you commit to them full-time. The cheaper canned foods work well as a treat or to use on top of dry food as a gravy, but they are full of fats and carbohydrates. Feeding your pup these cans cause several stomach issues and turn them into furry barrels of fat.

Vet-approved canned foods are a much better option, although quite a bit pricier. They are formulated for full-time use and contain the necessary ingredients your dog needs to thrive.

How Much Is Too Much?

Each bag of food will come with a recommended feeding chart. This chart will tell you how many ounces your puppy should be fed each day depending on their current weight. More expensive and specialized foods will have three columns and will recommend how much food your puppy should get based on their activity level.

A low-energy puppy that wouldn't be able to burn off the food as quickly may get 5 ounces a day, while a high-energy puppy will get 7 ounces a day. The amount per day should then be split up equally into the number of feeds you give them.

These measurements are incredibly important, especially during their growing years. They are especially vital for large and giant breeds that are prone to hip dysplasia, as it ensures they grow at a normal pace.

This also means that you are going to need to get a scale. Don't worry, you don't have to weigh your pup every day, but I do suggest you do it once a week so that you can increase their food regularly. Once their weight begins to stabilize, you should weigh them every one to three months.

Supplements

If you are feeding your pooch high-quality puppy food, you probably won't need to give them any supplements at all. That being said, there are some nice ones that are worth having on hand for when they are feeling a little under the weather.

A good stock of probiotics is in order. This powdered supplement can be sprinkled over food or mixed into water. It helps to keep your pup's stomach working correctly and is especially useful if they are recovering from an illness or injury. If you have a dumpster-diving puppy, you may want to use these more regularly.

Mobility supplements that contain glucosamine and antioxidants are a great supplement for large and giant breeds that are prone to hip dysplasia and arthritis. The glucosamine will help keep their joints healthy and in good working order, while the antioxidants will keep inflammation and swelling down. It's best to use these supplements throughout your dog's life to get the best results.

Omega oil supplements promote healthy skin and fur. This is a wonderful supplement to give to puppies that suffer from skin conditions, ticks, and fleas.

Immune system and antioxidant supporters should be used for puppies that are recovering from any medical issues. These boost the immune system and work at easing any inflammation and pain.

All puppy foods are rich in calcium, but occasionally, your vet may recommend that you give them an additional supplement. This is usually the case for very young puppies that are still being bottle-fed or for puppies that have had any issues with their bone growth.

You can never go wrong with a good multivitamin! These promote overall good health and can be used throughout your dog's life.

You can buy gummy or chewy health supplements, although they may be a bit more expensive. It is worth it, though, especially if you have a pup that can smell medication from a mile away.

Be careful not to mix too many supplements together, as they can have negative effects.

Treats

I wasn't kidding when I said relationships are based on treats. Whether you're training your dog, you want their attention, or you just want to buy their love, give them a treat. However, a treat should be used as a treat. Continuously giving your pup treats will take away their significance, and your dog is unlikely to be as excited or motivated when they get one. Never mind the weight they will gain!

Make sure that you don't let them manipulate you with their big puppy eyes for more. However, let's be honest here, who can actually resist them? For this reason, it's a good idea to invest in a variety of treats.

Training Treats

During training, you will be giving your dog plenty of treats. Seriously, you will be going through them like tic tacs. When choosing your training treats, you will need to find ones low in fat and sugar. Dogs prefer quantity over quality during training, so try to get the smallest ones available.

I personally like to have two or three types of flavors on hand during training. I switch to a different treat type when I notice that my dog is getting bored or when they do something superb and deserve a big reward.

Tasty Treats

Sometimes dogs deserve treats for no other reason than existing. This kind of sweet reward is great to build up your relationship and keep them busy. These need to be high-quality, absolutely irresistible treats. Large, chewable treats or peanut butter is a great way to keep your dog stimulated during their downtime. I won't lie; I like to use low-fat peanut butter because it ends up entertaining both of us. That chewing face is just too funny. If you just want to build up your relationship, smaller treats work well as you can give more of them.

Dental Treats

These are my favorite. They are large chewy treats that contain several natural ingredients that help clean your dog's teeth. They are made in such a way that your dog will have to chew on them for a good few minutes to get through. Keeping them entertained at the same time.

Liver Bread

If you are worried about what goes into store-bought treats, I have the solution for you. You can make your own! Liver bread is pretty disgusting, and I can't imagine eating it myself, but dogs go absolutely mad for it. It's easy to make, and you can bake large batches at a time and freeze them for later use.

Ingredients

1. 500g Raw liver

2. 3 Eggs

3. 1 Cup flour

4. 1 ⅓ Cup whole-wheat flour

5. 1 Teaspoon baking powder

6. Onion, beef, or chicken seasoning or stock cubes (optional)

7. Grated raw butternut, baby marrow, broccoli, or pumpkin (optional)

Method

1. Blend the eggs and raw liver together

2. Mix the blended mixture with the dry ingredients

3. Add in vegetables and seasoning

4. Place mixture into a large flat baking tray

5. Bake at 356° F for 15 minutes

6. Allow to cool and cut into squares

7. Bribe your dog into doing whatever you want them to do!

If you are worried about any of the ingredients, swap them out! If you are worried about the flour, you can change to a gluten-free or rice flour option.

Mom Says Chocolate Isn't Good for Dogs

Ever dealt with the consequences of a dog stealing some cake? Trust me. You never ever want to. It involves plenty of paper towels, boiling water, and an air freshener. It's not just chocolate, either. Dogs LOVE food and will take a slice of anything that is left out.

Absolute No, No's	Toxic but Not Deadly in Small Doses	Not Toxic but Certainly Not Good
Alcohol	Avocado	Milk and Dairy
Chocolate and Coffee	Citrus	Raw Meat
Grapes and Raisins	Coconut	Raw Eggs
Macadamia Nuts	Onions and Garlic	Yeast
Xylitol	Salty Food and Snacks	Uncooked Bones

These are just a few of the most harmful foods your dog may get into. In fact, there aren't actually many human foods that are safe for dogs to eat. While the first little bite won't harm them, continuous access can cause immense weight gain and upset stomachs.

Every time I hear an owner say, "Well, I give them the leftovers that have been in the fridge for a while, I would rather not waste food!" I could pull my own and their hair out. Your dog is not your trash can, and this can cause severe, sometimes fatal consequences.

Helpful Tools

Mealtime doesn't have to be a hassle, and there are several tools that make preparation and feeding quick, easy, and much more enjoyable.

Food and Water Bowls

Don't limit yourself to one of each. Otherwise, you will be constantly moving them around the house. I suggest buying a nice big water bowl for outdoors, a smaller one for their play area, and one to go with their food bowl. Stainless-steel dishes are your best bet. They are much more hygienic, durable, and can easily be washed in the dishwasher. But they can get hot in the sun, and dogs aren't particularly fond of tea, so make sure the water is in the shade.

When picking out a food bowl, make sure that you get something suitable for your dog's size. A large dog bowl is not going to work for small breeds, and they will spend half their time searching for their food. For giant breeds, I recommend that you get a bowl stand, which lifts the bowls off the floor and brings them closer to your dog's height. Constantly leaning down to eat can put pressure on your dog's neck and joints, which can be uncomfortable and potentially cause issues in their later years.

Food bowls should be cleaned after every meal, and water bowls should be rinsed and refilled at least once a day to reduce algae and bacteria buildup.

Slow Feeders

If your dog is a glutton, it's time to get a slow feeder. Puppies that suck up their food like vacuum cleaners can become bloated and, in some cases, throw up their food. They are less likely to actually chew their kibble, which can cause constipation.

These bowls have bumps and ridges inside of them, which makes your pup work a little harder for their food, and it gives their stomach time to register that it is full. You can go one step further and buy an interactive feeding bowl. I love these as they make dinnertime fun.

Lick Mats

Lick mats are a super fun enrichment tool that is great for dogs of all ages. These silicon mats have various textures, which makes it difficult to lick the food off. It also just feels great to lick them; you should try it sometime. Layering soft canned foods and treats such as peanut butter on them is sure to keep your dog entertained for a while.

Scale, Measuring Scoops, and Cups

Depending on the dog food you buy, you may get a measuring cup. These have gram or ounce measurements on the side, which help you to easily measure out your dog's food. Just remember that these cups are food-specific. Larger or smaller kibble of another brand will weigh more or less than the cup indicates. I prefer to weigh my food in a transparent cup on a scale. When I have the right amount, I mark it with a line and my dog's name. Since I have a multi-dog household, I use the same cup and mark off each dog's food amount. This makes dishing up meals so much easier!

Food Bin

Many brands have started fitting their dog foods with reusable seals to keep the food fresh between uses. I don't really trust these, and I find that they constantly snap open by themselves, and large bags of food for big breeds don't have them equipped. An airtight food bin is best. It stops spilling unwanted creepy crawlies, and honestly, it just looks better. My neat freak brain is in love with the fact that I don't have to have the food bags sprawled around the kitchen. Instead, I have three food bins stacked next to each other, with my dog's bowls and measuring cups on top.

Chapter 6:

Smiles, Not Snarls!

Dogs are (mostly) highly social creatures and have never quite shaken off the pack mentally of their ancestors. Even though you have now become a part of their pack family, it's not quite the same as having another furry friend who doesn't mind being chased around and jumped on. Puppies are still getting used to not having their littermates around, and the lack of constant canine attention makes them extra eager to make new friends and enjoy some dog-on-dog playtime.

Sometimes, a little too eager. While you would think it would be easy to socialize a puppy, you need to consider your dog's social intelligence and the personality of their new playmate. Puppies that are taken away from their mom and littermates too early don't quite learn how to speak dog and can be overly clinging, which annoys their playmates. Especially older dogs that don't have much patience. Because of this, it's important to learn how to safely introduce your bundle of joy to other dogs and keep them from having negative experiences that may cause fear and aggression later in life.

Learning to Speak Dog

So, you have already learned a little bit about puppy body language and how they communicate with us. Now it is time to learn a bit more about how they communicate with each other. These signs and signals are vital during socialization attempts, as they will allow you to avoid potentially dangerous situations and fights.

Positive Body Language

Positive body language indicates that your pup is relaxed, happy, or excited. Their entire demeanor should look loose. Muscles relaxed, ears flopping around, and their tail should be hanging or wagging in long slow movements.

When excited, that tail speeds up, and their whole body begins to wag with it. They may even seem like they have a smile on their face! If they are bouncing from wall to wall and bowing down with their butts in the air, they are feeling extra playful.

A relaxed puppy stays loose but is happy to relax on a bed or in the sun. They are still confident in themselves and will hold their heads high when they aren't lying down. Their ears may perk up now and again if something interesting happens around them, but they aren't too worried about getting involved.

Negative Body Language

Negative body language indicates that your puppy is either scared, aggressive, or overly dominant. Their bodies are noticeably tense, and you can see their muscles through the fur. Aggressive and dominant dogs will stand tall and still with their ears erect. Their tails will stand upright and sometimes wag in rapid, short motions, which indicates arousal. You will notice that they are fixated on a target and won't take their eyes off it unless you drag them away.

Depending on the situation, they may start to produce a low growl and bend down slightly as if to stalk prey.

A scared dog, on the other hand, will try to make itself as small as possible so that it is less of a target. They will hold their tail between their legs and cower. Their ears will be flat against their head, and they try their best to avoid eye contact with whatever is terrifying them. If the situation becomes too intense, they may whimper or cry out before running away.

Excitable behavior can often turn into dominant behavior quickly if you aren't monitoring them. The more hyped up they get, the more boisterous the play becomes, and in due time, somebody is going to become frustrated and nip. The adrenaline coursing through their veins from the excitement can turn to dominance or aggression.

If your puppies are roughhousing and getting a little too excitable, call them back to you and give them a second to refocus and relax before letting them play again.

Socialization Goals

First, figure out what your actual socialization goals are, and train your dog according to them. Going too far in your training can cause you and your pup unnecessary stress. Remember, puppies are just as good at forgetting as they are learning. So, whatever your goal is, you will need to stay consistent.

Introverts and Extroverts

Some dogs are the ultimate extroverts. They will bound up to any stranger or dog and give them a big sloppy kiss hello. They just love attention and snuggles! This behavior is fantastic and will give you a head start in training. However, that doesn't mean that no training is required. Such behavior can be viewed as bad manners, and if you don't teach your dog recall, you are in for trouble. Not everyone wants to be greeted that way, especially reactive or nervous dogs. Children especially can be knocked over like bowling pins if your dog is on the larger side.

On the other hand, you get introverts. These aren't as rare as you may think. No matter how much you try to socialize them, they simply aren't interested in the company of others and prefer to keep you all to themselves. This is okay. The important thing is to ensure that you train them well enough to not fear or react negatively during social situations.

Family Comes First

A family-friendly dog is easy enough to raise, especially if you already have a partner and children. Children that treat a dog well will be treated back with respect. If your dog is less friendly to your child, you should investigate the situation further, as they may be making some serious pet care mistakes.

If you do not have children but plan to one day, or if you plan to take your pup with you to family events, you will need to get your dog used to being played with. Believe it or not, some dogs are petrified of children. Who can blame them? They terrify me, too, sometimes. Dogs can't quite understand why they are so small yet so loud. They almost seem to be the same as them, but they have no tails or fur. It can be difficult for them to adjust to that kind of attention.

In this case, the only option is to have regular little visitors so that your pup can get a chance to interact with them and learn their ways. Be sure to reward them for good behavior and remove them or the child from the situation if your pup becomes a little too hyped up. It's best to give them both a short rest to calm down.

A Confident Walker

This is a non-negotiable goal, especially if you are planning to walk your dog. A confident and happy dog will be able to casually walk down the street with you with no fuss at all. Even if they are not quite a social butterfly, you don't want them to react negatively to any strangers or strange dogs. It can become pretty embarrassing when you walk out the gate only for them to bark at the neighbors and passing cars.

What Could Go Wrong?

Safety is a priority. This goes for you, your dog, and those around them. If you find that your dog is becoming more reactive with every walk, it's time to put a halt to the whole operation and go back to the basics. An aggressive encounter is the quickest way to create a reactive and fearful puppy. It can be difficult to bring them back from this point, but there are some foolproof solutions if you are consistent enough in your training.

No dog is inherently aggressive, and they don't take pleasure in the act. When your dog reaches their threshold, they have two options. Fight or flight. If they can't flee, they are going to try their hardest to scare the living daylights out of whatever is triggering them.

Working through this fear before you get back to walking is vital. If this is something that you are struggling with, don't worry. I will be covering the solution in Chapter 10.

Puppy Illness

Puppy daycares, regular walks, and any interactions which involve other dogs can invite some unwanted illnesses. This is why vaccinations exist! Even if the dogs around you are not protected from these illnesses, you can ensure that yours is. Illness is not the only thing to worry about. If your pup enjoys sniffing poop or other dogs' butts, they can become vulnerable to parasitic infections. Again, this can be controlled, and as a responsible pet owner, you should be taking all the preventive steps you can.

Say Hello to My Little Friend

Introducing your puppy to humans is effortless. Your pup is open to new and exciting things, and they have already figured out that you were worth the effort; why not everyone else?!

The only problem with human introductions is the humans. You will need to be confident and speak for your puppy before somebody else gets to touch him. Let them know what they are allowed and not allowed to do. Immediately picking them up and swinging them around is a definite no, no. Roughhousing and play fighting with them is a no, no! Children, especially, struggle to understand how to meet a dog, and many will go straight in for a tackle or a shout.

Any over-excitable or potentially scary experience like this can affect your dog in the long term. They can develop associations of fear with the person who scared or hurt them, and this not only affects that relationship but many others.

You may find that they suddenly have an issue with meeting men, people with blonde hair, or people that wear hats. It seems strange at first until you remember that a man with blonde hair that was wearing a hat gave them a smack when they were younger.

Calm and collected introductions are the only way forward. Allow the stranger to kneel to their level, pat them gently and speak to them in a calming voice. Add in a few treats for luck, and your pup will have a new best friend in no time.

Dog Introductions

Very young puppies don't seem to have any issue meeting and making new friends. They are still in littermate mode and will readily jump on the first fluff ball they find. However, your puppy is going through their learning phases, and it's difficult to socialize them when they go through their cautious, fearful stage. Try to get them used to new puppies before this, as it will allow them to learn good doggy etiquette.

Important Considerations

It might not be the best option to introduce a tiny toy puppy to a larger, boisterous one. Large dogs don't really know their size, and as puppies, they are clumsy and playful and may just trample your pooch into the ground like a tent peg. It is not impossible to introduce them; you will just need to monitor them carefully.

Age gaps and temperaments also need to be considered. While most adult dogs are more accepting of a puppy over another adult, puppies can be quite annoying. If the dog you are introducing them to has a short fuse, your pup may end up having a bad experience. Do not introduce your puppy to a known reactive dog at this point!

Puppy Parties

Dog parks can be incredibly overwhelming for an under-socialized puppy, and you will need to proceed with caution if you notice that they feel uncomfortable. Imagine throwing an introvert on stage in front of hundreds of people! The standard response is panic, babbling, and then sprinting away. That's precisely what your pooch will do, although the babble may turn into a bite. Only go to the dog park when you are sure they are ready.

Obedience school is a fantastic way for them to socialize, as all the pups in the class will be focused on their owners and training. This breaks the ice a little, as they can become comfortable in each other's presence before meeting properly. However, obedience school is open to a lot of less knowledgeable pet owners, and you will need to stand your ground if they cross boundaries. Some owners may find it perfectly acceptable to let their dog run off leash and straight into your dog's mouth!

Puppy daycare is another great way to socialize your puppy. It's best to start them off at a young age and ensure that the daycare only has dogs that are of similar age. The best part of using a daycare is the staff. They are trained in caring for dogs and are always available to monitor the puppy party.

The Right Way to Introduce

As your pup gets older, you will need to take some extra steps when introducing them to a new friend. You should ALWAYS introduce dogs on mutual ground. Using one dog's territory will automatically create a bit of tension, which you don't want. Set up a puppy play date with a friend and organize to meet them at a park or a quiet lot.

1. Stand a couple of meters away from each other. Far enough that your dogs can't approach each other but close enough that they can see and smell each other.

2. Keep your dog's focus on you by playing a game or practicing some tricks.

3. Once they are calm, you can begin clicking and treating them every time they look over at the other dog. This will create a positive association with the other dog. Be careful not to reward them if they are displaying any negative behaviors.

4. Start to walk a bit closer and chat with your friend. Your confident, calm and happy state will become contagious, and your pup will be more intrigued than worried.

5. Keep rewarding them whenever they are relaxed or sitting obediently.

6. Once you're close enough, allow the two dogs to give each other a good sniff and then walk away. Don't let this interaction go over two to three minutes.

7. Distract your dog again by playing some fun games!

8. Repeat the steps until your dogs are comfortable with each other.

9. If you notice that either of them are becoming distressed by the situation, call it quits for the day and try again another time.

If your dog doesn't like another dog, it doesn't mean that they are unfriendly or aggressive. Just like us, they have preferences, and it's not their fault if they don't find the other dog funny or smart.

Chapter 7:

Training A, B, C's

A is for apple, b is for BALL!, c is for CAT!, and d is for DOOR! Thankfully, your dog doesn't need to learn the alphabet except for a few of the most important words. One of which starts with a T! Treat is probably the most dangerous word your dog could ever learn. Once they make the association, there is no stopping them from doing what it takes to get the reward. While this is remarkable in training sessions, it's less so when you are on the phone with a friend and find yourself saying. "Let's go out tonight, it's my t-r-e-a-t." It's easier to spell it out than deal with the fallout of your dog's tantrum.

Okay, enough jokes. Let's get serious. Puppies do need training, and the behaviors you will be teaching them are a lot more than neat little "tricks." These are foundational commands that are used to teach your dog basic manners. Without them, you won't be able to untrain negative behaviors such as jumping or proceeding to more advanced training. There are tons of ways to train a dog, but there are only a few ways to get the training to actually stick. Let's get to it...

Pawsitive Parenting

Positive reinforcement is the most popular method of training, and most trainers and behaviorists will recommend it over others. It forms one part of the four quadrants of training, and you will need to have a good understanding of each to make the right calls. Learning each section can be a little tricky at first; the names, in particular, can make things confusing.

The Four Quadrants

In this context, positive refers to adding or including a stimulus or item. Negative refers to subtracting a stimulus or item. Reinforcement refers to motivating your dog to keep displaying the behavior, while punishment refers to stopping your dog from displaying a behavior.

Positive Reinforcement

Positive reinforcement is easy. This involves rewarding your dog with a stimulus when they display a positive behavior. By rewarding this kind of behavior, your dog is more likely to repeat it, as they have developed a positive association with it.

Example: Giving your dog a treat when they walk calmly next to you.

Negative Reinforcement

By removing an item or stimulus, you can increase your chances of your dog displaying a behavior. Confused yet? Let's put it in a more understandable example.

Your dog likes to pull on the leash, so you decide to put a choke collar (stimulus) on him. When he pulls, he gets choked, but when he stops pulling, he is rewarded (stimulus removed) by not being in pain or discomfort. This makes it more likely for him to walk without pulling.

Positive Punishment

Positive punishment involves adding in a stimulus to stop your dog from displaying a behavior. The added stimulus is generally something painful or scary. Sadly, too many of us use this method when we are frustrated.

Example: You tug back forcefully when your dog pulls on the leash. Others include hitting them when they bark or shouting at them when they chew on something.

Negative Punishment

This involves subtracting a stimulus or reward to stop your dog from displaying a behavior.

Example: Your dog is pulling on the leash, so you stop walking. You have taken away the reward of them going for a walk. Once they display good behavior or stand calmly next to you, you reward them by continuing the walk.

Negative reinforcement and positive punishment are sadly still used in the training world, but it has become less common. While these methods may produce immediate results, they come with side effects, and most dogs that are trained through this are found to be more fearful, less obedient, and less likely to be interested in learning new things.

Positive reinforcement and negative punishment are, however, two methods that can and should be used throughout your training journey.

Clicker Training

During positive reinforcement training, the goal is to reward your dog at the exact moment they display good behavior. However, that is a little difficult if they are on the other side of the room. By delaying giving them the treat, your dog may be unsure of which behavior they are actually being rewarded for. Was it for sitting? Standing up? Or walking toward you? This is where bridging or marking comes in.

It's pretty simple. The dog does something good, you bridge (confirm) the behavior, and then you treat them. Bridging is usually vocal, and the word "good!" is commonly used.

Clicker training makes this much easier. The small handheld device will make a clicking noise when you press it, and this noise is used to mark or bridge the exact moment that your dog displays a good behavior, which means you never miss a beat.

In order to use clicker training, you first need to get your dog used to the clicker and what it means. All you need to do is get their attention, click, and then treat them. Continue doing this until they associate the click with a treat, but make sure they are focusing on you when you click so that you don't accidentally reward a different behavior.

Training Tools

You don't really need much more than a bag of healthy treats to begin training your pup. However, if you would like to go a step further, there are some helpful tools that make your experience easier.

Rewards

Rewards shouldn't just be treats. These may seem like the most obvious and tastiest option, but some dogs actually prefer to receive a toy as a reward! Incorporating a toy into your routine will also help stop your dog from putting on all those extra calories. A tug rope or fluffy toy is usually the best for training as these are interactive and keep their focus on you.

Treat Bag

Scratch what I said earlier. A treat bag is an absolute necessity. There is nothing worse than having loose, damp treats falling out of your pocket or having your dog tackle you down for the bundle you are trying to hold in your hand. A treat bag is waterproof, clips onto your belt or purse, and has a drawstring that makes it easy to open or close.

Yoga Mat

I like to use a yoga mat during training, especially if I am teaching my dog behaviors that require them to sit or lay on the floor. Hardwood floors, tiles, asphalt, and concrete are all very uncomfortable and can hurt your pup's paws and elbows if you ask them to lean on them too long.

Patience

The most important tool in your arsenal. Take a couple of deep breaths and get yourself into the right mindset before you start training. Don't bring bad energy into a happy space. If you feel frustrated, scrap the training for the day.

Thinking Caps On!

This is probably one of the cutest parts of owning a puppy. Seeing that tail wag and their minds working overtime to figure out what you want from them. They are trying so hard, and when that little lightbulb goes off and they succeed, their joy could just make you cry. Your happiness and excitement are contagious, and if you treat their success like a big deal, they will too.

You want to constantly make training a fun and exciting experience. If your pup gets tired or bored, stop it there and give them a break. If they struggle to master a new behavior, they switch back to an old one they have already mastered to build their confidence up. Set them up to succeed by training them in a quiet space with no distractions. The moment their minds wander, your training becomes ten times more difficult.

Below are the six most important behaviors that every pup should master!

Sit

The absolute bare minimum behavior that your dog should know. It's generally used as a calming and refocus cue. If your pup's butt is on the floor, they can't jump on you! If they are sitting, they are more likely to focus their full attention on you. Until your dog knows how to sit on cue, you cannot advance to training new behaviors.

1. Get their focus on you calling their name. Show them the treat and then give it to them when you have their attention.

2. Pull out another treat and slowly move it toward their face and then up above their heads, just out of their reach. Say "Sit" as you get the treat into position. If you do this too quickly, they will jump for it.

3. They will need to tilt their heads further and further back to keep the treat in view. This action will automatically require them to sit down. Repeat the word "Sit."

4. The moment that fluffy butt hits the floor, click and treat!

5. Repeat this method a few times until you can stand up straight and get them sitting without having to move your hand.

Bow

This is a simple, fun, cute trick that is relatively easy to train. I like to start off training these playful, easy behaviors first as it gets your puppy comfortable obeying your commands, and they end up with a deeper understanding of training in general. Which greatly helps when it comes to the more difficult things.

1. Get them to focus on you while they are standing up. Click and treat.

2. Touch your treat to their nose and then move it down between their legs, sliding it toward their belly. Say the word "Bow."

3. As soon as they start bowing to get the treat, click, treat, and get them moving. You don't want them to sit or lay down, as it defeats the purpose of training.

4. Keep repeating these steps until you are confident enough to remove the luring aspect. Once you can place the treat directly on the floor and use the cue "Bow," you are all set!

5. If you find that they automatically sit down when you try to refocus them, take two steps backward so that they have to stand up and walk toward you. Then try again.

Down

This is an adorable behavior, and it is the start of teaching your pup to roll over and play dead. Yet, it actually plays a much more important role than being cute. It works well to calm down an anxious or excited dog, and it is a prerequisite for teaching them to "Go to bed" when they misbehave.

Teaching your pup this behavior can become a bit confusing if you have also taught them to bow. I suggest that you master your bow training first, as it can give you a head start in training down if used correctly.

1. Get them into a focused sitting position. Click and treat.

2. Take out a treat and touch it to their nose, move it down to the floor in a straight line until they're standing, bending down. Say the word "Down"

3. Slide the treat across the floor away from them so that they have to lie down to take it. Repeating the word "Down." If you move too quickly, they will likely stand up and try to walk to the treat. You need to master your speed to get it just right.

4. The moment that fluffy tummy hits the deck, click, and treat!

5. Get them back up into a sitting position and repeat the steps above until all you need to do is hold the treat to the floor.

Stay

This is a goodie and so very helpful. Asking your pup to "stay" is not just useful when you want to run into a not-dog-friendly shop during your walk. It can be used for day-to-day activities to stop negative behaviors. I use it during every mealtime.

The moment 4 p.m. hits, my dogs can be found standing by their food bin, waiting in anticipation. This excitement can sometimes get the better of them, and every now and then they may try to jump the line and stick their heads in the bowl before the food is on the floor. By telling them to sit and stay, I can calmly prepare their food without any trouble.

1. Get them into a focused sitting position. Click and treat.

2. Lift your hand up and place your palm out toward their face. Say "Stay" while slowly backing away from them.

3. Take two steps and wait five to ten seconds. Click and treat!

4. Repeat this step, but start taking more and more steps backward before bridging their behavior. See how handy that

clicker is becoming? Once bridged, walk back toward them to treat them.

5. If they start to get up and walk toward you, ask them to sit. Once they are sitting, click and reward them for obeying your cue. Start moving back again when you have their focus.

6. You want them to succeed. So, if you find that seven steps back is a bit too much for them to comprehend, stick to six. Once they get the hang of that, you can walk away further.

7. If you would like to incorporate some recall training, you can add the cue "Come!" For this, you will need to repeat the above steps, asking them to stay, walking backward, and using the clicker to bridge the behavior. The only difference is that this time, you are going to say "Come!" the second after you click. They should bound toward you, and you will need to reward them big time. Hugs, a ton of praise, a treat, and even a toy if you would like. This is a big moment, as that little baby genius has just mastered three different behaviors in one go!

Shake or Paw

Shake or Paw is a super easy trick to teach your dog. It's not one of the most important, but it is absolutely adorable! This trick goes against what you are trying to teach them with "leave it." Attempting to train the two at the same time is going to cause mass confusion, and your pup won't be able to learn either. Once you have mastered the one and don't need treats, then you can start the other.

1. Get them into a focused, sitting position. Click and treat.

2. Close a treat in your hand and place it in front of their face. Say "Paw or Shake." They are probably going to get messy now and try to lick and chew their way through your hand. You want them to be frustrated enough to hit you with their paw to get it out.

3. Once they lift their paw to your hand, quickly click and give them a treat from the treat bag. Do not give them your practice treat.

4. Repeat this a few times until they ditch the slobber and only give you their paw.

5. Now you are going to open your hand with no treat it. Tell them "Shake or Paw," and once they give you their paw, click, and treat.

6. Do this a few more times before adding in the shake, and you're done!

Leave It

This is a bit of a difficult one for an impulsive puppy to learn, and if you intend to teach them to shake as well, I suggest you start with that. You need your pup to be a bit more mature and well-versed in other commands to get this right.

Even though it is a little more difficult, it is well worth it, and you can quickly stop your dog from eating some questionable items. This training will become beneficial when you start teaching them to walk nicely!

1. Get them in a focused sitting position. Click and treat.

2. Close your hand around a treat, let your dog sniff it, and ask them to "Leave it." Now you can see where the conflict comes in when teaching them to shake. You will likely be getting quite a few paw hits before they figure it out.

3. Once they stop trying and choose to wait patiently. Click and give them a treat from the treat bag. Your practice treat shouldn't be used, as it gives them the impression they can still take the item you have asked them to leave, as long as they wait patiently for it.

4. Let's kick the difficulty up a bit by showing them the treat. Open your hand flat with the treat on your palm and say, "Leave it." You are going to need to be quick now, and if they try to take it, close your hand.

5. Once they wait patiently, click and treat!

6. Keep making it more difficult by adding space between the two of you. Put the treat on the floor and take a step back. If they come for the treat, cover it with your foot. When they wait, you guessed it, click and treat.

If your puppy is becoming frustrated, don't push them too hard. Stick to close contact until they master it and then move further away. Switch it up by adding a toy into the mix.

Chapter 8:

Little Legs, Long Walks

It doesn't matter whether you have adopted a 30-pound Olympian or a 4-pound ball of fluff; your pup is likely overflowing with energy. Who can blame them? Everything around them is so exciting and new! This energy can become a little overwhelming, and if not released, your pup will find other, more destructive ways to keep themselves entertained.

Regular walks and runs are a great way to release this energy while keeping your dog fit and healthy. This gives them an opportunity to explore and use all of their senses to take in the enormous amount of information floating in the air. Social interaction and play with other dogs are just an added bonus.

However, it is simply impossible to fit in enough walks in a day to release this energy and keep your dog's mind sharp. You will need to find another way to keep them entertained. This is especially important if you are at work during the day and they are left alone.

Toys, Toys, Toys!

There are so many different types of toys on the market. Thank goodness, because our dogs can be extremely picky when they want to. You may find that your dog is an avid chewer, a ball addict, or one that likes to snuggle up with a fluffy toy. It's best to buy a range of toys to test out, and once you know which ones your dog likes most, invest in a few more of that kind.

Solitary Toys

Solitary play toys are made with just your dog in mind. These keep them entertained during their downtime and give you a second to relax. These include chew toys, squeaky toys, fluffy toys, and puzzles.

They generally come in different sizes to better suit your dog. A small, soft chew toy may be great for a Yorkshire terrier, but it will be torn apart or swallowed whole by a mastiff. You will also need to consider the strength of your toys. A fluffy toy will not be a good idea for a chewer, and some of the more serious chewers might need something a lot stronger than your standard plastic bone. Thankfully, there are brands that make tough toys specifically designed for these kinds of dogs.

Interactive Toys

These can be used for human and dog play or dog and dog play and are great bonding and training tools. Knotted ropes are one of my favorites. They are available pretty much anywhere, or you can make them at home. They come in a variety of sizes, and the fibers and shape of the toy help with teeth cleaning. It was designed for tug of war or toss and catch, but it is fantastic to use as a reward during training as well. If you have a multi-dog household, your dogs can play together.

Balls, balls, balls. You either have a dog that is mind-blowingly obsessed with a tennis ball, or one that gives you that "Are you stupid?" look when you throw one. I have one of each. The best part of playing fetch is the amount of exercise your dog gets in just a few minutes of the game. If you're feeling a bit lazy, you can even buy an automatic ball thrower and teach your dog how to use it. Although, this may not be as exciting for them, as half of the fun comes from you being involved.

Toy wands are not just for cats. Yep, you heard me right; you can actually buy doggie toy wands. The string is much stronger, and so are the toys and feathers on the end. This is not exclusive to small dogs either; buying or making wands that have long ropes can bring a lot of joy to a large pup.

Puzzles and Games

Hide and seek is one of my favorite games to play. I lock him in my bedroom while I hide several treats in and around the house. When I let him loose, he spends hours trying to find them all. This game really gets their minds and noses working and is surprisingly exhausting.

Food puzzles are a fun interactive way to get your dog thinking. There are plenty of different ones on the market, but I like to go old school and use colored plastic cups. I turn them upside down, put a treat under one, and then shuffle them while my dog watches. When he chooses the right cup, he gets the reward. When he selects the wrong cup, the shock on his face is enough to send me into a giggle fit.

Feeder balls make a good solitary play game. These come in different sizes to suit your dog, and they have various holes cut into them. You can fill up the ball with treats or dog food, and your dog has to push the ball around until the right hole is exposed and drops a treat. Most of these toys are adjustable so that you can increase or decrease the activity level for smarter dogs that figure it out too quickly.

Training for Stimulation

Training doesn't just have to be work; it can be fun as well. Dogs thoroughly enjoy cooperative activities, especially ones that lead to your excitement and a treat for them! Working through some of the old tricks they have already mastered is a great way to get them engaged and stimulated. Using these tricks ensures that there is no way your dog can fail, and you are less likely to get frustrated. It's also a fun way to bond, and if the opportunity arises, you can teach them a new trick.

Must-Have Walking Tools

Indoor stimulation is not quite enough. It's time to work on getting those little legs moving and exploring the wild world outside your door. Before you start, there are some important items you will need to have on hand to make the experience as fun and safe as possible.

Leash and Lead

A leash is around 6 ft long and comes in different thicknesses to cater to different-sized dogs. Pick the right one, as one that is too thin is likely to snap if a big dog pulls too hard.

Leads are much, much longer than leashes and are generally used in training. They are perfect for recall training, as they allow your dog to go off quite far from you while you still have control. Leads are also great for secluded outdoor activities such as parks and hiking.

If you are ever in a populated area or dog park, it's best to keep your dog on a leash, especially when they aren't fully trained. You don't know which dogs are reactive or social, and allowing your pup to run up to strange dogs is very irresponsible. Not only does this endanger both dogs, but you could be messing up somebody else's training.

Harness

I much prefer walking my dogs on a harness than a collar. When they pull, the harness applies pressure to the chest rather than the neck, which makes it more comfortable. This allows you greater control over your dog, as they can't slip out of one as easily as a collar. Some come equipped with handles, which are great during emergencies as you can gain full control over your dog immediately.

You can buy front clip or back clip harnesses or ones that come equipped with both. Back clip ones are generally used for dogs that are already pretty good at walking without pulling on the lead. Front clip harnesses work well for training as they allow you to redirect your dog and stop them from pulling.

A harness feels pretty weird at first. I mean, a dog is not exactly used to wearing clothes. So, it may take a little time for them to get used to it.

When you slip it on, adjust the straps so that it fits correctly. You should be able to comfortably fit your fingers under the straps and move them up and down your dog's body. Remember, the more exercise your dog does, the heavier their breathing will become, and their chest will expand. You have to have a bit of space between the harness straps and their chest to accommodate this.

Leave the harness on for an hour or two and regularly reward them when they are calm. Check the sizing again and adjust it if need be. You will need to keep adjusting the harness as they grow, and I suggest buying one that is adjustable enough to at least last their first year. Only once they are comfortable in their gear can you start walking them.

Car Seat Covers

These are an absolute must-have. Whether you and your dog constantly travel, or your car trips are few and between. These will protect your seats from fur and claws while also protecting your pup. The back-side clips on the backseat headrest, and the front piece clips onto the driver and passenger headrest, essentially turning your back seat into a box.

This prevents your dog from jumping over into the front seat while you're driving.

If you have a tiny dog, you can buy smaller, box-like covers which confine your dog to a single seat. This will stop them from slipping and falling in the car.

Tools to Avoid

Retractable leads should be avoided at all costs. The constant pressure it places on your dog's neck can be harmful. Despite what the marketing says, they do not actually stop your dog from pulling on the lead while walking. If anything, it worsens it. Your dog will get used to that constant pressure around their necks and think that it's normal. The moment you swap to a normal leash, they will try to replicate the feeling by pulling.

Choke collars were all the rage at one point. Sure, they are a great way to stop your dog from running away, but it's also a great way to cause some serious damage to their spinal cord and windpipe. Other than injury, using choke collars will ruin what should be a fun experience, and I will be surprised if your dog gets excited to go for a walk again.

Can We Go Yet?

Before you head straight out that gate into the big, scary world, you will need to do some practice and preparation. If you are lucky, your dog will take to it immediately, but let's be real here; they are probably going to tug on the leash in a panic when they realize they can't actually get away from you.

The steps below may seem long, boring, and unnecessary. Even if you do find them boring, I promise you; they are definitely necessary. Taking your puppy out on a walk too early and with no training can lead to a traumatizing experience for both of you. You need them to be confident and feel safe with you before they explore new areas.

Baby Steps

Training your puppy to heel is easy enough as long as you have enough time and patience. The goal of this training is to get your dog to walk in a controlled manner at your side. This training will greatly decrease the chances of your dog pulling on their leash when you get to walking.

Step One: Peace and Quiet

Puppies have the attention span of a goldfish, so when it comes to training, you don't want any distractions, loud noises, other pets, or human beings. Find a quiet spot in your house or yard. The quieter it is, the more your puppy will be able to focus on you.

Step Two: Get in Position

Stand with your dog on one side. If you choose for them to be on the left, then hold your click in your right hand and your treats in your left. Ask your dog to sit and focus on you. Click and treat to reward them. Try to keep this focus for at least a minute before you start moving.

Step Three: Bait Them!

Hold a treat in front of their face, but don't let them have it just yet. Walk two steps forward while saying "Heel" and wait for them to follow you. After these steps, click and treat. You want to keep them as close to you as possible, so try to hold the treat right by your knees. Higher or lower is fine, depending on your dog's height.

Step Four: Rinse and Repeat

Keep your sessions short; ten-minute sessions spread throughout the day should be more than enough. You can now spread out your treats a little more. Reward them every five steps, then every ten, and so on until you can cut the treats out completely.

Once you are happy with their progress, you can introduce the leash.

Toddler Steps

You want to teach your pup that pulling on the leash is the fastest way to get them nowhere at all. The moment they pull, and you allow it, the behavior will continue and become harder to fix. Let's go through some simple steps to get your pup walking like an angel.

Step One: Pulling Gets You Nowhere

Clip the lead on and start your heel training. After a few meters, quit the treats and continue to walk as normal in a straight line, giving them the full length of the leash. When they stay by your side, and the leash is loose, click and treat.

If they start to wander off from your path, let them but stand still just before the leash tightens up. They are going to turn around to try to figure out what on earth you have stopped for, but you will need to stay in position.

When they pay attention to you or return, reward them and start walking again. You will need to practice this in short but consistent sessions for the next few days.

If you find that your dog is struggling to understand what they have to do when you stop, go back to your heel training again. You want to set them up to succeed, and if that means repeating the basics, so be it.

Step Two: Hold Your Leash Correctly

Your dog is not a mind reader, and if they are walking in front of you, they don't know that you intend to turn until they feel the tug at their neck to bring them back.

Save yourself the hassle and your dog the confusion by using your leash correctly. If your dog is on your right-hand side, you want your leash in your left hand. Your right hand will steer your pup in the direction that you want them to go in. When you want to turn, you will move your hand down the leash until you reach your knees. Applying some gentle pressure will bring their focus back to you and direct their bodies in the direction you would like to go.

Step Three: Keep Their Focus

Dogs are creatures of habit, and if you only train in a straight line, they will continue to walk that straight line. They begin to anticipate your movements and aren't actually focusing on you at all. This can become problematic if they catch sight of something more interesting or if you want to quickly change your routes.

The best way to train them to focus is by making your movements unpredictable.

Start your training as normal, walk forward until you can see they have gotten into their old routine, and then suddenly turn them and walk back the way you came. When you turn, you will need to steer them using the method in step two. I prefer to use the vocal cue "U-turn!" as well to make sure that I have their full attention.

Whenever you feel you are losing their focus, try this trick and make sure to give them a reward for obeying.

SQUIRREL!

One of the things we don't prepare for is the sudden, extremely exciting moment that your dog catches sight of prey. If you have a dog with a high prey drive, prepare to run. If you aren't a great runner, make sure you are wearing knee and elbow pads; you are going for a ride. Even if you have adopted a soft nature pooch, the intrigue will be enough to stop them in their tracks, and it can be really difficult to get them out of the trance.

This is where recall training is beneficial.

Step One: Teaching Manners

To start recall training, you need to teach your pup that they can't barge through and take whatever they want. This is difficult and requires a lot of restraint from them. This training should be started early in life, but don't be surprised if very young puppies aren't capable of containing their excitement.

What you are going to do is repeat your walking training as usual, but this time you are going to add in multiple exciting objects such as toys, food, and treats. These should be far enough away from you that your pup can't snatch them when they walk past but close enough that they can see them.

As you walk, your pup will veer off course and head toward the closest toy. Stand dead still. They will realize they can't get further and turn and look at you for guidance. Call them back, click, and then reward them with the object they were going for.

This basic training teaches them that they can get what they want as long as they have enough manners to ask you first.

Step Two: What's My Name Again?

Time for actual recall training. You need your dog to feel that coming back to you is more rewarding than what they are trying to run after. For this, you will need to pull out your long lead and allow them some extra freedom.

Wait for them to move far off, and then, in a super excited, crazy voice, call them back to you. You should be patting your legs and shouting their name, and doing a little dance. Whatever it takes to get them excited enough to come back.

When they do, click and reward. This time, your rewards will not be one boring treat. Give them something special! I like to use a toy as a reward and have a short game of tug and war. Give them treats and toys if you need to.

Step Three: Rinse and Repeat

Keep this up for a few sessions and then increase the difficulty by putting them into a more distracting environment. Your lead is still on, which means that if they do decide to try to bolt, you still have control and can bring them back if needed. You may find that in these situations, your dog returns to you but struggles to maintain focus. If this happens, grab the lead and start to walk them in the opposite direction until you get their full attention.

Recall training is not a once-off. You will need to keep this up throughout their life. Do it during your walks and at home, even if you don't need to.

Which Way Should We Go?

Alright, you are now confident in your training and your dog's abilities. It's time to venture out. I suggest that you pick out a nice, quiet route. One that can accommodate a quick, short walk but can be lengthened as your training advances. Walk the route alone at first and take note of anything that might be frightening or intriguing to your dog. For example, do you walk past any parks, is the road very busy, or are there any dogs that bark at you from their yard? If you answer yes to any of these, figure out how you will help your puppy to remain calm when they walk past these obstacles. If you can't, it's best to pick out another route for now.

This might sound a little paranoid, but I find that it helps me to feel confident on my walks, and that's what you need to be to keep your puppy feeling confident as well!

Rinse and Repeat

Keeping up a routine is the next step and one of the most important ones. Not only is this routine sure to keep you and your pup healthy, but it will also keep them comfortable with the activity. Your puppy is in a vital learning stage, and the associations they make at this point will continue with them through life. Allowing too much time between walks allows the growth of fear, and a puppy that felt comfortable walking two weeks ago might feel different about it today!

Chapter 9:

Powering Through the Toddler

Stage

Okay, I knew it would be a bumpy road to success, but this road is full of potholes! I obeyed the rules and hid my shoes to remove the chewing temptation, but nobody told me I would have to hide my toilet paper, sofa, and water bottle too. Yet as I find myself on the verge of screaming and evicting this infuriating pup of mine, he shoots me the most adorable, apologetic look. How could I not forgive him?

There is a very popular saying in puppy training, and that is, "Just relax; they will grow out of it." I am here to assure you that they won't.

Your pup is currently in their boundary-pushing toddler months, and what they are doing is completely natural. If they were still with their mom, she would warn their behavior off with a growl or even a nip! Inviting them into your family means that you need to take control, become that mother figure, and help them to figure out what is wrong and right.

Don't worry; there are tons of positive ways to create boundaries without you having to bare your teeth and nip them…

Stop That!

Puppies are adorable, and even when they do something wrong, we can't help but forgive them when they flash us those big puppy dog eyes. The thing is… puppies grow up, and the behaviors you thought were cute are suddenly extremely problematic. Each time you reward their negative behaviors and choose not to fix them, you are reinforcing the idea that what they are doing is right.

Imagine the turmoil they will go through later in life when they find out that what they have been doing for all these years is actually wrong!

My Mouth Hurts

Chewing is a super common behavioral issue in puppies, and generally, it's due to teething. This can be incredibly painful, and chewing on things around the house can relieve the pain. While plenty of puppies do actually grow out of this behavior once the pain subsides, others continue to do it out of habit and because they simply don't know better.

By providing them with an alternative solution to the problem, you can save your Louis Vuittons and reduce the chance of the behavior reoccurring in the future.

Chew toys are the obvious solution here, but not all of them will work in this situation. Shoes are usually the first casualty in your dog's murder spree. This is because they are soft and pliable, which makes them gentle enough to chew without causing pain but hard enough to relieve the pressure. Purchase chew toys of a similar texture and softness. If they need a little more motivation to move over to their new toys, spread some peanut butter over them to entice them!

There are other ways to help your pup through this painful stage. Giving them ice cubes can soothe their gums, and it makes for some fun play time. Rubbing teething gel onto their gums will help stop the pain for a moment. Do this regularly if you find that they are really struggling.

Finally, kibble can be a bit harsh on those swollen gums. Consider switching them to canned or wet food for a while.

Your Hands Are Tasty

Mouthing is the ultimate puppy behavior. It seems so cute at first until their sharp little puppy teeth dig into your skin. I swear those little needles are more painful than their adult teeth! Mouthing usually occurs when your pooch is going through their teething stage. However, it also marks a critical moment in their social development. Puppies will mouth or nip to process information, test boundaries, and play.

You will need to teach them your boundaries and provide them with an outlet to release this energy. Chew toys are a great start, but the toys aren't as entertaining as you. Encouraging the behavior by giggling or turning it into a game is only going to worsen it! Ignoring their behavior and removing your hand or leaving the room entirely when they try to chew on you will show them that they will not get any reaction out of you when they do it.

Another way to discourage this behavior is by reacting dramatically when they mouth you. Allow them to chew on your hand without reaction for a few seconds and then shout OW! And quickly remove your hand. This will show your dog that what they have done has hurt you.

Pay Attention to Me!

Dogs will often seek attention by whining, nudging or barking at you. This can become very frustrating, especially when you are trying your best to concentrate on something important. Before you can remedy this behavior, you need to figure out why your dog is exhibiting it in the first place. There are basically four reasons why your dog behaves negatively, and attention-seeking can be caused by one of these. A lack of mental stimulation, a lack of socialization, a lack of physical stimulation, and a lack of attention in general from their owners.

Each of these problems are easily solvable, and I won't waste your time going over the obvious solutions. Instead, let's look at what happens when you reinforce their attention-seeking.

We often reinforce this behavior without knowing it. If your dog is whining, and you turn, pat their heads, then turn around and continue to ignore them, you have rewarded it. Your dog has not gotten what they needed out of that interaction with you, and you have not listened to what they were trying to tell you. They will continue to display this behavior and take pleasure in the small amounts of attention they do get from you.

This can become more difficult to fix, but it's best to start with the basics. By keeping your dog stimulated and emotionally satisfied, the attention-seeking will likely stop or at least slow. The remaining behaviors are just a consequence of habit, and it's best to ignore your dog completely when they start to beg.

This is called extinction training. Extinction training requires you to do absolutely nothing whatsoever. You just need to ignore the unwanted behavior that your dog is displaying. By ignoring it and not rewarding it, your dog will realize that it is useless to continue using this method to get your attention.

Extinction training requires a lot of self-control on your part, and if you give in, you will need to start the process all over again. I always recommend using extinction training with positive reinforcement. Reward your dog when they stop whining and sit calmly. This reinforces your approval of their calm, quiet behavior, and they are more likely to act this way in the future.

Hello, Can You Hear Me?

Yap, yap, yap! Just be quiet already!! We have all been here, and we have all screamed those exact words. That yapping, especially puppy yapping, for some reason. It feels like somebody is drilling into your brain. Puppies, much like kids, don't really have filters yet, and they are using every new bark they have in their vocabulary.

There are a few reasons why your pup may bark excessively; the first is due to attention seeking, which we have already discussed. The second is due to boredom. If your pup is bored, they are going to find a way to entertain themselves, and if that entertainment comes from you pulling your hair out, then so be it. This is easy enough to solve. Give them things to play with! When they become distracted, direct them back to their toy box and get them playing again.

Finally, this barking could be a fear response. Follow them when they bark and try to pinpoint what they are actually barking at. You may find that it's something as silly as an owl statue in your backyard. By removing the fear or showing your dog that they don't need to be scared, you can cure your barking madness.

This Is MY Food!

Food guarding is a common behavioral problem in dogs and puppies. This is just one type of resource guarding, and some dogs may go as far as to protect their beds, toys, and even humans! Rescued dogs will likely have a sense of abandonment and will try to keep what little they have protected. It can take a while for these lost souls to feel truly comfortable and relaxed in a new home.

Dogs that live in a multi-pet household are probably dealing with a lot of competition and are more likely to protect their special items. It's understandable for them to feel this way. We react the same way when our roommates take something that isn't theirs! Yet, when this happens, we, for some reason, still take away the toy they are guarding as a punishment. This is only making it worse as it creates an even stronger need for them to protect their things!

If you are dealing with this situation in a multi-pet household, then you will need to buy more of everything. Having enough toys, beds, and games to go around is the best option. If you have three dogs, and they compete for one toy. Buy two more of those. Don't let there be a need for the competition in the first place.

When it comes to food guarding, you may find that one dog is actually hogging the other's food, and your pup that ends up food guarding is doing so because they are hungry. Establish mealtimes and watch your dogs from start to finish, ensuring that everyone is able to get enough. If you need to, separate your dogs for the first few weeks so that they can become more comfortable.

Chapter 10:

Building Confidence and

Conquering Fear

Fears are generally only noticeable in dogs when they reach their adult years. This is mainly because their reactions to these fears are more prominent and destructive. In fact, the majority of these fears manifest when your dog is just a puppy. Puppies go through two major fear stages during their development.

The first stage occurs between two and three weeks of age, and the second between eight and eleven weeks. These periods are part of vital survival techniques, and the fears they developed in the wild would often become the difference between life and death. If they never learn to have a fear of fire, they would constantly be burned. A domestic situation is a little different, and they can end up being afraid of things they don't need to actually worry about. This is where we need to step in and ensure that they pass through these stages unharmed.

Understanding Fear

Before you can begin helping your dog to heal and overcome these fears, you need to figure out why they have developed in the first place. The cause is usually easy to identify when you really think about it.

Why is My Dog Scared?

Bad experiences are the top cause of fear. If your dog has been attacked or hurt by a person or dog, it's understandable that they will develop a fear and avoid social encounters. During their fear stages, something as simple as a smack from a ticked-off cat can trigger a lifelong fear response.

Isolation

Puppies that have been too isolated have never had the chance to actually experience positive and negative situations. They have never been able to learn and adapt their responses to these stimuli. Their emotional, mental, and social development has been stunted, and they simply can't cope with new experiences.

Isolation fears have become increasingly common in what we now jokingly call Covid-19 puppies. These puppies were adopted either just before or during the Covid-19 lockdowns, and their owners were unable to walk or socialize them correctly.

Incorrect Training

We all make mistakes; it's only human, and occasionally, our mistakes can instill fear in our pups. Using positive punishment and negative reinforcement is guaranteed to cause your dog to develop some sort of fear. It may not be noticeable at first, but the cracks will begin to show later in life.

Incorrect positive reinforcement can be just as bad. If you are rewarding your dog at the wrong time, you could be creating a positive association with the fear they are experiencing. Essentially, validating their negative feelings and allowing them to grow.

Common Fears

There are loads of different fears that your dog may develop through life, but it would be impossible to actually work through each one. While each dog has their personal experiences and trauma, their genetic makeup makes them more prone to the following common fears.

What Was That Bang?

There aren't many dogs that aren't petrified of loud noises or bangs. It's no surprise, their hearing is twice as good as ours! Even a car backfiring can send them into a barking frenzy. Some dogs begin to understand what these noises are and that they won't harm them. Others will live their entire lives with the firm belief that thunder has a personal vendetta against them.

Stranger Danger

This is not always a bad thing; you don't really want your dog to greet robbers with a cup of cocoa. However, it can become problematic when your pup fears everyone. There is no way for them to escape human and dog contact forever, and the constant stress can have some serious health implications.

Where Are We??

Again, a fear of strange new places is not unusual. All dogs should feel a sense of wonder and intrigue with a healthy dose of caution. As with all fears, there are levels, and an extreme fear can cause your dog to flee the scene or become aggressive if you hold them back. This type of fear usually occurs in dogs that have been isolated, and they are just so overwhelmed by the amount of new information.

Don't Leave Me Alone!

Separation anxiety is very common in rescue dogs that have been abandoned or given away to a new family. The trauma of being dumped like this causes them to have an unhealthy attachment to you, as they fear you may do the same. Although, boredom at home or negative experiences that you don't know happen when you are gone can also trigger separation anxiety as your dog looks to you as their protector.

Dogs with separation anxiety will often become destructive and destroy furniture. In extreme cases, they will become so desperate to get to you that they actually break through windows or scratch through doors.

What Happens If I Leave It?

Well, nothing good. A state of fear releases adrenaline, and your dog can only react in one of two ways when they reach their threshold. Fight or flight. The flight response is one of the scariest for us, as dogs can run at lightning speeds and scale walls like Spider-Man when they need to! At this point, recall training doesn't work, and it can be difficult to get them back.

Fight, on the other hand, can be just as dangerous. If you are holding your dog in a scary situation, they may turn and bite you to break free. Being stuck in a position with a strange person or dog, with no chance to flee, can cause your dog to attack. In their minds, It's their life or the strangers and in those situations, they will choose theirs.

Just A Big Ball of Anxiety and Reactivity

One fear leads to another, and another and another until your dog is a walking, barking ball of anxiety. A fear of strange people can suddenly lead to a fear of the dogs they are walking. This can lead to a fear of being in the park in the first place, which can lead to a fear of getting into the car. It's one big domino chain!

If your dog has hit this point, it is going to take a ton of work to get them back to the confident state they need to be in to be happy.

Shaping a Confident Puppy

Confidence is key! Your puppy will never be able to conquer their fears unless they are confident enough in themselves and their abilities to handle any situation. They require a lot of support and look to you as their protector. This means it's your job to guide them through this turmoil and show them that there is light on the other side of the tunnel.

Flooding

Flooding is a term used to describe overloading a dog with information or stimuli. It was once and still is used as a treatment for humans and dogs alike. The goal of flooding is to constantly expose them to a fearful stimulus until they are unable to be physically aroused by it anymore. Essentially getting used to the stimulus and losing their fear. An example would be locking your dog in a room and playing recordings of thunder until they stop reacting. The problem is that while the dog does stop reacting, it's because they are physically and mentally exhausted and have simply given up and accepted their fate.

While humans can understand and agree to such treatments, dogs are left in the dark with no idea what they did to you to deserve such a harsh punishment. Imagine trapping an unwilling person with crippling arachnophobia in a room full of spiders? They may stop screaming, but they will need a straitjacket and a trip to the hospital afterward. This is not a healthy way to treat fear!

In positive reinforcement training, we try our best to avoid flooding our dogs and instead use counter-conditioning or desensitization. This way, we can help them overcome their fears in a slow, comfortable way to build their confidence rather than destroy their spirit.

Love, Love, Love

There often seems to be confusion when you tell a person to love their dog during stressful periods. Love does not mean pampering them or soothing them when they are scared. Love means listening to them, protecting them and guiding them through the fear, and finding an appropriate solution.

An easy example would be a dog that is terrified during a thunderstorm. Sitting on the floor with them, rubbing their heads, and saying, "I'm sorry, baby, I'm sorry..." will only make things worse. You are focusing their attention on the stimulus and confirming their feelings of fear. They begin to react in an even more fearful way, which causes you to soothe them even more.

A better solution would be to take charge of the situation! You have listened to what they have told you; they are scared. Protect them by moving them to a quieter room and closing the windows and doors. Guide them through it by distracting them with a fun game or toy, and reward them when you see they are enjoying themselves and not as focused on the storm outside.

You have not confirmed their fear; you have lessened the stimulus and found a way to show them that life goes on and can be enjoyed, even when the wind is howling outside.

Counterconditioning and Desensitization

Counter-conditioning and desensitization go hand in hand. Desensitization involves slowly exposing your dog to a fearful stimulus, while counter-conditioning involves changing your dog's response to that stimulus.

Let's continue with our thunder example and work through how you could desensitize your dog to this sound. First, you are going to need some recordings of thunder. YouTube is here for you and will surely provide some fantastic ones. Then, grab some of the most delicious treats that you can find and pick up some of your dog's favorite toys as well.

1. Take your dog into a calm room with no distractions. Get their attention by giving them a treat. It's best to uplift their moods, so play a little game before you start.

2. Turn on the recording of the thunder at a very low volume. Your dog's ears are going to immediately perk up, and they will display their usual fearful behavior.

3. You are going to change your dog's reaction to the noise by creating a positive association with it. Give them tons of treats and play some games until they are relaxed.

4. Repeat this step with the recordings at this volume for a few days. If you play the recording and your dog immediately looks at you with a happy face, expecting a reward, you can advance to the next level.

5. Turn the volume up a little more, and monitor your dogs' response. Repeat the above steps and reward them continuously throughout the process.

6. Repeat these steps, increasing the volume a tiny bit each time.

7. If you notice that you are unable to get your dog's attention and the fear is just too much, turn the volume down again and work at a threshold that they are comfortable with. This is not a

quick process, and if you try to rush it, you can make their fear worse.

This kind of training can solve just about any fear your dog has. You only need to switch it up a little. If your dog is fearful of humans, introduce a stranger to them the same way you introduced the thunder. Keep them far away while you reward your dog. Ask the person to approach one step at a time while you continue to reward your pooch. After a few sessions, they may have just found their new human best friend!

You can also incorporate your clicker into this situation. The clicker means reward, so every time your dog glances at the stranger, click immediately and give them a treat. Use this method carefully, as you need to be quick! If you click too late, you may be rewarding the fearful response to that person.

Conclusion

Alright, let's swing right back into the happy stuff. Your book journey is over for now, but your puppy adventure has just begun. You are about to enter the most rewarding and downright adorable years of your life. I can't imagine anything more exciting!

Hopefully, I have been able to walk you through everything you need to know about finding your soul mate, how to feed them, and care for them when they are feeling ill. The foundations to become the perfect pet parent. The most important thing is that you have learned how to shape an emotionally stable, healthy, and obedient puppy that will be able to share years and years of joy with you. Everything you do together, whether it's car rides, training, adventures, or simple snuggles, should be strengthening your relationship, not breaking it down. If you find that you have made a mistake, which you are bound to! Don't let it get you down. Work through the steps to build your puppy's confidence back up and try again.

The responsibility of owning a pup can be quite overwhelming at first, and you should never feel ashamed to seek help if you need it. If you work long hours or if you are just worried about them being alone, save yourself the guilt and look into puppy daycare or a pet nanny. If grandma gets just as lonely, take advantage of the free labor and find out if she would be interested in caring for your baby while you're out! There are loads of solutions, and it is worth exploring each one before you become frazzled.

When you do feel like you have hit a wall, especially in training, take a deep breath, have a cup of tea, and come back for another read. There may be something you missed, and if I haven't covered it, there are tons of resources out there that can help you find the solution to your problem. If you find that you just need a shoulder to cry on, think about joining a puppy training class or one of the many social media puppy owner groups. These are fantastic safe spaces where you can share your struggles without judgment and learn new tips and tricks from others that have gone through the same thing.

The first few weeks are the hardest, but once you get into the rhythm of things, you won't even be able to remember the last time you felt unhappy. Cherish these puppy months, their adorable baby howls, their floppy ears, and those sharp little baby teeth. Embrace their mistakes, their successes, and all the unique behaviors that make your special bundle of joy.

If your puppy has enjoyed this book, please help to leave a pawsome review on Amazon!

Book 2:

Adult Dog Training Through Positive Reinforcement

Learn the Essential Skills Needed to Shape an Obedient and Well-Behaved Dog

Introduction

Picture this, you head to your local shelter, and you lock eyes with your soulmate. A large, furry, mixed breed named Sam. His tail wags and your heart is stolen. You take him home and get ready for the perfect life together, except he is anything but well-behaved.

You have heard that crate training is the best method, but he whines the entire time. The guilt takes over, so you let him out and give him free rein of the house. Suddenly, he has taken your bed, hogged the couch, and chewed up your favorite shoes!

You assumed that he would be housebroken. It's just common sense, right? However, Sam has never lived in a home situation and has taken a liking to your favorite rug as a toilet. He thinks he is being polite, only soiling one spot in the house. The solution? Walking! He will surely learn to potty outdoors then, and exercise is so important to ensure your pup is happy and healthy.

You have already picked out the perfect collar and leash. They were highly recommended by the local pet store. "These are the best on the market, guaranteed no pulling!" they said, but Sam doesn't seem to care. The excitement takes over, and he begins to drag you across the street. You are starting to panic. There are so many dangers around, and he doesn't seem to be aware of them. You immediately drag him back into the house.

The frustration begins to set in, but you try to remain calm and think. Maybe the park is quieter and less overwhelming. He may even meet a friend. You now know that he gets overly excited, but you have a plan! As soon as you pull up to the park, you secure his leash and command him to sit and wait. His tail is wagging, beating against the seat. With his tongue out and eyes wide, he actually sits! You slowly open the door.

In a split second, the sounds and smells of an exciting new world hit him, and what's that? Another dog? He's off! You realize right away this was a mistake. He is just not ready.

Exhausted and overwhelmed, you invite over Aunt Betty. She loves dogs. Perhaps she can convince you that you haven't made a mistake. As she enters your home, 80 pounds of furry, slobbery dog comes bounding up, and with one big jump, Aunt Betty is against the wall. Sam is convinced that these lovely licks and kisses are the only real way to say hello.

You have had enough. Being nice isn't working, and you start to yell, "Get down! Stop it! Bad Dog!!" The worst thought begins to flood your mind: *Should I take him back?*

These are just some examples of the challenges you may face when adopting an untrained adult dog. However, it is so important to take a deep breath and put yourself in their paws. Some dogs have not had the privilege of having an owner who is patient and kind and who followed through with their training. Some dogs have not had the privilege of having an owner at all. Sadly, some dogs have gone through trauma that you will never understand.

The idea that you can't train an old dog new tricks is simply a myth created by people who were not up to the challenge. Dogs are much, much smarter than you think! They have an amazing ability to heal from trauma, both physical and emotional, as long as they have the right support system.

Hope is never lost, and every dog deserves a beautiful life and the opportunity to shine.

I have always had a love for the underdogs, the ones that have been abandoned, mistreated, and forgotten, the ones that have so much potential but are so often misunderstood! This love became a burning passion when I adopted my first rescue dog. It was game over as soon as I saw those big puppy dog eyes.

For the last 30 years, I have dedicated my time to learning different training techniques from various professionals in order to help my dogs and others to adjust to their new environments and become the loving companions they desperately want to be.

My goal is to guide you through how to overcome these challenges and provide you with tried and true techniques which will help you to untrain negative behaviors and replace them with much more family-friendly positive ones.

It is important to remember that this type of training doesn't happen overnight. It takes time, patience, and consistency. Do not expect Sam to be doing circus tricks by the end of this book! My goal is to assist you in providing the best possible life for your companion through training processes that will ensure you have the most enjoyable time together.

Before you start training, you need to understand your dog. Let's get started.

Chapter 1:

Walk a Day in My Paws

Dogs come in all different shapes, sizes, and personalities! Each one is completely unique and gifted with a variety of quirks you learn to either love or hate. It's important to remember that you are never going to be able to train out their personalities, and why would you ever want to?

Just like us, dogs find pleasure in different rewards and activities. You may have a dog that will jump through hoops for edible treats or a picky eater that only enjoys a specific food. I personally have a dog that goes mad for a ball and a chew toy and another who couldn't be bothered with either. However, as soon as he gets his jaws on a squeaky toy, he is in absolute heaven.

In this chapter, we are going to focus on how important it is to have a thorough understanding of your dog. Without it, your training experience is going to be incredibly difficult, and implementing big changes will be near impossible. Let go of what you think you know and allow them to direct you.

Understanding Your Dog

Understanding a dog is no easy task. It's going to take quite a bit of time and a lot of effort on your part. Wouldn't it just be so much easier if they could just talk about their feelings? At first, you may feel like you simply aren't getting through to them, but the more you train and bond, the stronger your relationship will grow. Through this, they will show you more and more of themselves. You just need to learn to listen and try to understand what they have gone through.

Rescued Dogs

Adopting a rescued dog is not as easy as it seems. Yes, you know that you need to get their medical history, make sure their vaccinations are up-to-date, and get them a collar with a cute little tag that has their name on it. However, there is so much more to it, and some of the below factors can often be overlooked amid the excitement of bringing your new friend home.

Background

Background history is absolutely vital. The rescue shelter will typically be able to provide you with an up-to-date medical history, but be sure to ask a few more questions to ensure you have a complete picture.

Has the dog suffered any injuries, and if so, from what? If these injuries have been caused by people or other dogs, you can already expect to deal with behavioral problems.

Next up, how long has the dog been in the shelter and why? Adult dogs are not readily adopted as they are not considered as cute, but there could be other reasons that factor into it, and the dog could have been returned before. The length of stay in a shelter also affects the dog's ability to quickly acclimate to a new home environment.

Lastly, and most importantly, what is the dog's temperament? Does it get along with other pets and people, and have there been any aggressive occurrences? For most people, this is make-or-break information, and dogs that have shown aggressive tendencies or fear toward people are not readily adopted.

Get Ready for Trouble

Prepare for the worst and be pleasantly surprised! Sometimes the background history you get is incorrect or incomplete.

Keep in mind everything that could go wrong and get yourself ready. Any animal that enters a new home and environment for the first time is going to be a bit scared. It's only natural! Be sure not to overwhelm them, as this can quickly bring about negative behaviors you aren't equipped to deal with just yet.

Introductions should be kept to an absolute minimum for the first few days. This includes introductions to other animals and strangers. I do not recommend that any new dog is left alone with young children or other pets until you are completely satisfied that they have adjusted and are comfortable.

It is common for a dog to go from an angel in the shelter to a little demon in your home. Their lives have been completely turned over, and it can take some time for them to fully recover.

Special Considerations

If you have chosen to adopt or have inherited a disabled or geriatric dog, fasten your seatbelts, as you could be in for a bumpy ride. First, I would like to thank you. These are such special souls and are so worthy of a happy, loving home. They are often so full of attitude and have amazing characters.

However, you will need to ensure that you are able to fully provide them with the correct care and attention they need. This is going to include special housing, food, medical checkups, and potentially, an overhaul of your house.

Many of the training techniques listed in this book can be adjusted to suit your special dog, but on the rare occasion, you may need to accept that your pet is not capable of change. This is when you need to adjust your expectations and figure out a way to live together comfortably.

Untrained Adults

You skipped a few puppy school lessons and didn't quite have the time to socialize your dog as much as you should have. No big deal, right? Well, if you purchased this book, you have probably realized that it is a bit more problematic than you thought. The good news is that training is going to be much, much easier as an established relationship is already in place, and your dog is living in comfortable surroundings.

Adult dogs are also likely to learn new commands and behaviors more quickly than puppies. This is mainly due to the fact that they aren't quite as distracted by every blade of grass around them.

Most of the work you will be doing with your dog will be behavioral correction. This will involve changing the negative behaviors they have learned to positive ones through positive reinforcement. You are usually the source of these behavioral issues, as they have learned that it is perfectly acceptable to behave like a monster in front of you. That may sting a little, but throughout this book, I will show you how important it is to work *with* your dog. That means that you might have to change too!

Breed Specific

In the dog world, we have used genetics to our advantage and bred individuals that possess specific characteristics together in order to produce different breeds that suit our wants and needs. Some dogs have been bred as workers, and some simply as companions with unique physical traits.

Each breed possesses its own set of traits, some negative and some positive. It is important to understand these traits in order to cater to their needs and find the right training methods.

Exercise, good food, boredom relief, and adequate attention are the four dog basics. Every single dog, regardless of breed, needs to have access to these four things in order to remain mentally and physically healthy. However, your breed may determine how much of each you will need to provide.

There are currently 360 recognized breeds worldwide, which is just way too many to discuss in one book. However, each of these breeds are placed into one of seven groups, determined by the American Kennel Club. Their grouping is determined by the original job the dog was bred to do. Let's take a look.

Sporters

If you are looking for highly energetic, fun-loving dogs, the sporters are for you! This group includes the pointers, retrievers, setters, spaniels, and the absolutely lovely Brittanies.

As highly alert dogs with a stable temperament, they were originally bred to be a hunter's best friend and were trained for hunting game birds. Retrievers were particularly sought-after, as they were always happy to brave the cold water to retrieve their prey.

What to Expect

In a home setting, sporters are generally considered fantastic family pets, as their goofy nature makes for great playtime. They need to be provided with loads of exercise and activities to keep their minds sharp. Without this, they can begin to display destructive behavior out of boredom and frustration.

Hounds

Hounds can be split into two categories, scent hounds and sight hounds. Scent hounds are expert trackers that always have their noses to the ground. They are typically slower than sight hounds but more methodical. Bloodhounds, beagles, and bassets are included in this group.

Sight hounds are able to visually lock in on their target and use their long legs to reach amazing speeds in order to catch it. These breeds include greyhounds, whippets, Afghans, and wolfhounds. Due to their speed, these breeds are commonly used in sports such as dog racing.

What to Expect

Both groups are considered incredibly loyal and affectionate. However, their naturally strong prey drive can be difficult for some owners to navigate, especially if the dog has not been trained in recall. They are easily distracted by scents, sounds, and sights and will often become hyper focused on their target. Once a hound locks onto something interesting, good luck getting them out of it.

Workers

As the name suggests, these breeds were made to work! Although the jobs they were given may vary from family and farm security to pulling sleds, they are all powerful, loyal, and protective dogs, which is why they seem to be happy working for free!

This group includes breeds such as Great Danes, mastiffs, boxers, huskies, and Bernese mountain dogs. These breeds are generally bursting with energy and are considered highly intelligent.

What to Expect

They were bred to work, and they need to be kept stimulated at all times. Mentally challenging activities such as food puzzles and regular training are great at curbing boredom and frustration. As large dogs, negative and destructive behaviors are much more noticeable and devastating. Regular, extensive exercise and a large play area are absolutely vital.

Herders

These farm dog breeds were bred to protect, gather, and herd livestock. Some breeds include shepherds, collies, sheepdogs, corgis and Catahoulas. These are all incredibly smart and naturally responsive dogs. Their alert nature and willingness to train has made them invaluable working dogs. They are commonly used in rescue and recovery teams, with police forces, and as service dogs.

What to Expect

Boredom sets in very quickly, and they require strict structure, regular exercise, and instruction to keep them in check. They thrive on mentally stimulating tasks, making training incredibly easy and fun. Agility training is a fantastic way to work with herders, as it keeps their minds sharp and provides an invaluable amount of exercise.

As loyal dogs, they are very protective of their owners and families. Don't be surprised to find your border collie herding your kids.

Terriers

Terriers can be split into three main categories. The short-legged terriers include breeds such as Scottish terriers and Boston terriers. These dogs were bred to hunt and kill small animals such as vermin that may wreak havoc in a farm setting.

Long-legged terriers such as miniature schnauzers and Jack Russells are in a similar line of work, but their long legs make them great diggers, and they were also used for game hunting.

Bull terriers such as the American pit bull and Staffordshire bull terriers were originally bred for bull baiting and dog fighting. Thankfully, we have left this terrible past behind and these breeds are now welcomed, loving companions.

What to Expect

Sadly, there is a stigma surrounding many terrier breeds, and a lot of people avoid adopting them because of it. The idea that these dogs are an inherent threat is completely inaccurate. No dog is born aggressive! Many of the behaviors dogs display are a direct result of their owners' teachings and actions.

All of these breeds are known for their confident and courageous natures, which makes them loyal and protective companions. They are energetic, fun-loving dogs that love nothing more than pleasing their owners. This makes them amazing family pets and even greater nannies!

Like all other breeds, they need structure, mental simulation, and regular exercise. Without it, they can be prone to negative behaviors such as barking and chewing in order to curb their boredom.

Toys

Toys include all the small, lap-sized breeds that were bred to be companions. Some of the most sought-after breeds include pugs, Chihuahuas, Maltese poodles, Yorkshire terriers, shih tzus, and dachshunds.

They are affectionate, intelligent, and highly sociable with people and dogs alike. They adapt easily to different environments as long as they are introduced to that lifestyle when young. This makes them perfect traveling companions, and some breeds are even carried around in doggy handbags.

What to Expect

Small bodies, big personalities! These breeds can be stubborn and highly strung. They need regular exercise and mentally stimulating tasks to keep them happy. If you aren't an active person, you are in luck! Their tiny legs mean you only need to walk a couple of steps to keep up with exercise routines. They are highly affectionate and require a lot of attention. This makes them prone to destructive and attention-seeking behaviors if left alone without stimulation.

Teacup breeds can be prone to medical conditions such as physical injury, heart defects, and respiratory problems. This is due to their tiny size, and they should be fed a specialized diet to keep them healthy. It's important to keep an eye on them, especially around larger dogs and young children, and provide them with an appropriate play area as they can escape through small gaps.

Non-Sporters

Non-sporters include breeds that don't quite fit into the other categories. They are unique in the reasons they have been bred and can't really be compared to one another.

Due to the diversity of this group, we can't really discuss their common behaviors or what to expect when adopting. It's best to research each one to get a better understanding. For now, let's look at three different breeds from this group that couldn't be any more different from each other.

Dalmatians were originally bred as security guards for horses. They are extremely active and love the outdoors, making them perfect hiking partners. Their sensitive and playful nature makes them great household pets, though they may be a little too playful for small children. They are easy to train but require loads of exercise to curb destructive behaviors.

Poodles were originally bred as hunters but are now sought-after show dogs. Due to their highly intelligent minds, they are very easy to train and thoroughly enjoy mentally stimulating tasks. They crave attention and are prone to demand barking and destruction if left unattended for too long.

Bulldogs were originally bred for bull baiting. However, you would never think it with their sweet, easygoing nature. They are often mistaken for being lazy; however, they actually do enjoy walks when given the chance. They can quickly pack on weight if not appropriately exercised, which will make it much harder for them to curl up on your lap!

Start at Home

Now that you have a bit more of an understanding of your dog, you will need to figure out where you need to make changes in your life to accommodate them. These changes do not only apply to owners who have recently adopted or are planning to adopt an adult dog. These may also apply to those of you who are currently struggling with your lifelong pup.

Before you can even think of grabbing a leash and getting your dog out into the world, you need to focus on your homelife. Your home is your and your dog's safe place, and you need to structure it in a way that benefits both of you. That means boundaries!

Make the Changes

Dog proof your house! This is especially important for creating boundaries with new dogs. If there are certain areas of your home you would prefer your dog not to enter, find the best way to close off access. Many people do this through the use of baby gates, which are inexpensive and easy to set up. One of the benefits of using a baby gate is that your dog is still able to see what is happening on the other side.

This can decrease anxiety in protective or needy dogs and reduce whining if used properly.

Use the remaining space to create a safe environment and remove any temptations from your dog's view. There are some things in this world that a dog just cannot resist, and at the top of that list is food.

You should pick one spot for your dog to eat, and I recommend that you use an area where they are isolated and able to eat in peace to avoid food guarding behavior.

Set aside a quiet space for them to relax and sleep. Whether you are using a crate or a bed, choose this space wisely. You don't want to have to move your dog around the house. This is tiring for you and disruptive for them.

Your dog needs potty breaks and exercise, so you will need to grant them access to your yard. Whether you are planning to allow your dog out without supervision or not, make sure that your fence is secure and high enough to avoid jailbreak situations. Don't underestimate what they are capable of! For some dogs, all it takes is one curious squirrel to kick them into Olympic-level athletics.

It's Not Just About You Anymore

This is one of the hardest adjustments for new pet owners and parents. You can't just lock up the house and go on a three-day vacation anymore. Suddenly, you need to figure out how they are going to survive without you. Realizing that there is a little life that completely relies on you can be nerve-racking, and you are going to need to make some changes to your lifestyle to accommodate them.

Creating a routine will help both of you adjust to the new arrangement. Set a time for breakfast and dinner, a time for walks, and a time for play! You will be amazed at how quickly a dog can adjust to a new routine. If you set your playtime for 3:00 p.m. every day, don't be shocked when you look over and find your dog staring you down with a tennis ball in their mouth at exactly 2:59!

Building a Family

You are not the only one who needs to bond with your dog. Everyone in your household needs to play their part in welcoming their new furry family member. Introducing an adult dog to your children should be done calmly and slowly. Ensure that your children understand what they can and can't do and show them how they can express their love in a way the dog can understand. Pulling a dog's tail is definitely not the best greeting!

The Foundations

When you ask somebody what the foundations of training are, you will likely receive a hundred different responses. Some might say it's down to commands and reward types. Some might say it's establishing dominance and creating boundaries. To me, there are four core fundamentals every dog owner should know. If you can live by them, you can train by them.

Love

There is absolutely nothing more important than love! It is the glue that holds the world together, and in your dog's eyes, you are that world. The bond between you and your dog will be the basis of all training. They need to be able to trust that you know what is right for them, and with that, they will readily learn from you.

Patience

This is a hard one! It can be impossible not to become frustrated when you're on your third load of soiled laundry. Throwing away the pillow that was unfortunate enough to become your dog's latest victim can quickly become the last step to full-blown tears, and that's okay! It is only natural, but it's important that you don't take this frustration out on your dog. Find yourself a coping mechanism, take a deep breath, and relax yourself.

When working with your dog, you need to be patient and understanding. They can quickly pick up on when you're feeling tense. This can put a damper on the activity, so you need to ensure that you are in the right mindset. If you are not feeling it, your dog probably isn't either. Ditch the work and skip straight to cuddle time.

Consistency

Establishing a routine is a great way to build confidence in your dog and secure a good relationship between the two of you. Remember to take it slow and don't make promises you can't keep. There is nothing wrong with missing a game of catch on a rainy day, but ending routines, especially fun activities, can lead your dog straight back to their old bad habits.

Consistency is also vital for training. You can't train for an hour and expect it to stick. Many of the commands you are teaching them are foreign, and you can't verbally explain to them why they are important to you. Instead, dogs learn through practice and positive reinforcement. The longer you keep it up, the more ingrained the behavior will become.

Time

Take your time when training. There is no way you are going to see results in one day, so don't try to push it. Dogs can get as tired and frustrated as you and will stop responding to your commands and rewards if they have had enough. Attempting to train during this time is only going to discourage them from learning.

Schedule an hour every day before playtime to train. Stick to using one command until it is fully ingrained, and then move on to the next. Slow and steady is the only way to win the race.

Chapter 2:

Behind Those Puppy Dog Eyes

Did you know that staring lovingly into your dog's eyes causes your brain to release a chemical called oxytocin? Also known as the love hormone, it's vital for bonding and gives you a sense of euphoria! Dogs are very in tune with their bodies, and while they may not understand why it is happening, they know that they love it. That is one of the reasons why some dogs crave attention from their owners.

As amazing as this bond is, you may be struggling with some of the behavioral issues that come with attention seeking. In this chapter, we are going to take a peek into your dog's mind and work through some of the most common behavioral problems and their potential causes.

You may be quite surprised! Sometimes all it takes to cure an undesirable behavior, is to remove the stimulus that is causing it.

Common Behavioral Problems

It is important to remember that at no point are dogs displaying behavior to purposefully irritate or harm you. Most of the issues we are going to talk about are behaviors that dogs have learned or are displaying due to another underlying cause.

The most common and probably the most frustrating behavioral problems include jumping, house training, barking, whining, pulling on their leash, and poor socialization, all of which will be covered in depth in this book at a later stage. However, there are a few others you may be dealing with.

Chewing

This is one of the worst! Coming home to pillow stuffing strewn around the house or your favorite pair of shoes torn to bits can be aggravating. It's a very difficult situation, and it's hard to not get angry. This sort of destructive behavior is usually from anxiety and boredom due to a lack of toys or mentally stimulating tasks. Ensure that your dog always has fun activities to do before you leave your home.

Some dogs are just natural chewers. Provide them with a ton of chew toys, lick mats, and interactive feeders to keep them busy. I always recommend that owners of chewers remove any temptations from their dog's area. If you know that they enjoy chewing shoes, don't ditch your boots right next to their bed.

Food and Toy Guarding

When you head to the kitchen, full of excitement, getting ready to savor that delicious piece of cake that you saved, only to find that somebody has already eaten it. The fury kicks in, and if you could, you would bite! The next time you get a piece of cake, you make sure to hide it or gobble it down immediately. Sharing is definitely not always caring.

Dogs that live in multi-pet households often feel the same way and this can lead to food, bed, and toy guarding. Food guarding can be solved by providing your dogs a safe space to eat without looming threats. If you are only feeding your dogs once a day, you may find they are even more protective of their food as they know it will be a while until their next meal. Spreading the meals throughout the day is a great way to solve this.

In order to prevent bed and toy guarding, you will need to give your dog a safe space in which to retreat when they are feeling overwhelmed or if they just want some alone time. Try to spread out your dog's beds or crates if you find that they are getting irritated with each other.

Begging

This behavior is regularly overlooked by owners. That is, until you have a dinner party and realize that your guests are getting continuously harassed by big puppy dog eyes. The number one reason for begging is you rewarding the behavior! Let's not pretend that you haven't slipped your dog some leftovers or a piece of juicy steak off your plate, so how can you be upset when they ask for more? The best way to solve this is to stop rewarding it.

If the behavior continues, add in a new step to your routine. At dinner time, get your dog used to being isolated from you, either in their crate or bed with a fun toy to distract them. Provide them with something rewarding other than your food.

Rough Play

Doggy playtime is supposed to be fun, but it's less so when you come away with scratches and bruises. Rough play is pretty normal in the dog world, it just doesn't translate very well to humans. The best way to solve this problem is to approach it calmly. Teaching your dogs basic commands such as sit and stay can help you to refocus your dog and calm them before you continue playing.

Common Causes

There are tons of reasons your dog may be displaying negative behavior, and sometimes it is not easy to pinpoint. Trauma, medical complications, and abandonment are the most common causes, but other factors such as psychological disorders should not be quickly dismissed. You know your dog best, and it's important to trust your gut when it comes to identifying problems. If you feel as though there is something wrong that you are unable to fix, seek professional help from your veterinarian. They will be able to give your dog a full check-up and identify any physical or psychological concerns.

Nobody Taught Me Better

Dogs that have not been raised in a home environment are unlikely to understand your strange human rules. We live very differently from animals, and it can be a huge adjustment for them. When they see food, they eat it, not put it in the fridge and save it for later. When dealing with dogs like this, you need to go back to the basics and treat them the same way you would a puppy.

However, there are some dogs that have never really learned to be dogs! These are usually puppies that were removed from their mother and littermates too early. Their socialization skills are severely stunted, and they have never been taught boundaries. This is why it is never recommended to adopt a puppy under the age of eight weeks. During these fundamental weeks, your pup is busy testing the waters, biting their mom and littermates and getting put into their place. They learn to groom themselves and mom teaches them some basic safety rules. Most importantly, they receive their mother's love.

But the Others Dogs Do...

Most animals and humans learn through observation and imitation. As puppies, they learn important behaviors from watching their mother. As they grow, they become aware of the animals and humans around them and learn which behaviors and activities are treated as negative or positive.

If your dog sees another dog getting away with stealing food with no consequences, why can't they? This does not just apply to dogs that live in the same household. Some dogs may have never barked at people walking down the street or neighborhood squirrels, but when they see your neighbors' dog doing it, it seems quite fun, so why not join in?

Lack of Exercise and Mental Stimulation

Boredom is top on the list when it comes to behavioral problems. Dogs with no stimulation such as toys or interesting changes to their environment will be sure to find their own entertainment. The problem is this kind of fun could be tearing up the couch and scratching down the doors. The same goes with exercise! High-energy dogs are especially susceptible to behavioral issues when not exercised properly. There is no way for them to channel the energy that is bursting out of them, and they become increasingly frustrated. The way they display this frustration can be destructive and even dangerous. If they find that escaping the yard and enjoying an afternoon run is more rewarding than staying at home, it seems worth the punishment.

Thankfully, if this is the reason your dog is acting up, it is easily fixable with environmental and food enrichment and some good daily exercise.

Could It Be Medical?

There are many medical conditions that can contribute to undesirable behaviors. Some breeds may be prone to psychological genetic disorders such as obsessive disorders, while others may be prone to physical disorders such as hip dysplasia or hormonal imbalances.

No matter the medical cause, the concern remains that dogs are simply unable to communicate the issue with you! This is when you need to learn to listen through body language and carefully observe what they do when they don't know you are watching.

Pain

Dogs display pain in a few different ways. There are clear physical signs such as limping, visible injuries, and bleeding. However, internal pain is much trickier to communicate.

Whining is the closest way your dog is able to communicate with you. Think of it in the same way that you want everyone to know that you are miserable when you are down and out with the flu! This behavior can be very annoying, but if you continue displaying a negative reaction to it, your dog will stop trying to tell you what is going on.

Licking the same spot such as the stomach can indicate discomfort and pain. Dogs lick themselves to self-soothe, and if it brings them relief, this licking can quickly become obsessive. Licking and chewing paws can also indicate medical concerns like allergies, mites, and fleas.

Chewing on themselves or objects in the house is often a sign of a deep frustration, which can be brought on by pain. Puppies will typically chew everything they can get their paws on! This is because it brings relief during the teething stage.

Aggression is the most worrying sign of pain. This will usually occur when you touch a painful spot on their body, such as a sprained paw or a sore stomach. It can also be displayed if you are trying to get your dog to participate in an activity that they know will cause them pain.

Incontinence

A sudden onset of inappropriate urination and defecation in the house is regularly a sign of incontinence. This is typically common in aging dogs that are no longer able to hold it in for long periods of time. Your dog may also be suffering from a urinary tract infection. This will typically be accompanied by other behavioral symptoms such as whining and licking due to the pain.

Impaired Vision or Hearing

Being unable to see or hear properly is quite a terrifying thought. Dogs that are suffering from this typically become very alert of their surroundings, which enables them to navigate as normal. However, this can cause a lot of fear and anxiety, and if they get a fright, their body can switch them into fight-or-flight mode, and nipping can occur. Dogs with impaired vision are also prone to barking as they are unable to process the shadows they are seeing.

Rescue Trauma and Fear

Trauma can make us all do crazy things. Even if we don't realize what we are doing or why we are doing it, the fear can linger in your mind. Dogs feel the same way, but without having the ability to fully understand why they have been harmed, it can be difficult to bring them out of the pit and get them to trust again.

Dogs that have gone through trauma will often react in one of two ways when placed in the same or similar fearful situation: fight or flight.

Human-Inflicted Trauma

This can be the most difficult trauma to deal with! Dogs that have undergone trauma inflicted by humans can become wary or even aggressive toward owners, strangers, children, and even specific genders. More commonly, you may experience that your dog is fearful and cowers if you raise your voice or approach too quickly. Lying flat on the ground or belly up is typically a sign of submission, which is meant to tell you that they understand that you are in charge, and they don't want any trouble. This may seem harmless, but an overly submissive dog is not a confident dog.

Whichever behavior you are experiencing, it is important to take it slow and build up trust with your dog before introducing them to outside influences and strangers.

Dog-On-Dog Conflict

Trauma from a fight or attack from another dog can cause serious socialization problems. This is not always from a rescue situation. Inappropriate socialization methods can lead to arguments between dogs and cause them to become wary of others.

This can be a little trickier to fix. While you understand your dog and how they will react, you don't always know what the other dog may do.

Housing Trauma

This may seem a bit silly, but dogs can often display negative behaviors if they have been continuously displaced. This could either be due to a rescue situation or if you have had to move repeatedly over a short period of time. Your dog has not been able to fully settle into a place that they can call their home and territory, and as soon as they do, they are removed from it. This can cause increased anxiety as they never really know what to expect next.

Trauma can be healed through positive reinforcement, bonding, and love. However, it is not uncommon for owners to seek medical help for severely anxious dogs. This is a last resort, and you will need to work very closely with your veterinarian to ensure that your dog is receiving the correct treatment and making progress.

The Effects of Food

We read about it in magazines, watch it on TV, and are reminded of it on billboards. It's instilled in us when we are children. Healthy food is healthy living! Our bodies are organic machines, and without the proper food, we can run into all sorts of medical and psychological problems. We set out our eating routines, a protein-filled, grain-free egg and gluten-free toast for breakfast. Fruits packed with healthy sugars and energy for snacks sustain us throughout the day. A balanced meal of proteins, carbs, and vegetables that are full of vital nutrients fills us up for dinner.

Why do we not think about this when it comes to our dogs? Before you think about splitting your food with your dog, it's important to remember that their bodies require different levels of protein and nutrients to function correctly. They are simply not able to digest most of the foods we eat.

It can be a bit difficult standing in a pet store, staring at the shelves full of different brands of food. With so many options and so many price tags, how on earth are you supposed to choose? It's time to bring out the nutritionist in you and check the labels.

First things first, avoid dog foods that are high in carbohydrates, sugars, and filler ingredients. These are typically added to make the kibble seem more substantial at a much, much cheaper price. Eating this type of food is the equivalent to us living off of takeouts. Weight gain is always a concern, but you may find that your dog suffers from stomach upsets, urinary tract infections, and lethargy. Foods that are high in sugar can lead to hyperactive and destructive behavior, but once the sugar high begins to wear off, the crash begins and the moodiness comes out.

Protein is the most important ingredient in dog food. This is where your dog's energy comes from. Low protein foods will lead to lethargic or lazy behavior, which can often mimic depression. The right amount of fiber also needs to be taken into account, as this will keep your dog's tummy working the way it should. Without it, they may experience tummy upsets and constipation. Fatty acids and antioxidants are also common ingredients in high-quality dog foods, especially puppy foods. These are used to promote healthy brain function and have been proven to assist in training and memory.

There are quite a few brands that create specialized foods for specialized breeds. These are readily available for owners of toy breeds.

If you are still struggling to decide, chat with your veterinarian. They will be able to direct you to the best food for your breed.

The type of food you give them is not the only factor that needs to be taken into account. Feeding schedules are also very important. We all feel that energy crash when we haven't eaten for a while, so imagine only eating one meal a day. A dog should be fed two to three times a day, the same way we feed ourselves. High-energy dogs can even be fed four times a day. This reduces pigging out behavior and aides in proper digestion. It also keeps the metabolism and energy levels stable throughout the day.

Food should be correctly measured out for your dog's weight and energy levels, and this amount should be split evenly across all feeds. You will be pleasantly surprised at how a healthy, balanced diet can reduce behavioral problems in dogs. Only once their minds and bodies are healthy can you begin to work on correcting remaining behaviors.

Chapter 3:

Pawsitive Parenting

Negative reinforcement is a human nature default. When somebody does something wrong, you are confident enough to tell them that it's wrong, but how many times do you praise somebody for doing something right?

How many of you despise your boss because your hard work goes unnoticed, but if something goes wrong, you're immediately in the firing line? This is the same feeling many dogs experience. The only difference is that they can't leave the situation, go home, and vent about it to their partner.

In fact, it is often even worse for dogs, as they don't understand why the behavior they have exhibited is bad in the first place, especially if it is something they are doing to show you love. Negative reinforcement will typically lead to a strained relationship between an owner and a dog, which can negatively impact training. Positive reinforcement is all about killing negative behaviors with kindness. Promote the good, and the bad will soon cease.

What is Positive Parenting?

In order to truly understand what positive parenting is, you need to understand what it is not. In this chapter, we are going to run through a variety of parenting styles, conditioning, and training methods, and we'll discuss how to correctly manage your dog's behavior. It can get a little overwhelming at times, but don't worry! We will work through the methods again in the following chapters.

Parenting Styles

There are essentially three different parenting styles: authoritarian, permissive, and authoritative. Authoritarian owners use negative reinforcement, punishment, and dominance to stop their dogs from acting out undesirable behaviors. Permissive owners allow their dogs to do what they like without any consequence, essentially rewarding the undesirable behaviors.

Authoritative owners are in the middle, and this is considered the most effective, as it builds a strong bond between dog and owner while still maintaining structure and boundaries. Owners that use an authoritative parenting style will often follow the same principles of relationship-based training.

Relationship-Based Training

This training style incorporates a lot of different training methods which can be used to create a mutually beneficial life together. This requires having a clear understanding of how the dog feels when they are behaving negatively and trying to find and cure the source of the problem.

Training is done slowly, and the commands are usually taught in a quiet space so they are easy to retain. Once the command has been learned, the owner will begin to use the command in a more demanding setting. The difficulty of the training gradually increases as the dog becomes more comfortable.

Dominance-Based Training

This training is based on the concept of pack mentality within wild dogs and wolves, which relies on dominant and submissive behavior. In these packs, there is an alpha who essentially rules over the submissive individuals in the pack and directs them on what they can or can't do.

Dominance-based training mimics the same behaviors and reinforces the idea that you are above the dog, you eat first and walk through doors first. This also includes avoiding any behaviors that might make your dog see you as an equal, such as allowing them to sit with you on the couch or crouching down to their eye level. Some owners are known to hold their dogs down on their back to force submissive behaviors.

The biggest problem with this type of training is that you are not actually a dog. Why on earth are you acting like one? Your dog isn't fooled, and trying to mimic this behavior can cause aggressive responses resulting in bites. You are also reinforcing the idea of a pack mind, and if you are first, they will want to be second in command. If dominating your young child gives them an opportunity to achieve this goal, there is a good possibility they will try it.

This method is now considered outdated, and many behaviorists believe it creates a relationship of fear, which can be detrimental to training.

Operant Conditioning

There are four quadrants of operant conditioning. Positive parenting is all about using the least stressful, force-free methods which promote positive behavior. This includes positive reinforcement and, on occasion, negative punishment.

Positive Reinforcement

Positive reinforcement involves rewarding a desirable behavior with a treat or toy. In this way, the dog is more likely to repeat the same behavior. It is most commonly used in basic command training but is often overlooked when it comes to behavioral correction.

Negative Punishment

Negative punishment involves removing something desirable when a negative behavior is displayed. This training method can be useful if used correctly. A good example of this is closing your hand around a treat if your dog tries to jump up and snatch it instead of obeying the command you have given. An example of using this training method incorrectly would be removing your dog's access to food and water when they have a potty accident indoors.

Negative Reinforcement

Negative reinforcement involves removing something scary or aversive when a good behavior is displayed. This method involves the use of threats over actual punishment. Fitting a dog with a choke collar is a good example of this. If they display positive behavior by not pulling on the leash, you won't pull back and tighten the choke collar.

Positive Punishment

Positive punishment is the use of physical or vocal punishment methods to stop an undesirable behavior. This can be through yelling, jerking back on a leash, and hitting. Electronic training is unfortunately still widely used in today's society. It usually involves the use of a shock collar or similar device. When the dog displays a negative behavior, you can trigger the collar to shock them, punishing them for it. I highly suggest that anyone that purchases a shock collar tries it on themselves before inflicting it on their dog.

The only way for positive punishment to effectively work is by actively causing your dog enough harm or trauma to scare them out of a behavior. Otherwise, this method simply interrupts the behavior temporarily but never gets rid of it.

In some cases, positive punishment is a reward in itself. Dogs that are severely lacking attention may bark continuously. When you turn around and yell at them to stop, they may feel rewarded by getting your attention, even if it's negative attention.

For years, we have tried to train and command our dogs through negative reinforcement, punishment, and fear, but it has never worked as well as love and reward.

Dos and Don'ts of Positive Reinforcement

Do: Reward good behavior! This is how your dog knows they are doing something right. Rewarding your dog for obeying commands is not enough. You need to reward them for exhibiting positive behaviors all by themselves.

Do: Be consistent! Keep up with your training and routines and don't give in to temptation. You can't train your dog to stop jumping on the bed if you reward them for doing it when you want a cuddle.

Do: Be patient with your dog! They are trying their best, and this whole training thing is pretty confusing. Take your time and prepare yourself for them to make some mistakes.

Don't: Use force to train! This is not going to get you anywhere. If anything, you will be training your dog to fear the commands and behaviors you are asking of them.

Don't: Display negative energy! Dogs may not be able to talk, but they are very good at communicating through body language. When you are upset and tense, they are well aware of it.

Don't: Punish! I will say it again, using punishment to train a dog simply does not work.

Don't: Use harmful collars! Other than physically harming your dog, these collars can also cause great emotional trauma and make it very difficult for your dog to learn that walking is enjoyable.

Don't: Give in to frustration! You have got this. You are both trying your absolute best, and he is not doing these things to upset you on purpose. It's okay to feel upset; it's not okay to take it out on your dog.

Behavioral Correction Methods

When it comes to behavioral correction, there are a few different methods you can use. There is no one-size-fits-all style, and you will often find yourself needing to jump between different methods to remedy different types of behavior.

Extinction

Extinction is a type of nonreinforcement, which means that no negative or positive reinforcement is used to fix the behavior. All you have to do is ignore them.

By ignoring the behavior, you are not rewarding or punishing the act. You are simply reiterating the fact that what they are doing is not working. Once your dog realizes that they get absolutely no reaction from you, they will stop doing it, essentially rendering the behavior extinct.

This really doesn't work for dogs that are displaying aggressive or destructive behaviors, but it can be quite effective for minor issues. It has been used to remedy attention-seeking behaviors such as demand barking, jumping, pawing, and nudging.

The problem with using extinction as a correction method is that it is very difficult to keep up. The moment you acknowledge your dog when they paw you, you are reinforcing the behavior again.

Train an Incompatible Behavior

This method is very useful, and I recommend it over extinction, especially for attention-seeking behaviors such as begging. It involves training a positive behavior using something they enjoy, making it impossible for them to perform negative behaviors.

A very simple example of this would be training your dog to go to their bed and play with their toys. Each night before dinner, ask your dog to enact this behavior, and it will be impossible for them to beg at the same time.

Shaping

This is a great method to use for anxious and fearful dogs. It involves positively reinforcing everything but the undesired behavior. If your dog lies calmly in bed, reward them. If they sit and wait patiently without command, reward them. If they are fearful of a stimulus, reward them when they don't react!

This technique works by building up your dog's confidence, which allows them to comfortably complete normal activities and behavior while reducing the fear of a looming threat. If you plan to use this method, be sure to use vocal and toy rewards as well. If you only use treats, you are going to end up with a chunky dog!

Desensitization

Desensitization is usually used in conjunction with a clicker. This is most commonly used in dogs that are struggling with fear and fear-based aggression. The goal of this training is to desensitize your dog to the stimuli that scares or triggers them to react negatively.

This could include emotionally averse reactions to loud noises, people, animals, and even objects such as cars. Once your dog is comfortable using a clicker, you can begin to slowly introduce the negative stimulus. Each time your dog looks at you instead of the stimulus, you click and reward. This helps the dog remain calm and focused on you, and they will slowly begin to realize that the stimulus is not actually going to hurt them. This needs to be done gradually to avoid placing your dog into a state of high stress.

Change the Motivation

This is the easiest method of all, and it works almost every time. It involves changing the motivation rather than changing the behavior. For example, if your dog is restless and prone to barking and destruction at night, it is more than likely because they are still full of energy. This motivates them to display this behavior. Adequate exercise and stimulation throughout the day will tire your dog out. This sleepy feeling will motivate them to hop in bed and get some zzz's. Easy-peasy!

Model-Rival Training

Model-rival training makes use of observational learning. The idea is that if your dog observes you rewarding the model, a human or another dog, for a good behavior, they will mimic this behavior for the same reward. The model then becomes the rival, and your dog will try to compete against them to receive the reward first. This encourages your dog to complete the task quickly.

Management

Managing your dog's bad behavior can save you a lot of time and trouble. Removing the temptation that is causing the behavior will also remove the self-reward your dog receives from it. An easy example would be not leaving that delicious pepperoni pizza on the counter. If you are struggling with them wandering out the yard, fix your fence!

It seems so obvious, but we often forget that our dogs don't think the same way we do, and we need to be conscious of the temptations we are unknowingly putting in front of them.

Training Tools

Having the right training tools on hand is vital to the success of training. Dogs that feel uncomfortable or unmotivated are less likely to learn the behaviors you are trying to teach them.

Positive Parenting Tools

Treats

Having a variety of rewards is key, especially for dogs that can get easily bored. Not all dogs enjoy treats as a reward, and you may need to avoid them if you have a dog that is struggling with weight gain. This is where toys come in handy! Playtime is just as rewarding as any tasty treat.

Walking Equipment

Having the right harness, leash, and collar for your dog can make a world of difference during your walks. Find something that suits your dog's temperament and most importantly, their size! Ill-fitting equipment is going to make for a miserable walk as your dog will be constantly trying to readjust the harness.

Clicker

A clicker is not absolutely necessary, but it really does make training much easier. They are quite cheap to purchase, so I suggest you grab one and test it out.

Treat Bag

Always have your treats handy! Holding multiple treats in your hand can be a bit confusing for your dog and will promote jumping up and grabbing. At the same time, stopping your training in order to go and get more treats from the kitchen can disrupt the learning process. A treat bag is a great way to store your training treats and keep them accessible by clipping the bag onto your belt.

Attitude

A good attitude is going to take you a long way. Your dog will pick up on your energy and match it, so if you are feeling excited and eager to learn, so will they.

The Dangers of Negative Reinforcement Tools

The biggest danger of using aversive tools is that they work—for a limited time. This reinforces us with the idea that they are good behavioral correction tools, and we continue to use them. The problem is, the dog will only suppress the behavior when the aversive tool is present. These tools do not help in long-term behavioral change.

A dog may walk calmly while wearing a choke collar because it is well aware that the threat of punishment is there. However, when walked with a normal collar, the threat is gone, and it's game on!

Shock, prong, and choke collars have the ability to inflict not only physical damage to our pets, but psychological damage as well. The constant fear of being punished for doing something wrong they don't know is wrong can be extremely traumatic.

Shock collars used for barking are especially damaging, as it is punishing the dog for exhibiting completely normal behavior. The dog may also associate the shock with the object, animal, or person they are barking at, causing a fear response when they are in their presence.

The use of aversion tools is the death of motivation. When there is no excitement or reward, and the only reason your dog is training is to avoid punishment, they will give you just enough to leave them be. Nothing more.

Heightened fear responses and anxiety will often lead to an increase in aggressive behavior. Remember, all dogs respond to fear by either fleeing or fighting. If the dog feels as though they are truly stuck in a frightening situation, it can turn aggressive.

Chapter 4:

The Crate Is Great!

I know what some of you are thinking. You will never use a crate! It's simply cruel. How could you put your dog into a prison like that? Well, I am here to assure you that that is simply not true, as long as you do it correctly.

Dogs, just like humans and other animals, need a space where they feel safe. a space they can retreat to when they are feeling afraid, tired, or simply done with you. All the crate is doing is mimicking the denning behavior of their wild counterparts, the wolves. The only difference is that this den comes with a fleece blanket and a bunch of fun toys.

By learning to use the crate to your and your dog's advantage, you can create a comfortable and safe home. It can also make the training experience a lot easier as it's a fantastic way to teach your dog, especially puppies, independence and boundaries.

Still not convinced? Let's dig a little deeper.

Why Crate Train?

First things first, the crate is a training and behavior management tool. It's your dog's comfort zone. It is not an easy way to control your dog by placing them into it for the day. They need exercise, stimulation, and space to thrive.

Your crate is a fantastic way to manage negative behaviors. If you are expecting visitors or have a nice dinner planned, you can put them into their crate with their favorite toy. This will stop them from jumping on your guests or begging for their delicious food. Rewarding them during this time will reinforce the positive behavior of remaining calm.

This is an ideal training method for teaching them boundaries and correcting negative behaviors such as potty mistakes, chewing, and attention seeking. By starting your new dog in a crate, you know that your house is safe. As your training progresses, and you start to get rid of the negative behaviors, you can gradually grant them more space by using a playpen around the crate. Open this space further until they are able to move around the house unsupervised.

Getting your dog used to feeling comfortable in a crate will also make traveling much easier. Whether it's by plane or car, you can always ensure that your dog feels safe and comfortable.

It's Not for Everyone

If you know that you are not going to be able to correctly crate train, don't do it! It requires time, energy, and your presence at home. If you struggle with time restraints during the day, consider doggy day care or a dogsitter. Another option is to use baby gates or similar devices to block off access to certain rooms of the house.

Some dogs don't take to crate training, at least not without extra help. High-strung and anxious dogs will struggle to be in the crate for long periods of time and may try to chew their way out if left unattended. This can lead to a greater fear response and cause your dog to view the crate as a prison cell. If your dog is suffering from severe anxiety, take training very slowly and avoid using training methods that could trigger them.

Setting It Up

Choosing Your Crate

There are a lot of different crates on the market. Some are cheap, and some are down right expensive! It all depends on what you need and what you are willing to spend. If you are still unsure about crate training or you only want to use it for a limited time, I suggest purchasing a mid-range crate. If you are planning to use a crate on a regular basis, do yourself a favor and spend a little more to get something you won't need to replace.

Size Matters

Purchase one that will suit your dog's size or is a little bigger to make sure they are completely comfortable. This is especially important if your dog is still growing. If you have a tail sticking out of one end and a snout sticking out the other, it is too small.

Consider Everything

What are you going to use it for? Is it just for home? Do you want to use it for transportation as well? Would you take it traveling? Purchase something that suits your needs. If you are undecided, there are plenty of versatile crates that can be dismantled and put up easily. Some of them are even adjustable to better suit your location.

The Best Materials

Crates can be purchased in four different materials: wood, plastic, metal, and fabric. Fabric crates are collapsible and easy to store. However, they are difficult to clean and do not work well for medium to large dogs. Plastic crates are generally used for travel purposes but can be used at home as well. They are durable and easy to clean but can become quite hot and a little uncomfortable for your dog.

Wooden crates are great, but not commonly used in home environments. They are difficult to clean, especially if your dog has an accident, as the wood absorbs urine and odors. Dogs that are prone to chewing also tend to enjoy these crates as chew toys.

Metal crates are the most commonly used. They are durable and collapsible, so they can be easily moved. They are easy to clean and come with dividers or add on options which allow you to expand them as your dog grows.

A Safe Place

If the crate is not comfortable or in a good, peaceful location, your dog will not want to use it. It needs to be easily accessible so that if they want to, they can go and lie down on their own.

Location

Take your time to pick the right place in your house. You don't want it to be in a room that is very noisy, but you also don't want to isolate them completely. The living room is generally the best spot as this is where you will spend the most time together. Choose a shady spot. You don't want your pup to cook in the sun!

If you have two dogs that are besties, place their crates side by side so that they can keep each other company.

Making It Comfortable

Comfort is key! Use a soft padding on the base of the crate. This is especially important for heavy dogs. There is nothing worse than waking up with a sore back. Use your dog's favorite blanket and provide them with plenty of toys to play with. You will need to clean out the crate at least once a week and once a day if you are experiencing rain and muddy paws.

Training

Training your dog to use a crate is incredibly easy. As long as you keep your cool and reward the behavior, you can get them comfortable in just a few days. Before you start, make sure that your crate is fully set up and ready for use.

Step One: Introduction

Introduce your dog to the crate slowly; don't throw them in and close the door. Put treats into the crate or their favorite toy. Praise them each time they enter and give them a reward.

Some dogs may be apprehensive at first, and it can take some time for them to get in, especially if you are sitting behind them pushing their bums in. They need time to smell everything on the crate and ensure that it is not as dangerous as it seems. Lining it with blankets and pillows that smell like them will entice them in.

If they are really not interested, place something fun inside and walk away. Your dog may feel more comfortable to investigate when they aren't being intensely stared at.

Step Two: Close the Door

This is the trickier part. Only do this once your dog has settled in. Wait for them to get into the crate and provide them with something fun to do. You don't want your dog to focus on you at this point. If they are, they will want to push out the door to get to you. Once they are lying down and relaxed, close the door halfway. They may push back at first, and that's okay! Wait for them to relax and close it again.

Once your dog is calmer, close the door completely. I suggest sitting near the crate so your dog feels safe. However, keep your attention diverted. Read a book while you wait. If you focus on the crate, your dog will too.

Open the gate after a few minutes and repeat this step until your dog is comfortable.

Step Three: Walk Away

It's time to walk away! Your dog has felt safe with you near the crate, but as you walk away, they will quickly notice and try to follow you. At this point, I recommend that you put something really fun in with them. I love using lick mats as my dogs get completely engrossed in them.

Close the crate door and sit on the other side of the room. Again, don't concentrate on the crate or your dog. They may whimper for a second, but when they realize you are still there, they will relax and carry on playing. Repeat this step while moving further and further away from the crate until you are eventually out of the room.

Keep your cool. Your dog may start to whine, cry, and even panic when you leave the room. Resist the urge to don your superhero cape and sprint in to save them. Give it a minute or two and walk in calmly. Talk to them as you would just before playtime, and then follow through with playtime! You want them to think that what is happening is normal.

Common Training Mistakes

While mistakes are possible, they are also avoidable. Make sure you are training correctly and keep your dog's needs met.

Should I Be Worried Too?

Stop panicking and stop checking up on them! They can feel your apprehension, and they will match it. Keep up the encouragement and provide them with rewards. Make yourself some brownies and reward yourself if you need to. If you remain positive and confident, your dog will trust your decision.

I Don't Fit!

The crate is a relaxing, safe space where your dog can feel secure. It's not a prison cell. They need to be able to stand up, lie down, and move around in order to feel comfortable. A crate that is too small is going to lead to discomfort, body pains, and frustration.

I Need to Run!

Your dog needs to move. You need to let them out of the crate at regular intervals for them to stretch their legs, have a run, and go potty. Without this, you can expect weight gain, medical problems, and potty mistakes, not to mention a frustrated dog! With all that pent-up energy, you can expect them to burst out of the crate and never want to go back in.

This Is So Boring!

By not providing your dog with adequate stimulation, they are going to get bored! Don't expect them to sleep the day away. Bored dogs will begin to whine, bark, pace, and even try to escape. Give them their favorite toys and puzzles to play with to keep them happy.

What Did I Do Wrong?

It is important to remember that your crate is for management, not for punishment. Place them in the crate before your guests arrive, not after they jump! Using it as a punishment tool will cause them to have an adverse reaction to it, which can be difficult to fix.

Chapter 5:

Not on the Carpet!

Okay, let's be honest here. Is there anything more infuriating than standing in a puddle of an unknown substance? You close your eyes, take a deep breath, and try to pretend that it's anything else but pee, but you know the truth! The odor removers and sprays don't seem to be working, and you have never managed to catch your dog in the act to punish them.

We have all heard that rubbing your dog's nose in their urine is a sure way to get them to stop, but I mean, really? Imagine if somebody did that to you! This method is incredibly outdated, yet still widely used. Instead of fixing the problem, it instills your dog with fear, and all they understand is that urinating is bad.

This often leads to dogs feeling the need to hide from their owners when they need to potty. This can cause more accidents in the house and greatly affect their ability to potty during walks and playtime.

The good news is that there are very easy ways to potty train your dog, even when they are fully grown. However, it requires you to take a couple more deep breaths, prepare for a couple of accidents, and for the sake of your dog, avoid punishment!

Why Is This Happening?

There are many reasons why this behavior could be happening. We will go through a few of the most common ones and then figure out the best way to curb the behavior. Some solutions may be simple and some less so. It is all going to depend on how ingrained the behavior has become.

I Couldn't Hold It Any Longer

Incontinence is incredibly common in aging dogs. Some breeds may reach this stage in their life earlier than others. It's always important to keep up with regular health checks, especially when they are reaching their golden years, to ensure they are comfortable and happy.

If your dog is younger and has suddenly begun to display this behavior, it could be due to an injury or infection. Monitor your dog and check for any signs of uncomfortable or painful behavior that usually accompanies an infection. When in doubt, check with your veterinarian.

Where Is All My Stuff?

Moving may be exciting for us, getting to start fresh in a brand-new place, but this is absolutely terrifying for dogs. They are moving to an unknown location with no idea why. They don't know the new setup, their usual poopy place outdoors is now gone, and there is still the lingering smell of the last dog that lived there. It is perfectly acceptable for your dog to make a few mistakes during this time, so bear with them and help them navigate the new environment.

I Didn't Know It Was Bad

This is most commonly seen in rescued dogs. They have never had to learn human etiquette, so they have never had to learn to potty outside. Dogs that have lived in shelters for a long time are typically not provided with large enough areas to make the association to potty outside, sleep inside. Their outdoor area is just next to their resting place. So when they move into a new home, they think they are doing pretty well making sure that they poop 5 feet away.

How Do I Get Out of This Place?

Dogs that have never lived indoors are typically very uncomfortable pottying inside. While outdoors, they have had the opportunity to go whenever they needed to, no waiting and no permission needed. Indoors, they need to learn to grasp the new concept of asking to be let out and learning how to hold it in until they have the opportunity. Your dog is guaranteed to make mistakes indoors until you are able to establish a new routine.

This Is MY Space!

Dogs will often mark their territory during walks and while visiting the park. This is to show everyone they have been there and that they own that tree! At home, your dog does not feel the need to replicate this behavior, as their presence is already firmly established. However, this behavior can be triggered by bringing home a new furry family member.

Your dog may feel threatened and feel the need to reinforce the fact that this space is theirs and theirs alone. It's important to help your dog feel comfortable and safe during this turbulent time by providing them a private space they can call their own. Introduce the new dog slowly and keep them away from your dog's safe space in the beginning. Once the stress subsides, the behavior will generally stop.

I Missed You So Much!

Some dogs urinate when they are excited to see you. This is called submissive urination, and it is a perfectly natural behavior which is mostly displayed by puppies. As nice as it is to know that somebody loves you enough to pee themselves, you also really don't want to be the one that has to clean it up. This behavior usually subsides as your dog grows up, but smaller toy breeds may continue it into adulthood.

Why Didn't You Listen?

Let's be honest. How many of you have been lying comfortably in bed, about to fall asleep, and your dog begins to whine? You wrestle with the pros and cons of ignoring it and by the time you finally get up, you realize your dog couldn't wait any longer. You need to take responsibility in situations like this. It's your job to create a structured routine that ensures your dog has enough time outdoors to do their business—especially before bedtime!

How to Tell When Your Dog Needs to Potty

Most dogs are relatively vocal when it comes to telling you they need to go outside. They will often whine, bark, or scratch at the door. Quiet dogs may pace around the room, circle certain areas, or sniff around the floor looking for the best spot to potty. The quietest ones are the ones that suddenly sneak out of the room after making sure you aren't watching.

Get to know your dog and their tell-tale signs so that you can judge when you need to take them outside. If they realize that whining gets you to open the door for them to potty, they will learn to continue using that cue to communicate with you.

The Solution

When it comes to training or correcting any kind of behavior, we need to give a little to get a lot. Typically, the giving part involves changing parts of our environment and routine to accommodate our dogs and assist them in their learning. It's important to find a mutually beneficial way to do this so that you don't end up feeling uncomfortable.

Organize Your Home

Start inside and work your way out. You need to make a few small changes indoors to disrupt the habit. These changes are usually reversible once the behavior has been corrected.

Sterilize, Sterilize, Sterilize!

First up, clean up the mess. The smell is gross enough for you, but any lingering scents can trigger your dog to potty again in the same place. There are lots of commercial pet odor products you can use to clean these areas, but a homemade mixture of white vinegar and water works just as well! White vinegar contains acetic acid, which can be used to remove alkaline odors. Soak any linen items in this mixture as well before washing them with normal laundry liquid.

If your dog has messed on items you cannot remove or soak, such as a couch or a carpet, you can use baking soda. Sprinkle the baking soda over the area and leave it to absorb the urine for at least five hours. You can then vacuum the remaining powder and clean the area with a normal upholstery or carpet cleaner. If you find that the smell still lingers, you can repeat the baking soda trick and spray the area with vinegar.

Restrict Access to Certain Areas

Dogs are creatures of habit and will often use the same spot to relieve themselves. If your dog has taken to pottying in certain areas of the house, especially carpeted areas, it's time to revoke their access. If possible, keep these areas blocked off either by closing doors or using baby gates. Make sure that your dog still has adequate space in the house to play and access to the yard.

Restricting access to their usual toilet will disrupt this routine and open up the door to learning a new one.

Indoor Potties for Aging Dogs

If you find that your aging dog is struggling to hold it in at night, it's time to make them an indoor potty area. It's not ideal, but it is much better than scrubbing a carpet every morning! Choose your spot wisely. You don't want it right next to your bedroom, and you want to be able to sterilize it daily. If your dog has taken to using a certain area already, it's worth turning that into their nighttime potty.

At night, lay down newspaper, artificial turf, or puppy training pads. Use anything that is absorbent, and your dog will readily take to it. In the morning, clean and remove the items to encourage your dog to potty outdoors.

Routine

Routine is everything! You need to provide your dog with enough opportunities to display good potty behavior to develop a routine together. They can't pick and choose when they need to potty. Their bodies are doing that for them based on the food you are providing them. At the end of the day, they are going to be the ones dictating the routine, you just have the opportunity to slightly adjust it.

Feeding Schedules

Get your feeding schedules right. Dogs should be fed two to three times a day, the same way that we eat. Food goes in, food gets digested, food comes out! This all happens in the space of a couple of hours, so meals should be given at a reasonable time every day. If you only feed your dog at 9 p.m., they are going to need to potty by 1 a.m., and if you are not awake, you can't blame them for messing in the house. The same goes for breakfast. Feed them as soon as you wake up and allow them outdoors for a final potty break before you leave for work.

Don't Be Lazy, Open the Door!

Set up a regular schedule so that your dog has options. The most important times are going to be as soon as you wake up, after every meal, a midday break, and just before bedtime. For dogs that are still struggling to get into routine, give them an opportunity every one to two hours.

This does not have to be a full walk. It can just be taking them outdoors. If they don't need to potty after five minutes, bring them back inside.

Keep Track

Get yourself a notepad and make a doggy potty book to keep track of your dog's poops. Okay, you don't really need to go that far, but at least make mental notes of when your dog does its business. This will help you get a better idea of when you need to schedule your walks and potty breaks. Once you figure this out, you can slowly wean off the hourly potty sessions.

Nighttime Potty Breaks

Let your dog out to potty right before bed, and I mean right before! Once you shut the door, you should be turning the lights off and getting into bed. Letting them out an hour before bedtime is not enough, especially if they have decided to drink some water or nibble on food before they go to sleep. If you sleep for eight hours, your dog needs to hold it in for eight hours. Keep this time gap consistent with the amount of hours you're asleep, and this should be enough to avoid any nighttime mistakes.

You are going to have to avoid the luxury of sleeping in, at least until your dog is fully trained.

Reward the Behavior

Always reward the good behavior. Don't punish the bad. When your dog successfully potties outdoors, make a big scene! Tell them how fantastic they are, give them a treat, and reward them with some playtime after each potty break. They will soon learn that you really like it when they poop, and they aren't too fussy about asking why.

By ignoring this behavior when it happens indoors, your dog will learn that they get no reward, and it's not worth their time if they have an opportunity to go out and get praised. Punishing the behavior when it's indoors and praising it when it is outdoors is very confusing. They are not sure if they are being punished for being inside, the exact spot inside they chose to potty, or if you changed your mind about being happy that they pottied at all. Sometimes, they don't even associate the punishment with it!

It is helpful to use a clicker or a cue word such as "go potty" when training. Clickers are great because your dog will identify the exact behavior they are being praised for. Keep it on you when you leave the house and use it the moment they are finished.

Use a Crate

If you have decided to crate train your dog, the steps above are going to be a lot easier. As discussed in the previous chapter, the crate allows you to restrict access, which means your dog doesn't have the option of sneaking off to potty. They will have to communicate with you.

Put your dog in their crate when you are not playing or working with them. Give them a break every hour and take them outdoors for an opportunity to potty and stretch their legs. As your dog starts to learn that this behavior is rewarding, you can start granting them more access to the house.

Do this by adding a playpen or baby gates around the crate. This now gives them the opportunity to potty outside the crate. However, they should have learned that this is not acceptable behavior. If they continue to display good toileting etiquette, you can expand their indoor space!

Chapter 6:

Eyes on Me!

Now it's time for the fun part, training your dog to obey commands. This is one of the most rewarding experiences, and most dogs are able to pick up what you want from them very quickly. This is not just training; it is bonding as well. The two of you will learn invaluable information about each other through the process and build a much stronger relationship.

While "sit" and "lie down" are usually viewed as cool little tricks you can teach your dog and use on the odd occasion you want to show them off, they are actually much more meaningful. These commands are going to form the basis of the rest of the training covered in this book.

Dogs, just like people, learn through repetition, and they are perfectly capable of forgetting something that has not benefited them in a long time, which is why it is so important to continue training these commands throughout your dog's life.

Choose Your Rewards

Picking the right reward will make all the difference in your training efforts. Treats are usually the go-to reward, but if you are trying to get active and train an overweight dog, these are going to be a big no-no. Some dogs will also respond better to toys or vocal rewards. Believe it or not, dogs can get bored when they have had too much of a good thing. Keep a variety of rewards on hand and alternate between them to keep the excitement alive!

Treats

Pick your treats carefully. You want them tasty but healthy! Avoid treats that are loaded with sugar and carbohydrates, and opt for protein-filled grain-free ones which promote mental and physical health. Larger treats such as biscuits and chew strips are great options for home. However, when it comes to training, your dog is going to gain a ton of weight if you are offering them a full biscuit for every good behavior they display.

Purchase specialized training treats, make them at home, or break up your larger treats into small pieces. Your dog is not looking for a gourmet meal to savor. Lots of small rewards work better than one big one, and pieces a little bigger than a grain of rice work perfectly.

Toys

Choosing toys can be a little trickier because different dogs like different things. I am sure you have purchased some toys that you thought were great, but when you offered them to your pup, they just gave you a blank stare, wondering how you could be so stupid to think they would like things like that. I suggest that you buy one toy of each variety and test them out with your dog to see what they enjoy. You will need to purchase toys for solitary play and communal play.

Chew toys are for solitary play. They are great for natural chewers, puppies, and dogs that are easily bored when alone. Squeaker toys are also fantastic for solitary play, but this depends on how much squeaking your ears can actually take.

Enrichment toys such as food puzzles and treat dispenser balls are vital for dogs that need constant mental stimulation. I am looking at you, border collies! Most of these have an option for adjusting difficulty levels to ensure your dog does not get bored with them too quickly.

Communal play toys such as balls or Frisbees for fetch provide your dog exercise, and the fun playtime can help you bond. Tug toys are very popular options to use as rewards when playing. You still stay in close contact with your dog, and you can easily remove the reward when you want to perform the behavior again.

Vocal Rewards

Vocal praise is just as important as any treat. Pair your praise with rubs and pats to get an even better response from your dog. Try to use the same phrase and voice pitch to praise your dog. This will help them associate the words with the good behavior.

Clicker Training

Clicker training is incredibly useful when using positive reinforcement methods. When a dog displays a good behavior, you click and reward. The advantage of using a clicker is that it immediately signals that you approve of the behavior. This allows for quicker learning as there is no gap between behavior and reward in which the dog could get confused.

In order to use a clicker, you need to first teach the dog that the click means reward. All you need to do is click, treat, click, treat, and within minutes, your dog will understand exactly what it means. Once they have been conditioned, you can begin to use your clicker in conjunction with other training methods.

Command Foundations

Sit

"Sit" is definitely the most frequently used command in dog training. Dogs are basically preprogrammed to obey this command. That's how easy it is to teach. This is usually taught to puppies as a cute little trick, but it is actually much more important. Not only does it form the foundation of all other training methods, but it also immediately stops any unwanted behavior. Your dog can't jump, pull on the leash, or sprint out the door while they are sitting! Using this command immediately calms them and brings their full focus back to you.

How-to

1. Grab some treats and move into a quiet space with no distractions.

2. Stand in front of your dog and get their attention by showing them the treat.

3. Hold the treat up over their heads out of their reach and slowly move your hand toward the back of their head.

4. Say the word "sit."

5. As you move the treat further back, they will be forced to sit in order to keep it in view! Repeat "sit."

6. When their bum hits the floor, click and treat!

7. Repeat these steps until they choose to sit before you get a chance to say your cue.

Down or Lie Down

Now that your dog is sitting like a champ, you can move onto the "down" or "lie down" command. It is up to you to decide which cue to use. I prefer to use "lie down" to avoid confusion, as I use the cue "down" for when my dogs try to jump. This command also forms the foundations of the tricks used in agility or sport training.

It is a lovely command to use for anxious or overly excited dogs, as it's a quick way to get them to relax. It works especially well for car rides and vet visits. The effectiveness of this cue, of course, depends on your dog's personality.

My pup is so eager to please that he will often perform "sit," "paw," and "down" in a matter of seconds. This voids the idea of using this cue to produce a calming behavior. When practicing multiple commands, I now say, "Hit the deck!" I use the cue "calm" to get him to lie down and relax in everyday scenarios.

How-to

1. Grab your treats and move into a quiet location.

2. Show them the treat and ask them to sit.

3. Touch your treat to their nose and move it down to their paws.

4. Once they start to bend down for it, slide it along the floor in front of them and say the commands "lie down" or "down."

5. When they lie down to reach it, click and treat!

6. If they stand up to follow the treat, move them back into the sitting position and start again.

If your pup is still struggling to understand what they should be doing, place your hand on their lower back and gently apply pressure at the same time that you move the treat away from them.

Stay

Sit and down are pretty pointless if your dog doesn't understand that they need to stay in that position! When you want your dog to remain calm, get them into a lying down or sitting position and ask them to stay. When practicing "stay," you can also incorporate the command "come," which will better prepare them for recall training.

How-to

1. Get your dog into a sitting position and hold your palm out toward them in a stop motion.

2. Say the command "stay" and slowly back away from them, repeating the cue word.

3. If they get up to move toward you, tell them to stop with the command "uh-uh" or something similar. I don't really like to use the word "no," but you may if you choose. Once they are sitting, continue to move back slowly.

4. When you are ready, tell them "come" or "okay" and reward them!

5. Repeat the steps above while increasing the distance between you each time.

Come

Recall is not optional. It is vital! If you are unable to get your dog's attention back onto you, you are in for a world of trouble when you start walking. This is especially important if you have a reactive dog or if you want to get to the point that you can walk without the leash. It is often overlooked in training, which is ridiculous, because it's so easy to teach. It just takes some patience.

How-to

1. Find a quiet spot outdoors where there are no distractions.

2. Hold your leash but keep it loose. Grab a handful of treats and face your dog.

3. Hold them in a sitting position and tell them the command "stay."

4. Move back quickly and say, "Come!" They will run toward you, and you are going to need to give them a big reward. I'm talking, cheers, jumps, treats—everything you have in your reward arsenal. You need them to think that coming back to you when called is the best thing since sliced cheese.

5. Repeat this a few times. Making your runs a little further each time.

6. Change from rewarding them with treats to one of their favorite toys. When they come to you, play with them for a minute or so.

7. If you are practicing this in your backyard. You can start to repeat the steps without your leash.

8. When you feel confident that your dog is obeying, add in some distractions. Start by getting a friend in, they should be standing a few paces away and doing something intriguing. They cannot call your dog toward them, as this can cause a bit of confusion.

9. Once your dog starts to walk toward them, say, "Come!"

10. Practice this during your walks, especially if you find that your dog has become interested in something.

11. When they return to you, reward them! Remember to reward your dog only when the leash is loose.

Heel

Want to get your dog walking nicely? Teach them to heel! If you can get this down before your walk training, you have won half the battle. This is a great way to create a bond between you and your dog, as they will learn to trust your decision-making and keep their focus on you.

How-to

1. Clip your leash onto your dog's harness, grab your treats, and find a quiet space outdoors.

2. Stand with your dog on your left-hand side. You want your leash in your right hand and your treats in your left so that your dog can see them.

3. Hold a treat close to your body but in front of your dog's face. Take a step forward and say the command "heel." When they walk with you, click and reward them.

4. Take some more steps, giving them a reward each time they obey the "heel" cue. If they wander off, call them back and get them to sit before you start again.

5. Once they get the hang of it, place your treats into your pocket so that they are out of view. Increase the number of steps you take before you use your command and reward.

6. Up the difficulty by practicing this in a new setting that has more distractions.

Drop It!

This command is fantastic to get your dog to stop trying to kill themselves! Use it to stop negative behaviors, such as chewing, by getting them to drop the shoe they were about to destroy. Or use it to stop them from stacking up expensive vet bills by getting them to drop the batteries they wanted to eat for lunch.

This training session is going to be about trading. You will need to give them something nice and ask them to drop it for something better.

How-to

1. Start by giving your dog a toy. It should be something they enjoy, but it also can't be their favorite one. Allow them to play with it for a bit.

2. Whip out the delicious treats and place one in front of their nose while saying, "Drop it."

3. If they drop the toy, click and reward them with the treat.

4. Take the toy away from them while they are enjoying their tasty snack.

5. Give them back their toy and repeat the process as many times as needed.

6. You can start upping the difficulty by replacing the toy with something they like better. If your dog loves playing fetch, practice getting them to drop their ball.

Leave it!

Once your dog has figured out that they need to drop something, you can start to use the cue "leave it" to prevent them from picking up the object in the first place. If you own a dog that has a strong prey drive, this command is vital, especially when they catch sight of another animal.

How-to

1. Move to a calm location and ask your dog to sit.

2. Close your hand around the treat and allow your dog to sniff your fist. They should start trying to take it from you.

3. Say the command "leave it," and when your dog stops trying to take it from you, click and treat!

4. Repeat this a few times until your dog gets the hang of it.

5. You can now up the difficulty by showing them the treat! Open up your hand and say, "Leave it." If they try to take the treat, close your hand until they sit back down.

6. When they leave the treat in your open hand, click and treat! Don't reward them with the treat you are holding. Grab another one with your free hand.

7. Make it a little more difficult by placing your practice treat by your feet. If they try to grab it, cover it with your foot.

8. When they leave the treat alone, click and treat!

9. If they are doing well, you can start to back up a little so that the treat is fully exposed. If they try to go for it, make sure you get there first!

It's important to always reward your dog with something other than your practice treat. If you allow them to take the treat that you asked them to leave, they will think it's fine to pick up any object you ask them to drop after they have obeyed you.

Rinse and Repeat

You are going to need to practice these commands over and over again for your dog to fully understand what you are asking them to do. This means that you can't just use these commands during practice sessions or to show off how smart they are to your friends. You need to incorporate them into everyday situations. Leave a plate of food on the table, and when you see your dog approaching, tell them, "Leave it!" If they obey, reward!

These little exercises will not only ingrain the commands, they will also be great opportunities for short bonding sessions, especially when your dog is getting rewards out of them.

Some dogs take a little longer to figure it out. Don't give up! They aren't stupid; they just don't speak human. If you have another dog that performs the behavior you want, you can practice with both of them at the same time. Dogs are brilliant at learning through observation.

Chapter 7:

Painful Greetings

There is nothing like being slammed against the wall by a raging 80-pound dog that can't contain their excitement to see you. While we wish that everyone in our lives would be this happy to see us, it can get to be a bit much, especially when you're wearing your new white pants.

While this behavior is frustrating, you need to remember that most of the time, your dog is just doing this because they love you. Let's be honest, how many times have you encouraged it when you were just as excited to see them?

We have all heard that the best way to stop a dog from jumping is to pull your knee up and hit them in the chest. Imagine getting punched in the ribs by somebody you love because you were trying to give them a hug. It doesn't seem as reasonable as when you turn the tables.

As with all my training methods, we will focus on killing the negative behavior with kindness. There are loads of ways your dogs can tell you that they are happy to see you. You just need to teach them how.

Why Is This Happening?

Why is my dog committed to tearing me to shreds with those sharp claws? Let's take a look at some of the most common reasons and then try to figure out how to make it stop, preferably while you still have some good clothes left.

Hi! Hello! Hi!

The excitement of seeing their owner after they've been gone for years (okay, it was just five minutes) is often too much for your dog to take. Your dog loves you, and they want you to know it by giving you a big, slobbery lick on the face. This is typically very rewarding for us, at least until it starts to hurt, or when you're in a sour mood. This is generally a bigger issue in large dogs, especially heavyweight champions such as Great Danes, who can knock you off your feet. Let's not forget that their small counterparts jump just as much. The only difference is that they can only get up to your knees.

I Just Want You to Know That You Are Mine

Jealousy makes you nasty. If you are in a multidog household, you have most definitely dealt with jealousy jumps. You give one dog a quick loving glance, and sure enough, you have three more dogs on your lap looking for some of that sweet affection.

This kind of territorial behavior can transfer onto people as well. Yes, your dog can become jealous of your spouse! They want to make sure that everyone around knows that you are theirs and theirs alone. This often occurs if you have allowed your dog to take over or share every aspect of your life, like allowing them to sleep on your bed, eat from your plate, or display any behavior they want and get away with it. When somebody comes in and threatens that relationship, they are going to fight to save it.

Boundaries

Getting your dog to understand that you are allowed to love other people can be tricky. You are going to need to set some boundaries, but these need to remain consistent. You can't go back on the rules you have put into place when your spouse leaves for work.

Stop your dog from performing activities that could create a rift between you and the person you love. An example of this would be your dog jumping on the couch and sitting between you. The solution would be not to allow the dog on the couch or to make your dog sit on a designated seat. Allowing behavior like this or laughing it off as cute is going to reinforce your dog's jealousy.

When you play or train, you all need to work together. Allowing your dog to develop a relationship with your partner independently is vital. Leave the room and allow them to get to know each other.

Please Play With Me!

If you ignore them long enough, you're sure to receive a slap. Or a kick? A nudge, perhaps. Regardless, your dog may find assaulting you the easiest way to get your attention, and oftentimes it works. One of my lovely rescued pups immediately took to nudging me under the arm when he wanted a cuddle. However, just like all bad behaviors, it started out cute, and then I found myself covered in boiling hot coffee.

The best solution, here, is to ignore the behavior and stop rewarding it. Turn away from them so they can't jump. If the jumps are becoming a bit much, you can gently push them down by applying some pressure to their chest.

I Am So Excited, I Could Jump!

Dogs get pumped up when they know something exciting is about to happen. They need a way to express how they are feeling. They might jump or bark or zoom at light speed around the house. It just depends on their personality. It is really unfair to take away their feelings of excitement, and it's important that you allow them to express themselves. Of course, it becomes a problem if they're jumping on you, but if they aren't harming you, and it's not an excessive behavior, then let them enjoy life!

Don't Get Caught up in the Excitement

Enjoying your time with your dog is one thing. Riling them up to display negative behavior is another. Remain calm and treat them the way you want them to treat you. If they get too excited during play, slow it down a little. You both need to refocus and take a breath before starting up again.

Oh, You Like This Now?

Consistency, consistency, consistency! If you don't want your pup to jump on you, don't encourage them to. A lot of owners encourage jumping when it's beneficial and rewarding to them. Lapdog-sized pups are irresistible and, of course, you want to pick them up and get a heartwarming cuddle. You can't blame them for trying to get back into your arms the next day. No jumping means no jumping!

This means that your family and friends need to be aware of and on board with your training methods. It's not okay to jump on one person and not the other. Some dogs may make the connection, but most do not, especially when the excitement hits. Whip out that whiteboard, get your laser pointer and give your visitors a full military briefing on what to expect and what not to do.

Please, Just Stop

Most of the behavioral causes above are based on love. Do not punish your dog just because you've had a hard day! Direct them on the best way to show their feelings by rewarding the good behavior.

Manage It!

Keep your treats on hand or leave a tub of them near the door. When you arrive home, and they start to bounce off the walls in excitement, grab a treat! Give them a command to do something positive, such as "sit," "get your toy," or "go to bed," and reward them for obeying it.

I personally found that using the command "toy" has worked wonders for my dog. He used to jump and kiss everyone that walked through the door. Now he grabs his favorite squeaker toy and shows it off before heading back to bed to play. The excitement is still very much there! His tail wags so hard that his entire body moves with it. We are still able to greet him with excitement so that he knows we missed him too. The only difference is the energy is now directed into the toy.

If you have a crate, use it! Before your guests arrive, pop your dog in, and voilà! You have avoided disaster. If you have designated a specific area for your dog to stay in while you are away, make sure they don't have access to the front door. Block this off so that you can walk in peacefully. Greet them over the gate and reward them for sitting calmly.

Sit Means Sit

Now, it's time to get down and dirty with training. Your leash is going to be an important component here. It allows you to easily control your dog's behavior and redirect them when they display negative behaviors. Put on some dog proof pants and grab your treat bag.

Step One: Gain Control

Get your dog into a sitting position and stand on their leash. They need enough leeway that they can move but not enough so that they can jump up onto you. Greet them. If they jump, ignore them or gently push them down by applying pressure to the chest. This is not reinforcing the behavior. It's managing it.

Step Two: Reward Good Behavior

When they sit, treat! Greet them again. Reward them for easy wins at first. When they start to get the hang of it, you can wait a little longer between treats, but make sure that you are not taunting them. Keep the treats in a treat bag or in your pocket and take out one at a time. If you are holding a bunch in your hand, and you are not rewarding the behavior, you are asking for a jump.

Step Three: Up the Difficulty

It is time to ditch the leash and add in a little more excitement. Greet them as usual. If they sit, reward them! You can start to move around the room, turning to greet them at semiregular intervals. If they jump on you, you now have two options. You can either turn around and ignore them until they are sitting, or you can gently push them down as before. Wait for them to sit and reward them. Rinse and repeat.

Remember, this is not going to stop the behavior immediately. This takes time and practice.

Step Four: Bring in a Guest

If you are feeling confident in your training and the way your dog has behaved, you can add a guest to the equation. Gather up the leash and stand with your dog next to you.

Get your visitor to stand at a distance. When your dog is sitting or looks at you for direction, treat them. Ask the visitor to approach slowly. If your dog stands up, your guest needs to stop, and you need to redirect your dog into the sitting position. Once that bum is on the floor and they look at you, treat them!

Continue this until your guest is able to walk up and greet them with some gentle pats.

Bring It All Together

When you know your guests are arriving, start by managing your dog's behavior. Distract them with a toy or a treat, or by placing them in their crate or another room. When it is time for the dog to greet your guest, put them on the leash and calmly walk into the room.

Get the dog into a sitting position and keep rewarding them for remaining calm. Your guests can now approach and say, "Hello!" Stop the greeting and the rewards if your dog tries to jump. Refocus them and ask them to sit before carrying on with the greetings. Once your dog is calm and has greeted your guests. Give them more freedom on the leash to mingle.

Chapter 8:

Alright, Already!

What is worse? The sound of your neighbor's car alarm going off in the middle of the night or going into your third hour of listening to your dog whine. For me, it's the whining! Ignoring it doesn't work, shouting doesn't work, and as soon as you reward the behavior by showing them attention, they realize it works in their favor.

Dogs generally don't just bark or whine for fun. They are usually trying to communicate what they think is vital information to you. The problem is that our definition and their definition of "vital" may be very different, and most of the time, we really don't need to know that there is another dog walking down the street.

While the thought of having a silent dog sounds like bliss, it's very important to ensure that they don't stop communicating with us completely. In this chapter, we are going to work through some common causes and fixes. The goal is to teach your dog what information you need them to relay and what is of no use to either of you.

Why Is This Happening?

Dogs communicate through barking, whining, and moaning. They even have different barks to tell you different things. You need to learn your dog's noises and the body language that is paired with it to understand what they are trying to tell you. Some of it might be more important than you think!

I'm SO Happy to See You!

Barking is quite a normal greeting for dogs. It is especially common when greeting their favorite human friend. They have heard the way that the pitch of your voices changes when you are excited to see them. You get to say, "Hello! I missed you!" and they like to mimic your excitement and reply in the same way. The problem is that this barking can become excessive when they begin to greet everything, including their shadow, with high-pitched barks.

Excitement barks are usually paired with happy body language such as wagging the tail, perking up the ears, and jumping. In no way is this a negative behavior, and you should never punish it. It's simply bad manners, and you can teach them other ways to show you they missed you.

Isn't My Voice Beautiful?

Some dogs are more vocal than others. Breeds that are used to living in packs, such as Siberian Huskies and Malamutes, often communicate with each other through howling. They are highly sensitive to the communicative noises other dogs make and will typically respond with a nice big "Awwooo!"

Dogs that were bred or trained as security or guard dogs are on high alert all the time. Their job is to keep you safe and let you know if there is any suspicious activity happening around the house. There is not a drop of water from a leaky tap that can evade their detection. If they are unsure in any way, they will let you know by barking until you arrive at the scene. The key is to teach them what they are barking at is not actually a threat.

I'm SO Bored!

In case you missed it the last hundred times I said it, boredom is one of the biggest contributors to behavioral problems. Keep your dog busy! Dogs that don't have enough mental or physical stimulation will be packed with energy. Barking is a great way to release this energy. They may also bark at you to let you know that they are bored and frustrated.

Why Don't You Love Me?

Mom! Mom! Mom! Mom! I don't know about you, but when my dog does this while I am working, I close my eyes and pretend I'm asleep (or dead if I'm having a bad day). Sometimes it works; other times I get a paw in my mouth. If you shout at them, they are rewarded. They might even think you are trying to bark back! If you give them attention, they are rewarded. The next time you stop scratching them, you can expect a bark to get you started again. As annoying as this behavior is. You need to try to ignore it. Close your eyes and pretend you're asleep.

Attention seeking can also be a sign of separation anxiety. This is a big problem if your neighbors are less than understanding. If you struggle to get this behavior under control, you may need to look into using a doggy day care facility.

There Is Something Out There!

These are the barks you don't want to ignore. Most owners can tell when their dog is barking a warning. Their voices suddenly go low. Their bodies are rigid, the hairs on their back stand up, and their ears are flat. My body ends up doing the same thing, and I am tempted to push them through the door first to save me from the boogeyman, especially when it's late at night. You need to be the grownup here, pretend you're not scared, and investigate the situation. You don't have to respond to your dog, but you do need to respond to what they are barking at. If you find that the stimulus is not actually a threat, such as the mailman or the neighbor, you will need to work at desensitizing them.

You will need to correct this behavior as soon as possible, as the longer it continues, the more ingrained it will become. If your dog barks at your neighbor every morning when they walk to the car, they are rewarded when the neighbor gets into the car and leaves. Your dog has learned that the bark works, and they will continue to do it.

Help! I'm Scared!

Barking at a stimulus that is making them feel anxious or scared can be similar to warning barks. The body behavior will likely be slightly different and is usually accompanied by a tucked tail, shaking, and crouching. Whatever they are barking at, it is clearly quite frightening. These barks may not be directed at an object or person, it could just be a fear response to a thunderstorm or fireworks.

This kind of behavior needs to be corrected through desensitization and should never be rewarded. The more you reward the fear, the more fearful they will become!

Dogs that are suffering from vision or hearing impairment are also prone to fear barking. This may be a little more challenging, but there are changes you can make in your home to help them.

Please Keep Quiet!

Before we get into how to make it stop, you need to know what not to do!

Electronic collars, spray bottles, and rattle cans are a definite no-no. If your dog is barking out of fear, this is only going to make it much worse. A muzzle is not a cure for barking and is considered cruel if used for extended periods of time. Your dog won't be able to eat, drink, or pant.

Don't shout! This simply rewards the behavior as they have achieved their goal of getting your attention.

Don't encourage it. Saying, "What's that?" or howling back is encouraging the behavior. You need to be as consistent as possible when training.

Don't reward it! If your dog is barking for food, wait for them to stop before you give it to them. If they are barking to get out of their crate, patiently wait for them to stop before opening it up for them.

Now that we know what not to do, let's work at fixing it.

Curb the Boredom

I am so bored, I could scream! Bored dogs are going to find a way to get their energy out. Keep them as busy as you possibly can. Use interactive toys like snuffle mats, lick mats, treat dispensers, and food puzzles. Tired dogs aren't going to be interested in barking. Ensuring your dog has had enough exercise is a sure way to curb the barking behavior.

Remove the Motivation

Sometimes the easiest way to cure a fear response is to remove the source. If you live on a busy road, and your dog feels threatened by the amount of people walking past the house, close the curtains! If they bark when outdoors, go outside with them and play a game. Some dogs may even be triggered by silence. If this is the case, put on some background noise such as music or their favorite TV show. In my house, *The Lion King* works pretty well.

Desensitize

If you are unable to remove the source of the fear, you will need to desensitize your dog to it. This can take a while, but it is definitely worth it to provide your dog a comfortable and happy life. Desensitization works best if you use a clicker. If you have already trained your dog to respond to the clicker, you will need to start introducing the stimulus.

Your dog has a threshold. When they reach this threshold, they will emotionally react to the stimulus as they become fearful or stressed. When using desensitization training, you always want them below this threshold. If they are reacting to a specific loud noise, such as fireworks or thunder, you will want to introduce this noise very quietly.

Take your dog into a quiet, calm room and click and treat. When they have started to focus on you, begin playing the noise softly. You will notice that their ears will perk up. At this point, you want them to refocus on you! Click and treat when they look at you and continue until they feel confident again. You can now raise the volume a little more.

As soon as you see your dog is reaching their threshold, stop training! That is enough for them for the day. Continue it again tomorrow. As you work through this, you will find that your dog becomes less and less reactive to the noise.

Train an Incompatible Behavior

This works well if your dog barks when guests come over. Figure out what triggers the bark. Is it the doorbell? The gate opening? The sound of a car driving by? Bribe a friend to help by replicating the stimulus. A glass of wine may be needed. It can get a little boring!

Train your dog to produce any behavior that will distract them from the stimulus. This could be the command "toy," which would direct them to go play with their toys. "Place" or "bed" works well, and your dog should respond by going to their special place or bed.

Practice this until they are obeying your commands and producing the behavior you want. Then, introduce the stimulus. Get your friend to ring the doorbell and tell your dog the command "bed." If they obey, treat!

Repeat these steps until your dog is displaying this behavior by themselves. Continue to reward them when they exhibit this behavior, even without your command. Keep up the tasty rewards for the next few months.

Stop training if you can see your dog is becoming irritable. Slow and steady wins the race. You can continue tomorrow!

Extinction

Extinction works well for curbing attention barking. However, this training only works if you stay consistent. Stop reacting to the barking, and your dog will learn that it doesn't work.

Using extinction can often lead to extinction bursts, which can be incredibly frustrating. Dogs that demand bark for attention will begin to bark louder and more often in a last attempt of getting what they want from you. Once this peak has been hit, and you have managed to keep your cool and not give in to acknowledging it, your dog will stop.

Quiet Training

Train your dog to understand what the word "quiet" means. When they start barking at you, say the command in a calm, firm voice. When they stop barking, click and treat. Wait a few seconds to ensure there is no lingering bark in that throat before rewarding. They will start to figure out what you want from them, and the next time they bark, you can use the command to make them stop.

Put It on Cue

You can also put the barking behavior on cue. Teach your dog to speak. Encourage them to bark by saying, "Speak." You can do a little bark yourself if it helps to get them going. Click and treat the behavior when they do it on command. Do not reward when they do it without command.

You can now bounce between commanding them to speak and commanding them to be quiet. The most important thing here is to make sure that your commands and rewards are crystal clear! Wait a few seconds between using the next command.

Chapter 9:

Where Are the Brakes on This Thing?

There is nothing quite as fun as turning a relaxing afternoon walk into a sweat-inducing sprint, and the great part is if you start to get tired, your dog will drag you the rest of the way. All jokes aside, this is probably the most common behavioral problem that dog owners deal with, and it's exhausting. A lot of owners quickly give up and accept the fact that walking is no longer an option.

The issue is that they aren't able to keep up with the exercise routine their dog needs to stay fit and healthy. Playing catch in the yard can only do so much, and the dog becomes less and less desensitized to the outside world. Sometimes a little chubbier too! This, in itself, can lead to a ton of new difficulties.

The good news is you aren't the only one experiencing this, and over the years, trainers have come up with new, more effective training methods that can solve the trouble quickly. As with any undesirable behavior, there is always a root cause. Figuring out that cause is key, as it enables you to decide which training method will work best.

Why Is This Happening?

This Hurts

Your dog is not going to want to walk if they are feeling miserable. Arthritis and injuries to the leg or paw are the most common health reasons, but even tummy aches and illnesses can affect them. Make sure your dog is feeling up for it. You shouldn't have to drag them out of the house.

Another factor that many owners don't take into account is how sensitive their little paw pads really are. When you head out for a walk on a hot day, put your hand down on the asphalt and check the temperature. If your hand burns, their paws are going to burn! You can seriously injure your dog by forcing them to walk on hot roads or sand. Opt for the park or a similar area so that they enjoy the cool grass.

If you can't avoid hot pavements or freezing cold snow, consider buying a set of booties. These are specially designed to protect your dog's feet and come in a variety of sizes and colors. This ensures a comfortable fit, and your dog can maintain their fashionista reputation.

Health Check

You can give your dog a brief health check at home. Sit calmly together and gently feel up and down each of your dog's legs. Start at the hip and work your way under their paws. Push gently on their joints and see if your dog reacts in any way. Pulling away from you, whimpering, or giving you a warning look is a clear sign that you have touched a sensitive spot. This could indicate a sprain or arthritis. If you suspect an injury, it's time for a trip to the vet!

This Is Not Comfortable at All...

Does your dog get the jiggles when you are walking? That means they are uncomfortable! Their harness is either too loose or too tight. If your leash is too long, it can wrap under their legs. Collars can also become quite annoying if you have connected your leash directly to it. If it's too tight, your dog is going to feel like they are choking. Loose collars will move around the dog's neck depending on how they move their heads. This constant friction can be very annoying, and you won't be able to direct your dog with as much control.

Choose the Right Equipment

The equipment you choose needs to fit comfortably and provide support. Make sure to select items that work for your dog's size and temperament. Without this, your walks will become a miserable affair.

Leashes and Leads

Every dog owner should own one leash and one lead.

A lead is a type of long leash which ranges anywhere between 20–100 feet long. It gives them the freedom to move away from you, but you still have control if they decide to run too far. This makes it a great tool for recall training.

Short leashes are awesome for walking and close contact training. This gives you more control over your dog as it keeps them at your side. It also allows you to softly pull back and stop walking when your dog is misbehaving. Using long leads for walking is guaranteed to end up with one of you flying through the air!

While I suggest you opt for a harness over a slip-leash. These do have their place. They can be used for reactive dogs and are much, much kinder than choke collars. Slip-leashes can be compared to lassos. The leash fits around the dog's neck and loops through a ring which sits comfortably on the back of the neck. If the dog pulls, the leash tightens, but as soon as they stop, the leash loosens back to a comfortable position.

Retractable leashes should be avoided during walks as it can teach your dog bad walking manners. These leashes apply a constant pressure, which the dog learns is normal. When using a normal leash, your dog will continue to pull to replicate the feeling.

Collars

Dogs should be comfortably fitted with flat collars on which you can clip their identification information. It's not recommended that you walk your dog with just a collar until you are completely confident that they are not going to dash off into the sunset.

Harness

Harnesses are highly recommended for walking reactive and untrained dogs. The harness allows you to have full control over your dog as it places pressure on the chest rather than the neck.

Front clip harnesses are a great option for dogs that pull, while back clip harnesses work well for comfortable walking and small dogs. You can purchase harnesses which offer both options. Some are even fitted with handles on the back. Handles come in handy if you are dealing with a reactive dog, as it gives you the option to hold them securely without having to pull back. If all else fails, you can even pick them up like a handbag.

Ill-fitting harnesses can cause chaffing, and your dog may struggle to breathe if it is too tight. Make sure that you fit it correctly and move your hand underneath the straps to ensure that there is enough space for your dog's chest to comfortably expand during exercise. Check how your harness fits before each walk and adjust it if your dog has gained or lost weight.

I Am So Glad You Like Running Too!

If you are rewarding your dog's pulling behavior by trying to keep up with them, they think they are doing the right thing. You must enjoy it if you're panting as much as they are, right? Be consistent in your training. If you want to go slower, you need to show them.

If you want to run with your dog, use a cue word like "run" to trigger the behavior and a cue word such as "heel" to end it. Choose your running phrase carefully and make sure it's not used in other training methods. If you use "let's go" for running and for getting in the car, you are going to end up having an awkward conversation with a very confused stranger that suddenly has a dog in their back seat.

This Place Is AMAZING!

Sensory overload! A dog's sense of smell is estimated to be around 10,000–100,000 times better than ours. Imagine the amount of information they are currently trying to process. Are you really that shocked that they suddenly stopped listening?

Allow Your Dog to Explore

Give your dog a chance to be a dog! There are so many new and exciting things around them, they can't help getting lost in their own nose. Give them a second to sniff around and process the new information. Take it slow, stay with them, and don't pull them back with force. If it's time to move, ask them to focus on you by giving them a command such as "sit." If they listen, treat and start your walk.

I Am Not Sure About This...

Dogs can get scared, and they are allowed to be apprehensive at times. If they haven't had the chance to get out into the world and experience different environments, it's only natural for them to be nervous on walks. If you are walking down residential roads, you may have neighbor dogs barking at you through the fence. It's an annoyance for you, but it is absolutely petrifying for them, and your dog may lunge at them or attempt to flee if they feel threatened.

If you have a chance to, change your route to a quieter one. If not, you will need to work on your dog's social skills to better prepare them for the outside world. We will discuss how to do this in-depth in the next chapter.

Come On, Let's Go!

If your dog is full of pent-up energy, it can be quite difficult to get them to slow down to your speed. I had a Greyhound that suddenly evolved into a rabbit when it was time to walk. If she couldn't go forward, she was at least going to go up! Prewalk playing used to help curb the excitement. They don't need to be exhausted before you get them walking, but they need to be calm.

Keep Calm and Walk On

Who let the dogs out? You! You! You! If you have an overly excitable dog that loves to bolt out the door the moment it opens, you have got a problem! Not only is this incredibly dangerous, but your dog is also getting the impression that they are in charge of the upcoming activity. This behavior needs to be corrected before you can even think of walking nicely.

Step One: Take Back the Power!

Harness up your pup, secure their leash, and get out that treat bag. Gather the leash up so that you have a firm grip and walk up to the door. By this point, your pup should be vibrating with excitement. Stand by the door and wait patiently. Eventually, your dog is going to turn around and look at you for direction. You need to ask them to sit.

Once their bum is on their ground, and their eyes are on you, give them a treat and tell them well done!

Step Two: All Eyes on Me!

Plant your feet firmly on the ground because now you are going to open the door. If they blast out, it's tough luck for them. Redirect them back inside, close the door, and start over. You want their bum on the floor and their eyes on you even after the door is open. Remember to reward your dog every time they sit and every time they look at you for direction.

Step Three: One Step at a Time

After a few repeats, you should be able to open the door without losing their attention. You can now walk outside. The same rule is going to apply here. If they try to run while you are walking out the door, you need to redirect them back inside and start from the beginning.

It's tedious, I know, but don't give in just yet. They will eventually understand what you want, and after a few tries, the two of you will be able to walk out that door calmly. This is not a once-off training session. You need to practice this behavior every single time you open that door.

Let's Get Walking

Now that your dog is not bursting out the door like an escaped convict, you can begin walk training. Start in your backyard or indoors if you have the space.

Step One: Use Your Leash

The way you are holding the leash is surprisingly important. If you have your dog walking on your left-hand side, you want to hold your leash firmly in your right hand. You will be using your left hand to pull the leash and direct your dog. When it's time to turn or redirect, slide your left hand down the leash to your knee. This provides enough horizontal tension and will gently pull your dog to where you want them to be. Hold this position until your turn is complete.

Step Two: Keep Their Attention

The world is jam-packed with new and exciting sights and smells, which makes you the most boring aspect of the walk. It is only natural for your dog's attention to drift off to something more rewarding. Walk forward, use your leash, and turn. All their attention is suddenly going to shift straight back to you. By being unpredictable, you can ensure that your dog will constantly keep you in mind and focus on what you are doing rather than what is around them.

Step Three: Ignore the Bad

When your dog begins to pull, stop walking and wait for them to redirect their attention back to you. When the leash is loose, and they are focusing on you, reward and keep walking.

Step Four: Reward the Good

Reward, reward, reward! When your dog successfully turns, give them a treat, a vocal reward, or even a toy! When they sit and look at you for direction, reward! When they are walking with a loose leash, reward! By rewarding all the good behavior, they will forget all about the negative behaviors that previously felt good.

Step Five: Up the Difficulty

Start to incorporate new distractions. This could be people walking down the street, cars driving past, or even ducks swimming in the local pond. It doesn't matter what you choose, just make sure you start at a distance.

Take it slow and walk calmly past the distraction. If the leash stays loose, reward them. If they start to focus on the distraction, redirect them by turning. The moment their focus is back on you, give them a reward!

If your dog has done well, walk past the distraction again, but this time, go a little closer. Only do this if you are absolutely sure you have your dog's full attention. Don't set them up for failure; you can try again tomorrow.

If only two ducks get to float away bark free, your dog has done well! Redirect them and walk back the way you came. Always celebrate the little wins.

Off-Leash Walking—Is It Okay?

Off-leash walking is the dream! You get to prowl around town with your pup in tow, no care in the world. As lovely as it seems, it is almost always a bad idea. Off-leash walking is only possible if you have a dog that is well-trained in recall. If your dog does not come running when you call their name, put that leash back on. If they do not obey recall, you can be assured that a time will come when they dash off after something unknown, and you will be sprinting after them screaming their name like a maniac. Some communities also have leash laws, so you'll want to abide by those as well.

Different dogs also have different social skills. Be aware that there are other people out there trying their best to train their dogs. If your pup decides to run up and give a reactive dog a sniff, there may be a fight. Not only does your dog stand a chance at being injured, you have also just ruined that other dog's training. "But my dog is friendly" is not a good enough excuse.

Don't be a buzzkill! If you are determined to walk off-leash, train your dog to obey recall and only remove the leash when undertaking isolated activities such as hiking.

Chapter 10:

Who Needs Friends Anyway?

If you are having problems socializing your dog, you are experiencing one of two things. Your dog seems terrified and desperately tries to flee the situation, or they go into complete attack mode and lunge at the nearest threatening target. Both of these, especially the latter, are likely to put you in a complete state of panic, as nobody wants to own an aggressive dog.

While it may seem easier to just stop taking your dog to the park or work out which times of the day your walking route is quietest, there will come a time when social situations are inevitable. These can quickly become dangerous as your dog will suddenly be stuck in a situation that they don't know how to handle, and their behavior can become unpredictable.

Getting your dog to socialize with other dogs can be a little tricky at first, but with time and patience, you can get it done. Even if it's just to teach an introverted dog that other pups are not as threatening as they may seem.

Is Your Dog Social?

Dogs may have been pack animals, but that doesn't necessarily mean that they are all happy in social situations. Just like us, dogs have their own personalities and preferences. There are certain things they enjoy and certain things they don't. When they meet a like-minded friend, they are sure to have a ball. However, that doesn't mean they will like everyone.

Social Dogs

Highly tolerant and social, dogs are more than happy to take a tail to the face if it means they get to play with someone else and have a great time. They are happy to meet new friends and quickly adapt to all types of play styles.

Tolerant Dogs

Dogs that have a midrange tolerance level are generally happier with a smaller group of friends. They know each other well enough to know how to play together and when to leave each other alone. They typically don't mind other dogs, but they can become irritable if approached by an excitable pup that doesn't know how to play by the rules.

Antisocial Dogs

Antisocial dogs do not play well with others. They will often become aggressive when approached and are much happier left alone. Aggressive, antisocial dogs are a product of previous trauma or a lack of socialization as a puppy. If they have been in a traumatic situation with another dog, they are likely to bite first and ask questions later in an attempt to keep themselves safe.

Dogs that were not socialized as puppies are typically antisocial because they are scared. They don't quite know how to deal with an unexpected lick from a stranger.

Introverts

Yes, there are introverted dogs, and no, they aren't necessarily aggressive. These pups likely received the right amount of socialization when young but have simply decided that they prefer humans. Introverts are usually tolerant of other dogs, and while happy to go to the park for a walk or game of catch, they are not too interested in playing with anyone else.

There is nothing wrong with this behavior. If your dog is happy and healthy and displays no aggression toward others, don't force them into social situations. Sometimes it's okay to not have any friends.

Understanding Body Language

Understanding your dog's body language is going to be the difference between a fun-loving greeting and World War III. By knowing how they feel, you will be able to judge the situation better and decide whether to continue with the introduction or raise your white flag and call it a day.

Posture

It's generally quite easy to gauge how a dog feels based on their posture. A relaxed body is a good body. If they put their chest on the ground and bum in the air, they are ready to play!

When your dog is feeling upset, you can actually see their muscles tense up. If they are cowering or hunched to the ground, they are definitely not feeling comfortable. They do this to make themselves as small as possible to indicate that they are not a threat.

If they go straight into the attack pose with their weight shifted forward and their heads lowered, you have got a problem, especially if this is accompanied by snarls and intense staring. This is equivalent to saying, "Come at me, bro!" If the intended target does not back down, you can expect your dog to lunge.

If you see that the hair on their back is standing up, it means that they are incredibly intrigued by whatever is in front of them. It's exactly the same as us getting goose bumps! This is not necessarily a negative behavior, but if it is accompanied by barking, growling, or negative posture, it can indicate a threat.

The Way of the Wag

Wagging tails aren't always a sign of happiness. They are just a way for your dog to display an emotional response. Long, sweeping wags that jiggle their whole bodies are the best kind of wags. This means that they are happy and excited to see you.

If your dog's tail is up and twitching quickly, proceed with caution. This doesn't necessarily mean aggression, but it does mean that they are having a strong emotional response to the stimuli in front of them. The higher your dog's tail is, the most assertive and confident they are. If this is accompanied by other negative body language, it is a sign of aggression.

Low-hanging tails, especially ones that are tucked in between their legs, are a sign of fear or submission. This is not a happy tail and most certainly not a happy dog. Retreat and do something they enjoy to distract them.

What Are You Doing With Your Mouth?

Snarling is the most obvious signal your dog can make with their mouth, and you already know that it means trouble. If this is accompanied by growls, it's time to retreat. Dogs do also smile. While this may seem similar to a snarl, their mouths are generally much more relaxed. This is their way of letting you know they are friendly.

Snarls and smiles are not the only way your dog communicates. If you find that they are yawning a lot, they could be feeling stressed out. This is often accompanied by lip licking and excessive swallowing.

If Looks Could Kill

If your dog turns their head and avoids eye contact at all costs, it means they are stressed or feeling uncomfortable. They will typically try to flee the situation, or if your dog is anything like mine, they will hide between your legs and ask you to sort out the bully.

On the opposite end of the spectrum, if your dog is staring daggers at another, they are trying to threaten them. If you are struggling to snap them out of it, you should remove them from the situation immediately. They are clearly too focused on the other dog to obey you.

Let's Get Sniffing

Before you start training, you need to figure out what you actually want to achieve and set yourself some goals. In this chapter, we are going to work on the following:

- keeping your dog calm when visiting a new area

- being able to walk without your dog reacting to other dogs or people on the road

- stopping your dog from trying to eat your guests

- helping your dog make a new friend

These seem pretty simple, but they are going to be the foundational steps to proper socialization.

Goal One: Keep Calm

If your dog does not feel comfortable walking in a new environment without people and dogs around, you cannot expect them to feel comfortable in the park! Dogs that have been isolated will often become incredibly anxious when faced with too many new things all at once. Start with the basics and avoid placing them in the middle of a terrifying situation.

If your dog is comfortable in your backyard, start there! Use this space to practice your command, walking, and recall training. Start introducing random items from the strange outside world that your dog hasn't been exposed to. This could include anything from plants to your dirty shoes and blankets that smell of other dogs.

Now, work your way out. Does your dog get nervous when the two of you are in the front yard? Then stop there. Turn this into a fun experience by playing a game. Reward confident behavior, and they will soon learn that this is not as scary as it may seem.

It's all about flipping their perspective. You want to change something they fear into an opportunity to get a reward or play a fun game. When they are a little more confident, walk out your gate.

It is so important to remember to keep your dog below their response threshold. If they stop accepting treats or responding to you, they are overloaded. It's time to go home and relax.

Goal Two: Stop Reacting

Now that your pup understands that the world outside your gate is not, in fact, an alien planet, you can begin working on desensitizing them to people and other dogs. Remember, they are not reacting negatively to strangers because it's fun; it's because they are frightened.

You may find that they react to certain people. If they have only been exposed to women, they will be understandably nervous of much larger, taller men. If they have never been exposed to children, they are probably trying to figure out what kind of strange, furless dog is in front of them.

Thankfully, the streets are full of people of different ages, sexes, sizes, and clothing preferences. Find a quiet spot where you can maintain at least a 20-foot distance from a frequently walked path or road. If your dog is still feeling uneasy, you can move a little further away.

Use their absolute favorite treats for this activity. If they love sausages, stock up on sausages! Every time they look at a person walking past, use your clicker and reward them. Stop rewarding when the person has walked out of view. Once they feel more comfortable, you can move closer to the road and start again. If your dog becomes reactive, redirect them and return to the 20-foot mark to start again. If they become unresponsive to the rewards, they are too overwhelmed. Call it a day and go home to relax.

You are going to be using the same steps to desensitize your dog to other pups. I suggest walking around a dog park first. Keep a reasonable distance so that your dog is not overwhelmed. You just want them to pick up on some smells and sounds. When the park is quiet, you can walk your dog along the fence line and give them a chance to sniff around.

When they begin to relax around the area, you can work on getting them a little closer. For this, I recommend finding a cooperative owner with a calm, well-socialized dog. Get them to sit calmly 20 feet away from you. Every time your dog notices them, you can click and reward. You can start to walk closer as your pup feels more comfortable, but remember, this is not an introduction! Redirect your dog before you get too close.

Repeat these steps at a 20-foot distance while the other dog is performing different activities. Ask them to walk past, play a game or make some noises. If at any point your dog is feeling uncomfortable, redirect them away from the situation and start again at a further distance.

Goal Three: Please Don't Eat My Friends

Assuming you achieved goal number two, and your dog is no longer reacting to strangers, you can start to let those strangers into your home. Please don't get real strangers, just friends of yours that your dog hasn't met yet!

I like to start the introduction by bringing home some of my friend's clothes for my dog to sniff. They gain a lot of valuable information from this, and they won't need to sniff as hard when my guests arrive. Choose a mutual setting that your dog can enter and exit at all times. They need to feel as though they can escape the situation without having to pull the fire alarm. A backyard or living room works well.

Place your dog in their crate or behind a baby gate until your guests are settled. When are you sure your dog is calm, open up and allow them to enter or exit the room. Continue your conversation as you normally would.

Do not get your guests to approach your dog first or get them to give your dog treats out of their hands. You want your dog to make the first move. If they decide to stay hidden, you can ask your guests to throw them a couple of treats to prove that they are friendly.

At the end of the day, if your dog decides not to come and greet your friends, that is fine too! There was no negative behavior, your dog learned some valuable information, and they will likely be much braver the next time around.

The same method can be used for a reactive dog, but you will need to ensure your guest's safety. Keep your dog on a leash at all times, and if you notice they are becoming anxious, remove them from the situation.

Goal Four: Making Some New Friends

If your dog has achieved the first three goals with flying colors, you can now attempt a dog-on-dog greeting! Find a friend or family member who has a calm, well-socialized dog and organize a doggy play date. It's best to meet on mutual ground, and a quiet park with no other distractions works well.

Keep both dogs on loose leashes and get confident. Your dog can sense when you are anxious. When you see your friend, you can begin to approach each other slowly. Chat as you normally would to keep yourself and your dog from getting tense.

When you eventually meet up, allow the two dogs to sniff each other calmly. Dogs' greetings are short and sweet. They don't need to spend an hour having a conversation over coffee. A five-minute sniff to size the other one up is more than enough. Once this time is up, redirect your dog a few paces and play a game to reward them.

If it all goes well, you can walk up for another greeting a little later. Repeat this a few times a week, extending the greeting period by a few minutes each time.

Keep an eye on your dog's behavior during the interaction. If you see that they are becoming at all jittery, redirect them a few paces back and play a game while the other dog is still in sight. You need to show your pup that they are not a threat before attempting another introduction.

Before you try this out, ask yourself, does your dog really need a friend, and is it worth a potentially bad experience to get them one? If your dog is still reactive and aggressive to other dogs that come near, stop trying. Sometimes the trauma goes a little too deep, and if you have managed to get your pup walking calmly with you, that is enough.

Professional behaviorists and dog trainers are great options in situations like this, especially if you find that you are becoming increasingly anxious. They have the knowledge and experience to calmly handle socialization scenarios and will be able to offer hands-on assistance.

For more serious cases, consider giving your dog calming medications before you begin your training. If you have chosen this route, be sure to work closely with both your veterinarian and trainer to ensure that your dog is getting the best possible care.

The most important thing to remember is not to push their boundaries. Keep working at getting them to feel safe and confident. Who knows? In a couple of months, they may be ready.

Conclusion

Time flies when you're having fun, right? Don't worry! Even though the book is finished, your journey with your best pal has only just begun.

If I have done my job right, you should be feeling calmer and much more optimistic about the future. You have been armed with up-to-date training techniques and behavioral correction methods. You should be bursting with confidence and prepared to share your expertise with your friends, family, and that one neighbor whose dog enjoys barking for hours on end, unless you are watching your dog chew up the couch right now... What a mood killer!

If that's the case, I would just like to remind you that everything is going to be okay! There will be good days and bad days, but it is important to remember that consistency and patience are key. Don't give up on your dog, because they sure won't be giving up on you. Take a deep breath and work through the steps. Watching your dog change and flourish will be the greatest reward you can imagine.

This is not a one-man job. You will need to work with your dog to figure out the best way forward. If you take the time to listen to them, they will tell you exactly what they like and don't like. If you find that some of these methods aren't quite working for you and your pup, don't be afraid to switch it up and innovate! Small adjustments can lead to huge changes.

This book should be used as your reference guide. When you are feeling unsure, scroll back to the chapter you need. Bookmark the chapters that apply to you the most, scribble in your notes, and read it to your dog! Do whatever you need to do to get the most out of the information I have provided.

On the worst days, when you feel like you just can't do it anymore, seek out a friend. There are tons of support groups out there for owners of aggressive and reactive dogs. If this is something that you are struggling with, I highly recommend that you look into joining a local group or one of the many online ones. Having the chance to talk to somebody else who is working through the same problems as you can be a lifesaver.

It's now time to pick yourself up, give your pup a big kiss and head to the local pet store to gear up for your adventure! Pick out a great harness and leash, grab some fun toys, and don't forget your pup's favorite treats.

If you have enjoyed this book, please leave a review on Amazon.

Book 3:

My Senior Dog

A Complete Guide to Caring for Your Old Dog

In loving memory of Gizmo. You turned my life upside down, and I thank you every day for it.

Introduction

Sam seems to be slowing down these days... You wake up in the morning and shuffle down the hallway, eager to greet your best friend. Sam is laying there, staring seamlessly at the wall with milky eyes, he didn't even notice you. As you get closer, he raises his head and wags his tail, but this is not the same ball of energy that used to bound down the hallway to greet you with kisses.

If there is anything that gets him going, it is food! His excited little tail beats against your leg as you prepare his breakfast. He has been losing weight, maybe it is time to give him lunch as well? He starts chomping down immediately, but he seems to struggle when it comes to chewing the bigger pieces.

After breakfast, it is time to potty. It's a beautiful day and a perfect morning for a game of fetch. Sam walks out the door with you but pauses at the stairs. The large grassy backyard has lost its appeal, and he decides that he would rather potty on the deck.

You throw the ball to start a game of fetch, perhaps that will get him moving. He stops and watches the ball bounce, but after a thoughtful moment, he turns around to go back inside. Something just doesn't feel right, but you're going to be late for work. You go to give him a quick kiss on the forehead and realize that he's shivering as he curls up in his bed. It's not that cold, is it? Grabbing a warm blanket, you tuck him in before you leave.

There is no better feeling than arriving home to an ecstatic dog, but today Sam is not waiting, he's asleep again. You wake him up, and he looks at you with all the love in the world. He tries to get up to greet you but quickly loses his balance. Not to worry! You are there to catch him and help him up.

It's time for the routine afternoon walk, an activity that Sam usually loves, but you can tell he is not up for it and the two of you snuggle up in front of the TV instead. Stroking him gently, you notice the tiny gray hairs growing around his muzzle, and you wonder, is Sam really getting old?

These are just a few examples of how your dog may act when they reach their senior years. Most owners are not prepared for these changes, and why should they be? Dogs aren't supposed to get old! The idea that you may have to say goodbye to your dog soon is absolutely terrifying, but it is important that you don't get stuck in this mindset. It may feel as though the end is near, but for your dog, this is just the beginning of their golden year's adventure.

My passion for dog training began when I brought home my first rescued dog. He was the epitome of chaos and my best friend. He changed my life, pushed me out of my comfort zone, and while I healed him, he healed me. He showed me my purpose, and together we set out to learn, train, and help as many people and pups as possible.

The day that I realized he was getting old, I was heartbroken. I immediately hit the books, searching for an immortality potion. Failing that, the least I could do was ensure that I would be able to provide the best care for him. However, even with my new-found knowledge, I still felt so overwhelmed and ill-equipped. Until, as always, he came to my rescue.

I learned to listen and realized that he was showing me exactly what was wrong and what he needed. The last few years we spent together were some of the happiest of my life. The knowledge I gained and the techniques I learned have proved invaluable, and I have been able to use and adapt them to suit the needs of any senior dog.

If you feel that your dog is slowly slipping into their senior years, and you are beginning to lose sleep over it, don't worry! I am here to help you both. This book is packed with all the information and techniques that I have used, adapted, and perfected over the last 30 years. From medical conditions and diet management to grooming tips and dog-approved life hacks, rest assured that you will find your answers here.

Let's dig in!

Chapter 1:

Is My Dog Old?

Believe it or not, the age of your dog is not actually an accurate way to tell whether they are old or not! We have all heard that one dog year is equivalent to seven human years, but this rule doesn't actually translate. Experts have since worked out that the first year of a dog's life is equivalent to fifteen human years. The second year is equivalent to nine human years. From there on, each year can be judged at around five human years.

However, even with this myth busted, there is still no set rule or age that marks your dog old. Just like humans, aging is slow and subtle, and the rate at which individuals age varies greatly. Genetics, trauma, illness, and lifestyle all contribute to the body's general health and the rate at which it declines. Dogs, from the same litter, can even age at a different rate. So, how on earth are you supposed to prepare for your dog's senior years, and how will you know when they get there?

Understanding your dog and being aware of the physical and mental changes they may go through is key. Let's take a look at some of the most common signs.

Aging Your Dog

With the exception of large and giant dogs, the general rule of thumb is to assume that your dog will enter their senior years at the age of seven. At this point, veterinary checks should be conducted at least once a year, and lifestyle changes need to be considered.

Size Matters

Yes... size matters. Small dogs generally live longer than their larger counterparts.

Small and toy breeds, under twenty pounds, typically reach their senior years when they are around ten years of age. Medium dog breeds, under fifty pounds, become seniors at seven years of age. Large and giant dog breeds enter their senior years at around five years of age.

Scientists are still unable to provide a concrete reason as to why this happens, but they do have a theory on why large dogs are more susceptible to age-related medical conditions. Their bodies need to grow at a much faster rate, which makes them more likely to experience abnormal cell growth. This cell growth places strain on the internal organs, which can cause early aging and a quicker decline of the immune system.

This is why it is so important to understand your dog's breed!

Effects of Injury and Illness

Injuries and illness can contribute to early aging or at least age-related conditions in pets. Dogs that have suffered injuries, particularly in the legs, are more likely to develop joint stiffness and arthritis at a much younger age. This will cause them to slow down earlier, which makes them prone to conditions such as obesity.

Severe and prolonged illnesses such as diabetes, cancers, and heart conditions put immense strain on the body. They suppress the immune system and can affect the health of internal organs. Making age-related conditions more likely to occur at a younger age.

Effects of Trauma

Mental and emotional trauma can also cause premature aging in dogs. Continuous fear and stress can cause hormonal imbalances, which can lead to a suppressed immune system and impact the heart and other vital organs. The short-term effects of stress, such as weight loss and vomiting, are the most noticeable and will often subside once the dog is in a happier environment.

Unfortunately, the long-term effects only show themselves later in life, and dogs can experience age-related conditions such as heart disease and diabetes before their senior years.

Premature graying in humans is a clear sign of stress, and studies have proved that dogs can experience the same thing! The little gray hairs that naturally form around their muzzles when they age can start to show in chronically stressed dogs as young as four years old.

Behavioral Changes

Behavioral changes in senior dogs are typically passed off as mental decline due to age. However, this is usually not the case. With the exception of cognitive dysfunction syndrome and canine dementia, most of these changes are a direct response to the physical changes they are experiencing.

Disinterest

General disinterest is one of the first behavioral signs owners notice in aging dogs. They will often become reluctant to partake in physically demanding activities such as walks or playing fetch. Their toys may become less exciting and the prospect of jumping up onto the couch to snuggle with you is no longer appealing.

This disinterest is likely due to a physical cause. If your dog is experiencing joint stiffness or arthritis, they will try to avoid going on walks, jumping, and other activities that are likely to cause them pain. Dental conditions, infections, and disturbed sleep cycles can cause disinterest.

How Can I Help?

Try to find out what is causing the disinterest and adjust your routine and lifestyle accordingly. Cut your walks shorter and pick up your dog when they need to jump onto the couch or into the car. Provide them with mentally stimulating toys, and swap out the hard chew toys for soft squeaky ones!

When to Worry

If the changes have not helped, and they become disinterested in more activities, food, and even people, it is time to visit your veterinarian. They may be struggling with a much more serious medical condition.

Disorientation

Disorientation is always worrying. You may notice that your dog is getting "stuck" or lost in areas that they should be familiar with. They will often stare blankly at walls, be unable to recognize familiar people, and have a harder time completing everyday tasks.

Depending on the behaviors they are displaying, this could be due to physical conditions such as a loss of eyesight or hearing. A more concerning cause is cognitive dysfunction syndrome and canine dementia.

How Can I Help?

Take your dog for a check-up to confirm the cause of the disorientation. You can then make the necessary lifestyle changes. Decluttering your home, keeping furniture in the same place, and closing off access to dangerous areas will help your dog to navigate their surroundings safely. Older dogs will struggle to adapt to frequent changes, so it is important to keep up a routine and avoid stressful situations.

When to Worry

If the disorientation gets worse or if you suspect that your dog is going senile, you need to speak to your veterinarian! They will be able to direct you on the next steps, medications, and lifestyle changes that you need to implement. Without proper treatment, your dog is at risk of harming themselves and others.

Aggression and Fear

Aggressive behaviors in senior dogs are linked directly to fear or pain. If your dog has begun to snap at you when you approach them, you may find that they are suffering from hearing or sight loss. They do not know that you are approaching, so they get scared when they suddenly sense you. If they have begun to bite or snap when you touch them, they are likely experiencing pain. This response is especially noticeable if you have other dogs in the household that like to play a little too rough with them.

How Can I Help?

Firstly, find the cause! If they are experiencing sensory decline, announce yourself before you approach them to keep them from getting scared. Provide them with a safe space to retreat to when they begin to feel uncomfortable with their surroundings. Crates, kennels, and even dog beds with sides work wonderfully.

If your pup is experiencing pain from an infection, injury, or underlying condition, your veterinarian will be able to locate the source and treat it accordingly. Be sure to keep younger, boisterous dogs away from your senior dog while they recover.

When to Worry

If there is no underlying physical cause and your dog continues to become more aggressive, it could be a sign of canine dementia. If this is the case, it is important to isolate your senior from other household pets and unfamiliar guests. This is especially vital if you are not there to supervise the interactions. This will reduce the risk of your dog harming others. Dementia is the worst-case scenario, and you will need your veterinarian to assist you with appropriate treatments.

It's important to remember that isolation is not a punishment! You should provide your dog with all the comforts they are used to, including plenty of toys and tons of love. Once you begin to see improvement, you can allow them more freedom to interact with others.

Abnormal Sleeping Patterns

This refers to dogs that have trouble sleeping through the night or tend to sleep for long periods during the day. Some dogs may do both. There are a couple of reasons why this could happen.

Dogs naturally lose their stamina as they age. If your pup sleeps well through the night but takes a few extra naps during the day, then let them sleep! It's completely normal behavior.

A lack of exercise can contribute to a sleepless night. Countless owners quit their regular routines as soon as their dog reaches their senior years. If your dog is sleeping away their boredom during the day, they are likely too energetic to sleep at night.

Dogs that are experiencing discomfort from stiff joints and limbs may struggle to get comfortable. The constant need to toss and turn will disturb their sleep patterns.

How Can I Help?

Heavy dogs should be given thick, comfortable mattresses to sleep on to ensure they are not laying on the hard floor. This will help to alleviate any discomfort they experience from aching joints.

Regular exercise and mentally stimulating tasks are an absolute must. You don't need to run your dog, but short, slow walks can make all the difference.

When to Worry

If your dog is sleeping for hours at a time and is struggling to wake up, it is time to visit your veterinarian. If they start to display symptoms of sleep deprivation such as irritability, disorientation, and forgetfulness, it is time to visit your veterinarian!

Most behavioral changes in senior dogs are subtle and take time to develop. If you catch them early, they can be remedied at home with little effort. However, if you ever feel unsure, it is best to take your dog for a check-up. Any extreme or abrupt behavioral changes should be treated as an emergency.

Physical Changes

As your dog ages, it is only natural for them to experience physical changes. Their bodies begin to take strain, their metabolism slows and their immune system degrades. Most of these changes don't require medical attention, but it is important to monitor them and make the appropriate lifestyle changes to keep them comfortable.

Cold Sensitivity

The ability to regulate body temperature is one of the struggles your aging dog may experience. This is generally age-related, but their weight, general health and fur can all contribute.

A dog's fur is a dog's clothes. Without it, they struggle to keep warm. As they age, their hair follicles age. You may find that their fur begins to thin out, and they develop graying around their muzzles. Muscle mass generates heat and provides insulation, and body fat is used as a backup energy source. Senior dogs that experience weight loss will likely lose muscle as well and without extra fat for energy, they have a harder time staying warm.

How Can I Help?

It's time to buy some sweaters! I like to have a range of sweaters, from thin indoor ones to thick outdoor coats. Booties and socks are a great way to keep your pup's feet and joints warm and are especially important in snowy weather. Warm blankets and heated beds will help them to stay warm throughout the night.

Now that their body doesn't need to work as hard at keeping them warm, it can focus on regulating important bodily functions. You will often notice a quick improvement in their general health.

When to Worry

If you find that your dog is shaking uncontrollably and struggling to get warm even with a sweater on, you should take them for a check-up. This could be due to an underlying medical condition, such as a neurological disease. Hypothermia, bronchitis, and pneumonia can develop if your dog remains cold for long periods of time. These are all dangerous conditions that can become fatal if not treated.

Vision Loss

If you notice that your dog has started to stare blankly at the wall, or doesn't recognize you until you walk closer, then they are likely losing their vision. Vision loss happens gradually, and most owners don't even notice it until their dog starts walking straight into walls! This can be caused by cataracts which reduce vision or by nuclear sclerosis which only affects depth perception. A white, hazy film over the eyes is apparent in both cases.

How Can I Help?

Vision loss can be treatable depending on the cause. If caught early, eye drops and minor surgery can prevent it from progressing further. Cataracts can be surgically removed, but this is not often done with older, high-risk dogs that have other medical conditions.

The best way to combat the effects of vision loss is by making your home blind friendly. Keep large items such as furniture in the same place and remove any clutter that could trip up your dog. Block off any dangerous areas such as pools and stairs to avoid any injuries.

If your pup is really struggling to see, it is time to take advantage of their other senses. You can mark different rooms in your house by putting down different textured mats or using different scents. This will help them to recognize where they are through smell and touch.

When to Worry

If your dog is losing their vision at a rapid rate, or if they are having frequent eye infections, you will need to take them through for a check-up. They could be suffering from diabetes or sudden acquired retinal degeneration syndrome (S.A.R.D.S.). Both of which can have incredibly painful symptoms that need to be treated immediately.

Hearing Loss

Hearing loss is another common symptom of aging that most owners don't notice until it is severe. Your dog may stop obeying your commands, and they will often bark for no reason. You may find that they are easily frightened and will snap at you or other dogs when approached too quickly. It happens gradually and while it is usually an age-related symptom, it can be worsened by ear infections, thick fur around the ears, and underlying medical conditions.

How Can I Help?

A check-up should be done to ensure that they aren't suffering from an ear infection. If this is the case, treatment should help alleviate any pain and can restore some of their hearing.

Deaf dogs can still detect vibration, and you can get their attention by clapping or knocking on a hard surface. However, this doesn't really help if they can't figure out what you are trying to tell them. Training hand signals from an early age can greatly assist in communication.

When to Worry

If you find that your dog is scratching their ears, often leading to wounds or bleeding, they could have a serious inner ear infection. Nerve damage from injuries can also contribute to hearing loss and an annoying pins and needles feeling. This needs to be treated as soon as possible.

Appetite and Weight Changes

As your dog's metabolism slows, you may find that they are losing or gaining weight. This can occur even when they are still eating the same-sized meals with the same calories.

Weight loss is generally due to a reduction in muscle mass or poor absorption of nutrients. A loss of appetite is a common symptom of digestive issues and dental pain. Weight gain is commonly due to a lack of regular exercise. Your dog is no longer expanding the amount of energy that they are getting from their food!

How Can I Help?

A change of diet and exercise routine is the best remedy here. We will work through this in-depth in the following chapters. If you are concerned that your dog may be suffering from a dental condition, it is time to visit your vet!

When to Worry

If your dog loses more than 10% of their body weight, it is time to worry! Internal parasites, organ failure and disease can all contribute to this drastic drop. These are serious conditions that should be treated immediately.

Incontinence

Incontinence is one of the most frustrating physical changes in senior dogs. Your dog may struggle to hold it in for long periods of time and in severe cases, they are unable to hold it in at all. The nerves that control the bladder will deteriorate with age, and the outflow valve is unable to fully close. In this case, you may find small puddles of urine around the house or in your dog's bed.

How Can I Help?

Regular potty breaks and indoor potty areas are usually enough to keep your house clean and your dog happy. In more serious cases, you can use specialized doggy diapers. If your dog is messing on themselves, it is important to keep up with regular baths. Not only is this uncomfortable, but the bacteria can also cause infections around their genitals.

When to Worry

If your dog is experiencing pain when they urinate, or you find blood in their urine, they are likely suffering from a urinary tract infection or kidney disease. Once treated, you should find that the incontinence actually stops.

Lumps and Bumps

The strange little lumps that develop on or under your dog's skin can be quite distressing and, let's be honest, kind of gross. The good news is that they are completely natural and commonly show up as your dog ages. They are called lipomas and are caused by an accumulation of fatty cells. They are not cancerous and are unlikely to cause any pain.

How Can I Help?

There is typically nothing you can do to help with these growths. Removing them is not necessary as they don't pose a health risk. The most important thing to do is ensure that your dog is not scratching and opening them.

When to Worry

If these lumps continue to grow, become infected, or start to ooze, you should seek medical assistance. Your veterinarian will likely perform a biopsy to check if the growth is cancerous, and they may feel the need to remove it.

Bad Breath

Bad breath is generally caused by a gum infection or dead teeth. It is very common in aging dogs as their teeth begin to break, file down and decay with age. Injuries can also cause dental disease, and you may experience bad breath in younger dogs and puppies. This is very uncomfortable, and your dog is likely to experience pain when they eat. An infection can spread to the body and affect internal organs.

However, bad breath is not always a sign of dental conditions. Dogs can be pretty nasty, and for some reason, they love to eat disgusting things. If they have had access to garbage, carcasses, and even cat poop, they may be enjoying some hazardous snacks when you aren't looking.

How Can I Help?

Dental check! If your dog has broken teeth or a gum infection, take them to your veterinarian for a check-up and dental cleaning. In some cases, they may even remove the broken teeth. Once this is done, you will need to keep up with regular cleanings, which can be done at home.

If your dog is munching on disgusting items, make sure that they can no longer access them. Move your cat's litter box and ensure that all your bins are sealed.

When to Worry

If your dog passes the dental checks and is still experiencing bad breath, you will need to ask your veterinarian to investigate further. Diabetes, kidney disease, and liver disease can all cause strange-smelling breath. Knowing the other symptoms of these conditions can help you identify the cause.

Chapter 2:

Medical Conditions and Disease

If you are anything like me, I am sure you have been monitoring your dog carefully, and taking notes of every little sneeze and stumble. The looming, invisible threat of health complications can drive you over the edge. The thing is, these threats have always been there and while aging does come with its set of challenges, most medical issues that senior dogs experience are minor. It is not likely that your dog is going to suddenly become inflicted with a life-threatening medical condition.

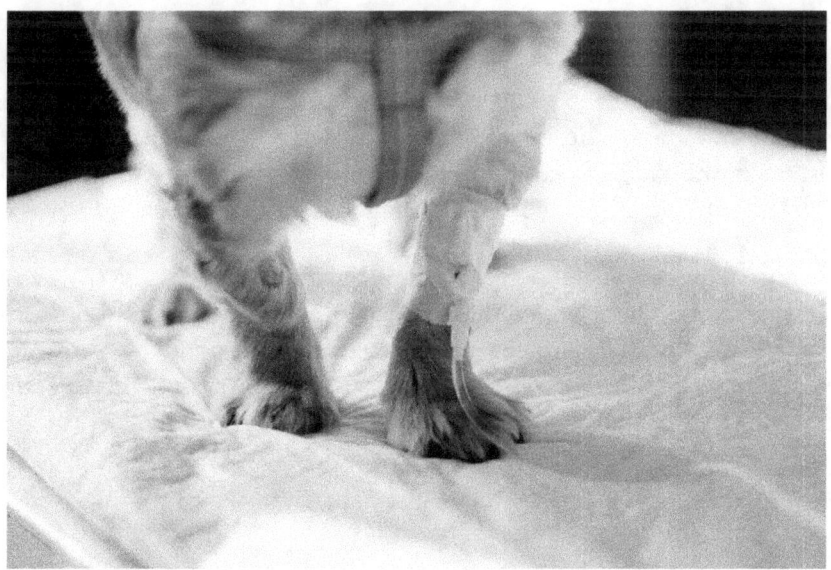

However, that doesn't mean that you shouldn't be careful. Understanding the threats and how to spot them is the best way to prevent any complications. It is also the best way to decrease your anxiety! Always remember that your dog can pick up on your emotional state, and they will often mimic how you are feeling. In this chapter, we will discuss a variety of ailments, from acute to chronic, known to inflict senior dogs. While some of these are treatable at home, it is important to remember that you are not a veterinarian, and you can only do so much before you inflict more harm.

Treatment Options

There are a few different options you can choose from to treat your dog. However, before you attempt any home treatments, it is vital to understand the condition you are treating and the possible causes. Home treatments can mask symptoms that indicate a much more serious disease. Be smart, and work with your veterinarian to provide the best care for your pup.

Chronic vs. Acute

An acute illness infects the body quickly and the symptoms are seen within a few days. These types of illnesses usually last a week or two. Although the side effects may linger in the same way that you may recover from a cold, the cough may linger for a few weeks.

Chronic illnesses develop slowly and will typically worsen over time unless treated. These conditions last for months to years and, in some cases, a lifetime. Chronic conditions will often trigger acute ones. For example, a chronic allergy can cause acute abscesses if your dog scratches their skin open.

What Is Holistic Veterinary Care?

Holistic care is a form of healing that incorporates the body, mind, spirit, and environment. It is non-invasive and puts the dog's overall health and emotional well-being first. The goal is not to just treat the symptoms. It is finding the root cause of the illness and removing it to ensure that the condition does not worsen or recur. Holistic veterinarians will combine modern medicine with holistic treatments such as homeopathy, rehabilitation, dietary care, and pain management practices such as acupuncture.

Surgery may be performed to fix a broken leg, but this is just one symptom. Holistic care would incorporate rehabilitation to help your dog regain muscle. Homeopathy can help manage pain and muscle stiffness. Nutritional therapy can keep your dog's weight stable while they heal. Grooming can keep your dog's claws short, which will reduce pressure on the joints. As well as a change in your home environment can accommodate your dog's temporary disability and keep them comfortable.

What Is Homeopathic Treatment?

Homeopathy involves using natural animal, vegetable, or mineral substances to produce a remedy that relieves, treats, or cures a medical condition. The principle of homeopathy is, if a toxic amount of a substance causes dangerous health symptoms, then a much smaller amount of the same substance should be capable of healing those symptoms.

While most homeopathic treatments are safe, there can be adverse effects if you mix certain substances with medications. It is best to speak to your veterinarian first if your dog is suffering from a chronic condition. Dogs cannot always digest the same substances we do, so be sure to check the ingredients first and make sure they are safe. For acute conditions such as upset stomachs, sprains, and short stress periods, homeopathic remedies can work wonders!

Rescue Remedy is the absolute bee's knees. This is my all-time favorite homeopathic remedy, and if you don't have a bottle, I suggest you go get one right now. You can use it to calm your dog before or during a stressful event. I give my dog two drops before a thunderstorm, and he sleeps through it like a baby. It can also be used to treat pain and discomfort. It won't take the pain away completely, but it definitely makes it easier to handle.

Acute Conditions and Disease

Most acute conditions are easy to treat and even easier to prevent once you are aware of them. However, they should still be taken seriously, especially with senior dogs that may be suffering from other medical conditions.

Ear Infections

Ear infections can be very irritating. They are itchy and painful and can disorientate your dog. If not treated, the infection can actually cause permanent damage to your dog's hearing.

They are usually caused by bacteria that thrives in moisture and wax build-up. So, it is important to dry your dog's ears after they bathe or swim. Dogs with ear infections will often paw and scratch their ear repeatedly, sometimes to the point of scratching open the skin. The ear is typically red and swollen, and you may find discharge or crusting inside it. Depending on the extent of the infection, there will be a strong odor as well.

While this is considered an acute condition, some dogs may suffer from recurrent ear infections as a symptom of a chronic disorder. If you notice that this is happening, speak to your veterinarian.

Treatment

The best treatment will be a course of antibiotic ear drops. However, you can treat the secondary symptoms at home. Use a disinfectant to keep the outside of the ear clean and free from any discharge or crusting. This will help stop the itch, but make sure that you dry your dog's ear well and do not get any disinfectant in the ear canal.

If your dog has long fur, I strongly recommend that you trim the fur around and in the ears to keep them clean. Once the ear infection has subsided, you should routinely wash your dog's ears every month or so to prevent it from happening again.

Vomiting and Diarrhea

Vomiting is not always a serious problem. Eating too much too quickly is the most common cause. If your dog has eaten something mildly toxic like plastic or plants, their bodies will reject it, and they will vomit it up. One or two vomits in quick succession are nothing to worry about. However, if your dog is shaking, drooling, and vomiting up large amounts, they have likely eaten something very toxic. This is an emergency, and you will need to get to your vet as soon as possible.

Diarrhea is commonly due to a dietary change. This can occur if you move your dog onto new food too quickly or overload them with treats. Mildly toxic foods can also cause diarrhea. The worst thing in the world is cleaning up after a dog has stolen a piece of cake! These types of stomach upsets don't last long, and if your dog is acting normal and eating and drinking as usual, you can treat this at home.

If the diarrhea lasts for more than 24 hours or has any blood in it, you need to start worrying. This could be a sign of gastroenteritis, parasites, and toxicity. A dog suffering from these will be weak, dehydrated, and tired. They will completely lose their appetite and there will be a noticeable weight change.

Treatment

If the condition is severe, you will need to take your dog to a veterinarian immediately. They will be able to hydrate them, flush the body of any toxins and administer the correct medications.

In mild cases, you can treat it at home and the first step is to take away all food for 12 hours. Keep them warm and comfortable, and make sure they have access to plenty of water. Be prepared to clean up some potty mistakes, and lay down newspaper or potty pads if you aren't able to give them permanent access to the yard.

Rice water is absolutely wonderful for treating digestive disorders. It alleviates bloating and lines the stomach. You can make this by boiling 1 cup of white rice with 4 cups of water for 20 minutes. Strain the water out and allow it to cool before offering it to your dog. Giving them probiotics will also ease the upset.

For the next week, I suggest splitting up their meals into four portions. This will make sure that their stomachs are not overloaded, and they will be able to digest the food easier. Do not give them any treats, high-sugar foods, or human foods!

Constipation

For some reason, dogs truly love to eat things that they shouldn't. Toys, plants, dirt and even hair can cause an impaction in the intestine which leads to constipation. If you suspect that your dog has eaten a foreign object, head straight to your veterinarian. They will do an x-ray to see if they need to remove any squeaky toys from your dog's intestine!

Constipation can be caused by reasons apart from stupidity! A poor diet, dehydration and chronic medications can inflame the gut and make it difficult for your dog to digest and pass food. Dogs that suffer from food allergies are also likely to experience consistent constipation. Dogs that are constipated are often noticeably bloated and will lick their stomachs excessively to try and self-soothe.

Treatment

Do not give your dog any food for at least 12 hours, piling food on food will only make the situation worse. Provide them with plenty of water, probiotics, and electrolytes. Dog-safe laxatives and liquid paraffin will help to soften their stool, making it easier to pass. These can be purchased from your veterinarian, who will be able to direct you on the correct dosages. You may need to continue using laxatives and probiotics for a few days, even if your dog has started to potty normally.

If the constipation was not caused by an impaction, you will need to make a few lifestyle changes. A good quality diet that is high in fiber, plenty of clean water, and regular exercise is usually more than enough to prevent constipation!

Urinary Tract Infections

Dogs that are suffering from a bladder or urinary tract infection will struggle to urinate or whimper when they do. Their urine will have a pungent smell and, in severe cases, contain blood. Female dogs are more prone to infections, and they can be caused by bacteria, holding it in for too long, hormonal changes, and strong medications. If your dog suffers from a chronic condition such as diabetes or kidney disease, they will become more susceptible to bladder infections.

Treatment

There is no way around it, urinary tract infections will need to be treated with antibiotics! However, there are a few things you can do at home to support this treatment, relieve the symptoms, and prevent it from happening again. Clean, fresh water is critical. Frequent walks and potty breaks will prevent your dog from needing to hold it in for long periods of time.

Antioxidants, probiotics, and dog-friendly cranberry supplements will help to fight the infection and keep the stomach and bladder functioning normally. Antioxidant supplements have anti-inflammatory properties, which will ease the discomfort.

Stiffness and Sprains

Stiffness is not isolated to senior dogs, although they do experience it more often. This could be caused by a fall, a pulled muscle, too much exercise, or an injury. This can easily be treated at home, but if you are worried that there may be a more serious cause, take your pup to the veterinarian.

Treatment

If your pup has sprained their ankle, you can support it by wrapping it up with a bandage. Just make sure that the wrap is not too tight. It's best to remove the bandage at night and when it gets wet or dirty.

Homeopathic remedies such as Arnica or T-Relief work wonders for sore muscles! T-Relief can be purchased in tablet or drop form and is perfectly safe for dogs. Arnica can be toxic if ingested, so if you do use it, make sure to wrap it up with a bandage. When you remove the bandage, wash off the Arnica as well.

Epsom salts have anti-inflammatory properties and work well for treating muscular pain and swelling. Put half a cup into a warm bath and give your dog a soak for 5 to 10 minutes. You really don't want to soak your dog multiple times a day. Instead, soak a cloth in the warm mixture and hold it against the sore spot to provide relief.

Coughing

A cough or two is completely normal. Dogs will cough, hack or gag if they have eaten something that disagrees with them or have inhaled an irritating allergen. However, if your dog is coughing continuously, they may have kennel cough. Kennel cough is a relatively loose term that refers to a number of viral and bacterial infections that can inflame the throat. They will likely show other symptoms such as nasal discharge and gagging.

The main causes of it are parainfluenza and Bordetella. These are extremely contagious and any dog with symptoms should be isolated. Vaccinations are available for both of these illnesses. While it is mostly just annoying for healthy adult dogs, it can have serious health consequences for young puppies and seniors that have lowered or underdeveloped immune systems. This is just one of the reasons why it is so important to keep up with your dog's annual vaccinations.

If your dog only coughs during physical activity, you should visit your veterinarian immediately, as this could be due to a number of chronic medical conditions or tracheal collapse.

Treatment

There is no treatment for kennel cough, but there are ways to relieve the symptoms. Buy a humidifier, or sit with your dog in the bathroom while the shower is on. The steam will provide relief and loosen up mucus. Some children's cough syrups can also be given, but make sure you check with your vet to see which one is safe. The best treatment is to support their immune system. Create a comfortable, warm environment for them, with good food and loads of water. It's best to avoid strenuous exercise for a while, as this can put further strain on their lungs and throat.

It usually takes around three weeks for the cough to subside, but older dogs can take up to six weeks or more. Older dogs are also much more sensitive to the cold and need to be monitored carefully, as kennel cough can lead to pneumonia.

Parasites

External parasites like ticks and fleas are easy enough to see. Mites, on the other hand, are microscopic. They cause the same symptoms, and you will notice that your dog scratches obsessively, chews their paws, and rubs their face and ears. Most mites are harmless but incredibly irritating and if not treated, your dog will begin to lose fur and develop wounds from excessive scratching.

Sarcoptic mites are the most dangerous as they cause mange, which is a severe skin infection. Dogs with mange will lose all their fur and their skin will be covered in sores and scabs. This is highly contagious and can spread to other mammals, birds, and even reptiles.

At some point, your dog will get internal parasites. It is inevitable! These parasites can be picked up from soil, dog parks, feces, and carcasses. If you enjoy giving your dog a kiss before bed, you should probably be dewormed too! In healthy dogs, these parasites aren't too dangerous, and you can treat them easily at home. In young puppies, seniors, or immune-compromised dogs, parasites can turn deadly.

Dogs that have worms will often scoot by rubbing their rumps on the ground. In more serious cases, you may notice a drastic drop in weight, dehydration, and blood and worms in their feces. If the infection has gotten to this point, it is best to get your dog to a veterinarian.

Treatment

There are a variety of different products on the market to kill internal and external parasites. Some products kill both in one go! However, you will notice that there is a big price difference between them. Regular dewormers will kill hookworms, roundworms, and tapeworms. Regular external parasite medications will only kill ticks and fleas.

I recommend purchasing one of the most specialized products at least once a year. These will also kill off ear and sarcoptic mites, heartworm, and whipworms.

Dewormers should be given every 3 to 6 months, depending on your dogs' exposure to contaminated soils and other dogs. Tick and flea medications are given every 1 to 3 months, depending on the brand. Avoid using parasite dips! These are very harsh on the skin and can cause severe reactions if ingested.

Abscesses

Abscesses are sneaky little pockets of puss that develop under the skin. This is generally due to a bacterial infection caused by a bite or wound. It can be difficult to see at first, but as the pus collects, the lump will become more prominent. They become increasingly painful as they grow and can develop anywhere on the body and inside the mouth. If left untreated, the infection will likely spread and cause necrosis and organ damage. In some cases, the abscess will burst by itself when it grows too large; however, if the puss is not completely drained, it will come back.

Treatment

There is no fun way to say it, an abscess has to be drained. In some cases, your veterinarian might find it necessary to lance it to get the bulk of the pus out. This typically leaves a large pocket under the skin which is susceptible to further infection. You will need to flush this pocket out every day to remove any debris, pus, and dirt.

Do not try to lance an abscess at home! It is incredibly painful, and you can cause your dog more pain. If you are dealing with a small abscess and your dog is not showing any other signs of infection, you can treat it with Epsom salts. Mix some in warm water and soak a cotton cloth. Hold the cloth on the abscess until it cools and then repeat it. This will help to open up the abscess and it will drain itself. Continue doing this a few times a day for the next week to completely clear it out.

If your dog shows any sign of infection, your veterinarian will need to prescribe a course of antibiotics to treat the bacterial infection.

Chronic Conditions and Disease

Chronic conditions should be taken seriously, regardless of your dog's age. The symptoms may not look as severe when your dog is young and full of energy, but as they get older, the condition will worsen if not treated. If your dog is showing any of the below symptoms, it is time to visit your veterinarian!

Obesity

Obesity and arthritis are the two most common chronic conditions seen in senior dogs. It is no surprise that the two are often linked. Stiffness and pain in the joints make your dog reluctant to exercise, which causes weight gain. A heavier body puts immense strain on these already painful joints, making it even more difficult to exercise.

Obesity, in general, has a considerable impact on your dog's overall health. It places strain on the organs, which exacerbates chronic conditions, and it can lead to diabetes.

Treatment

Obesity requires a strict diet change and exercise routine. It can take months to get your dog's weight back to a healthy level, and it is up to you to stay consistent. Treatments will be discussed more in-depth in the following chapters.

Diabetes

Diabetes can be separated into Type 1 and Type 2. Type 1 diabetes occurs when the body is unable to produce insulin. Type 2 diabetes occurs when the body is unable to use insulin correctly.

When your dog eats, the food is broken down and the nutrients are separated in the digestive system. One of these nutrients is glucose, which is carried to cells in the body by the hormone insulin. If the body is unable to produce insulin or use it efficiently, the blood sugar levels will spike and cause hyperglycemia.

This will cause a change in appetite, weight loss, excessive thirst, and dehydration. Most dogs will have strange, sweet-smelling breath, and you may notice that they urinate more often and develop urinary infections easily.

While there is no exact cause, it has been linked with autoimmune disorders, obesity, and even some chronic medications. Some breeds such as Poodles, Dachshunds, and Miniature Schnauzers are also more prone to developing diabetes as they age.

Treatment

Dogs that have diabetes will require regular insulin injections to keep their blood sugar levels in check. However, this is not enough to keep them healthy. Obesity is known to exacerbate diabetic systems, so it is important to feed your dog a healthy diet and continue with regular exercise. Avoid treats and foods that are high in sugar, and increase the amount of fiber in their diet. Fiber will slow down the absorption of sugar from food, which will keep your dog's blood sugar levels from spiking.

Arthritis

As your dog ages, their joints deteriorate, and they have an increased chance of developing arthritis. It can affect one or all of their limbs and is more likely to occur if they have suffered a previous injury.

You may find that your dog struggles to jump the heights that they once could. They struggle to get up and lay down without shaking and in some cases, they may develop a limp. These signs are particularly noticeable in cold and damp weather.

While it is quite distressing, it is not uncommon and around 80% of dogs will develop arthritis in their senior years.

Treatment

Strenuous and spontaneous exercise should be avoided at all costs. That means no more jumping in and out of the car! Short, slow walks will help them to stretch out and keep fit without the risk of injury. Foods and supplements that promote joint health and mobility are great options for relieving discomfort and combating weight gain.

Sweaters, socks, warm blankets, and heated beds can help alleviate joint discomfort during cold weather.

If your dog has developed a severe limp or struggles to stand up without falling, it is time to worry! A veterinarian will be able to assess the extent of the arthritis through an x-ray and provide you with an appropriate treatment plan. In most cases, you will be given a prescription for pain management medication, which will help take the edge off.

Allergies

Allergies can be caused by numerous factors. Environmental allergies are most common and include allergens such as pollen, grass, mold, and dust mites. These allergies are more likely to flare up in spring and summer. While you may see more conventional signs such as runny nose, watery eyes, and sneezing, these allergies mainly affect the skin. Dogs will often rub their faces, or bodies against the ground or grass to stop the itch. The worst itch occurs in the paws, and dogs will sit and lick and chew them for hours on end. Excessive licking and chewing on a certain spot can cause open wounds, fur loss, and inflammation.

Food allergies are a little less common but still account for 10% of allergic reactions. Dogs will display the same itchy symptoms, but can also experience bloating, constipation, vomiting, and diarrhea. The most common food allergens are beef, chicken, fish, dairy, soy, gluten, and general additives.

Treatment

Environmental allergies are very difficult to treat. The best thing that you can do is ensure that the house is clean and free of dust, mites, and mold. If there are specific plants that are causing the reaction, it is best to remove them from the yard. Pollen and grass allergies can't be cured, but they can be controlled by using antihistamines during spring and summer. If you suspect your dog is suffering from food allergies, you will need to change them to a hypoallergenic diet. These are free of common allergens and safe for the stomach.

Regular baths with a sensitive shampoo will relieve the itch and reduce any inflammation. Oatmeal has anti-inflammatory properties and works brilliantly for inflamed skin. Grind some up into a powder and mix it with water to make a paste. You can pack this paste onto any inflamed areas to soothe them. This works best for paws, and you can push the paste in between their paw pads. It is completely safe to eat, and your dog will have a great time licking it off themselves!

If your pup has dry, flaking skin from allergies, rub them down with coconut oil. It's edible, relieves itches, moisturizes the skin, and promotes beautiful soft fur growth. You can't go wrong.

Cancer

Cancer is terrifying and for many owners, this is the last diagnosis they ever want to hear. However, cancer is not always fatal, and many treatments are available to improve your dog's quality of life . This, of course, depends on the type of cancer and how far it has spread.

As your dog ages, the odds of abnormal cell growth increase. These cells surround and affect tissue, muscle, and organs. Localized cancers such as tumors are confined to specific locations in the body. Generalized cancers can spread throughout the body and damage everything in their path. There is no single cause for the growth of cancerous cells. A variety of environmental, genetic, and dietary factors can be responsible. Breeds such as golden retrievers, boxers, beagles, and Burmese mountain dogs are more prone to developing cancer.

The symptoms your dog displays will depend heavily on which part of the body is impacted. Lethargy, weight loss, muscle weakness, swelling, and lack of appetite are common symptoms, but these are not enough for a full diagnosis.

Yearly blood tests are vital for senior dogs as they will allow your veterinarian to pick up inflammation, infection, and abnormal hormone levels. X-rays, ultrasounds, and other tests need to be done before a diagnosis is made.

Treatment

Treatment will depend on the location and severity of the cancer. Early detection is key, as the further the cancer spreads, the more difficult it is to fight. Most localized cancers and tumors can be surgically removed. Chemotherapy and radiation are used for more generalized cancers, especially ones that affect internal organs.

However, when choosing a treatment option, it is important to consider your dog's age and their strength. A younger, healthy dog is strong enough to go through chemotherapy with a good chance of survival and recovery.

Elderly dogs will likely be too weak and in these cases, your veterinarian will suggest palliative care. This involves treating the symptoms and managing the pain to make your dog as comfortable as possible during their last few months or years.

Hypothyroidism

The thyroid is located next to the windpipe. This incredibly important gland releases hormones that control the metabolism. If too many hormones are released, hyperthyroidism occurs, and the metabolism is elevated. If the gland isn't able to produce enough, hypothyroidism occurs. This slows down the metabolism immensely. Dogs suffering from it will experience a noticeable increase in weight, yet no increase in their appetite.

The skin will often be dry and flaky, and their fur will become dry with dull fur. You may also notice bald patches along the body. As the condition continues, your dog will likely become sluggish and lethargic and show a reluctance to exercise. The chance of ear infections, high cholesterol, and muscle loss will also increase the longer it is left untreated.

This condition is usually caused by autoimmune diseases such as lymphocytic thyroiditis. While it isn't common, it is known to affect Labradors, Irish setters, boxers, and dachshunds.

Treatment

If your dog is displaying any of these symptoms, your veterinarian will take a blood test to confirm the diagnosis. Unfortunately, this condition is not curable, but replacement hormones can be given. This is a lifelong treatment, but it allows your dog to live a happy, long life.

To find the correct dose, the veterinarian will inject your dog with the thyroid hormone and then conduct a blood test a few hours later. This allows them to determine if the dose given was enough to stabilize their thyroid hormone levels. A blood test will need to be done every six months to monitor these levels and the dose will be adjusted accordingly.

Chapter 3:

Preventive Veterinary Care

Now that you are aware of the possible medical issues your dog may experience, it is time to learn how to prevent them from happening in the first place! Prevention is achieved by using every available resource in your arsenal, from dietary care and exercise to regular grooming. However, the most important and reliable resource you have is your veterinarian.

Some dogs are masters at hiding pain or illness and while you know your dog best, a veterinarian will be able to pick up on subtle symptoms that you may have missed. It is recommended that dogs over the age of seven undertake two health checks a year to ensure that any changes in their condition are noted. From there, your veterinarian will be able to guide you through treatments and show you the necessary changes that need to be made at home.

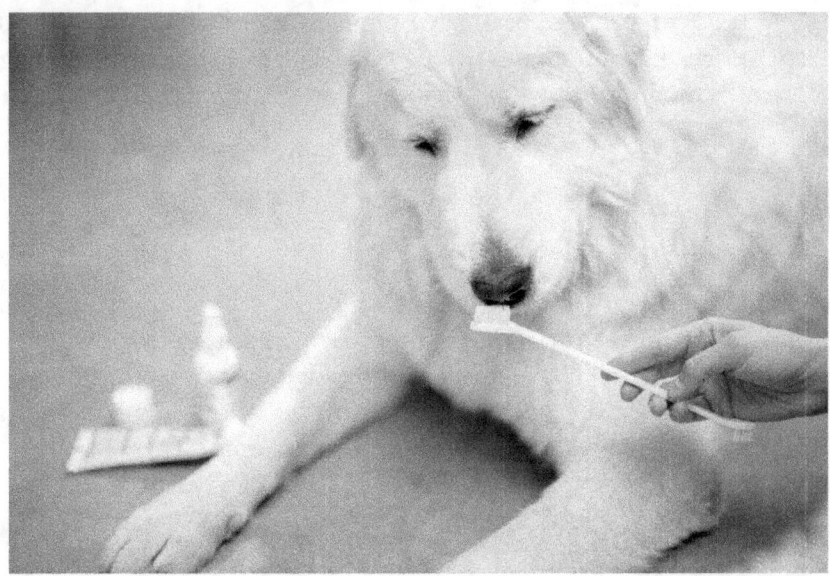

Let's take a look at what actually happens during these health checks, and what your veterinarian will be looking for.

Understanding Your Breed

For centuries, we have selectively bred dogs with specific genes to produce new and exciting breeds that possess unique physical, behavioral, and emotional traits. The problem is that we have allowed a couple of bad genes to slip through as well. These are responsible for the variety of genetic medical disorders that we see today.

Genetic disorders are commonly associated with purebred dogs, as mixed breeds have a much lower chance of two parents sharing the same recessive gene. Reputable breeders will ensure that their mating pairs are healthy and free of these genes. This is why purchasing a puppy from a breeder can be so expensive.

Backyard breeders and "puppy mills" value profit over their dogs. They can cut down costs by ignoring the breeding guidelines and voiding health checks and DNA sampling. Dogs from the same litter will often be interbred to produce as many puppies as possible for a much cheaper price. This rise in inbreeding caused an inevitable wave of dogs born with predispositions to medical conditions and sadly, it still continues.

Breed History

Reputable breeders will provide you with medical records and health certificates to prove that the puppies are healthy and possess no recessive genes. If you have not been provided with one or if you have rescued a purebred dog that has no history, it is time for some tests! Your veterinarian will identify specific worrisome genes through a series of blood tests. This can be costly, but it is worth it for some piece of mind.

Common Genetic and Chronic Disorders

Degenerative Myelopathy is a disease that causes the nerves in the spinal cord to deteriorate. This leads to weakness in the hind legs and, in severe cases, incontinence and paralysis. German shepherds are at the highest risk, but Bernese mountain dogs, boxers, and spaniels are also susceptible. Unfortunately, there is no way to prevent or treat this disease. However, the gene can be detected through blood tests, which allows you enough time to prepare your dog for it.

Dilated Cardiomyopathy is a disease that causes the heart muscles to weaken. Dobermans, boxers, Great Danes, and Irish setters are all high-risk breeds. Unfortunately, there is no way to test for this gene and therefore no way to predict it. While it cannot be cured, there are several supportive medications that can be used to provide your dog with a longer, more comfortable life.

Brachycephalic Syndrome is a respiratory deformity. This occurs in breeds such as bulldogs, pugs, and Boston terriers, which have rounded heads and flat faces. As a result of the much shorter snout, these dogs often have slit-like nostrils and a narrow trachea, which makes it incredibly difficult to breathe. This can be especially dangerous during exercise, stress, and hot days. As your dog's breathing increases and they pant heavily, the trachea may collapse.

English bulldogs are unfortunately the most susceptible due to an increase in inbreeding, and many require surgery at a young age to correct it.

Chondrodysplasia affects long, short breeds such as dachshunds and basset hounds. Due to their significantly short leg bones, their joints end up taking a lot of strain, which can cause severe arthritis as they age. Their spine is disproportionately long, and their legs are unable to properly support it. This puts stress on the spinal discs, which can lead to injury and disc disease.

Hip Dysplasia is one of the most common and well-known genetic disorders. It impacts large and giant breeds such as German shepherds, Labradors, Great Danes, and Saint Bernards being the most susceptible. These breeds grow rapidly. Sometimes, too quickly and the increase in muscle mass and weight puts too much strain on their still-developing skeleton. The hips and shoulders take the brunt of this weight and will shift and deform to accommodate it.

If it is caught early enough, there are surgeries that can be done to reshape the hip. Sadly, it is usually diagnosed too late and while surgeries are still available, the dog will likely end up suffering from severe arthritis.

These are just some of the many genetic disorders that can impact different breeds. However, it is important to remember that just because these breeds have a predisposition, there is no guarantee that they will develop these conditions.

Annual Veterinary Visits

Don't be a vet hopper! Going to the vet is scary enough, especially if your dog has had a painful experience there. Getting them comfortable with one veterinarian at one facility can greatly decrease their stress response.

Sticking with one veterinarian allows them to develop a good relationship with your dog and become familiar with their behaviors and physical condition. This will make it much easier for them to pick up on behavioral changes that indicate injury or illness. By using the same veterinary practice, you can rest assured that they will have all of your dog's medical information on file. If your veterinarian is ever away, the next one on duty will be able to take over without any hassle.

Annual Physicals

Regardless of age, your dog should go for a full check-up once a year. As they age, you will likely need to increase this to every six months. During these check-ups, your veterinarian will ask you if there have been any changes to your lifestyle and if you have noticed a change in your dogs' behavior, diet, and overall health. It is important to be completely honest, don't try to hide any embarrassing mistakes!

They will then begin a head-to-tail examination. Your veterinarian will check your dog's eyes, ears, mouth, and teeth. They will stretch out their legs to check their mobility and feel and prod along their stomachs to check for bloat or compaction.

Senior check-ups will take a little longer as your veterinarian will focus on identifying any age-related conditions. These may include arthritis, cancers, infections, and eyesight and hearing loss. If they do find anything peculiar, further tests will be done to confirm the diagnosis.

Annual Vaccinations

So many owners stop vaccinating their dogs as they grow older, which simply doesn't make sense! Senior dogs are much more susceptible to viruses and disease due to their lowered immune system. These annual vaccinations protect your dog from distemper, parvovirus, parainfluenza, and hepatitis. All of these are extremely contagious, and can be deadly for dogs with weakened or underdeveloped immune systems.

Annual Procedures

Your veterinarian will likely recommend several procedures to be done on a yearly basis to monitor the internal health of your dog. These can be quite costly and if money is tight, you should request that only the most important ones are done.

X-rays will be done to check the health of your dog's bones, joints, and the presence of arthritis. If your dog has been struggling with digestive or respiratory problems, your vet will likely take a gut and chest x-ray as well.

A complete blood count and chemical screening will be done to monitor how your dog's kidneys, liver, and heart are functioning. This will help your veterinarian to pick up on any cancers, infections, and disorders that may be hiding.

If your pup has not been dewormed, your veterinarian will do a fecal flotation, which will help them to pick up any signs of internal parasites.

Keep All Your Pet Documents!

This is a no-brainer. Get yourself a file and store all of your dog's medical information. This should include anything and everything from adoption and breeder certificates and vaccination records to x-rays and test results. If your dog has suffered from any injuries or illnesses, keep a record of the treatments and medications they received. Make sure to keep a list of allergies they may have as well. If, for whatever reason, you need to change to a new veterinarian, you will be able to provide them with your dog's full medical history.

I also recommend making a separate emergency folder. This should include your personal information, your veterinarian's contact details, and your dogs' information. Be sure to add in a list of any medical conditions and medications that your dog may be on. When you go away, you can hand this folder over to whoever is caring for your pup!

Emergency Care

Ideally, you want to avoid dealing with any emergencies. Through preventative care, you should be able to catch any condition early enough to treat it in time. However, accidents do happen and while you can't prevent them, you can be prepared for them.

If you don't have a pet first aid kit already, it is time to make one. You may never need it, but it certainly does come in handy the day that you do. This will give you the ability to treat minor wounds at home and administer emergency first aid to stabilize your dog until you can get to your veterinarian.

Your emergency information folder should be kept with your kit at all times, and I strongly recommend that you get a dog first aid guide. You can purchase them or source them online for free. These short pamphlets contain detailed instructions with pictures of how to administer CPR as well as how to deal with choking, poisoning, seizures, and more!

Pet First Aid Kit

These are some of the most important items to have. Excluding any medications that your veterinarian has given you, of course.

- Hydrogen peroxide—A fantastic wound cleaner that can be used to flush out dirt and debris.

- Antibiotic ointment—This ointment protects wounds and scratches from becoming infected. Depending on which one you get, it can also ease swelling and itchiness caused by allergies and insect bites.

- Styptic powder—Stops excessive bleeding by causing the blood to clot. Great for nips during grooming and claw cutting.

- Antiseptic wipes—It's always best to keep your dog clean. If they have scratched or injured themselves, you will need to remove any dirt around the wound immediately. If you don't, it can cause infection!

- Gauze—Stock up on a variety of sizes and lengths. These are great for stopping bleeding and wrapping up a wound to protect it from dirt. Use it to strap up a sprained leg and a makeshift muzzle if needed.

- Tape—You will need flexible tape to keep your gauze and bandages fixed in place. I prefer to use non-adhesive ones because the glues can get stuck in your dog's fur, making it painful to remove.

- Thermometer]—For doggy use only! This is one of the most important first-aid tools you can have. If you are ever worried that your dog is ill, take their temperature. A healthy temperature is between 101 and 102.5 °F. Anything higher usually indicates infection, while a low temperature indicates hypothermia.

- Gloves—Keep a pair of sterile latex gloves in your first aid kit. You should always wear these if you are dealing with open wounds, as you want to avoid spreading bacteria. If you don't have any, be sure to thoroughly wash your hands.

- Scissors—When is a good pair of scissors not handy?

- Syringes—Keep a couple of different-sized syringes in your kit. These are great for measuring out and administering medications and can be used for flushing out wounds.

- Tweezers—Tweezers are handy for removing splinters, ticks, bee stings, and any dirt or debris from wounds.

- Flashlight—A flashlight allows you to inspect hard-to-see spots on your dog's body. It's especially helpful for inspecting their mouth and paws.

- Towel or blanket—A good towel is extremely versatile. You can use it as a ground cover to keep your pup off the floor. Or wrap them up in it to keep them warm and calm. It can even be used as a makeshift tourniquet and an absorbent pad to stop bleeding.

- Soft fabric muzzle—Dogs that are in a high-stress mode after an emotionally distressing event are more likely to bite. A soft muzzle can help to keep them calm and prevent them from injuring you and themselves.

- Extra leash—It's not uncommon for dogs to snap their leash when they panic. You may just be unable to find your usual one. Regardless, having an extra one will provide you with immediate control over your pup and prevent further injuries.

Chapter 4:

Healthy Diet, Healthy Dog!

Food is your body's primary energy source, you use the nutrients and minerals from it to grow, maintain and heal. This is why it makes perfect sense to provide puppies with protein and calcium-rich foods. As our puppies grow, we swap them onto healthy maintenance food to keep their health in check. Yet, when it comes to senior dogs, a change in food is almost always overlooked!

As our dogs age, their teeth will often file down, break, or become brittle, which can make it much harder to chew the larger pieces of food they are used to. If your dog is struggling to eat, they will likely lose weight. Soft food is a great solution to this problem as it is much easier to chew. The only issue here is that many owners don't know how to correctly portion canned food, and too much of a good thing can cause excessive weight gain and plaque build-up.

Thankfully, there are plenty of dog foods out there that have been designed specifically for different-sized senior dogs. These foods contain the vital nutrients, at the right levels, that an old dog needs to thrive while still maintaining a balanced weight.

Should I Change My Dog's Food?

Yes, you definitely should. Specialized foods will help control medical conditions and remedy weight fluctuations. However, you shouldn't wait until these conditions arise. Moving over to an old dog diet when your dog first enters their senior years will promote a healthy immune system and prevent some medical conditions from occurring in the first place.

Dental Concerns

There is nothing worse than trying to eat hard foods with a sore mouth. Broken teeth and gum disease are the usual suspects. If you haven't been looking after your dog's teeth or if they like to eat or munch on hard items and bones, you can expect a tooth extraction or two.

Smaller-sized kibble can help tremendously and if your dog still struggles to chew, you can use hot water to soften it. I like to mix in a hot gravy to make my own style of soft canned food.

Canned foods are great, the small soft pieces are easy on the mouth and are highly digestible. If you want to swap over to soft foods permanently, you need to do your research! Cheap, store-bought brands generally lack vital nutrients and most are packed with sugars and fat. Opt for veterinary standard foods that are designed for senior dogs.

Weight Concerns

A drop in weight is pretty scary, but it is relatively easy to fix once you know the cause. Getting treatment for any medical conditions that are contributing to the weight loss is the first step. Thereafter, a change in diet, an extra meal a day and some added supplements will get your dog back to a healthy weight.

An increase in weight is a lot more difficult to fix. It happens gradually, so most owners don't notice until it is severe. Typically, this is due to overfeeding, excessive treats, and a lack of exercise. Basically, this comes down to you. However, some breeds are more prone to obesity than others. Pugs, golden retrievers and basset hounds are at the most risk.

The Dangers of Obesity

Obesity is a gateway to numerous health issues. A heavier body is heavier on the joints and if your dog is suffering from arthritis, this can be extremely painful. The extra fat will collect around organs, placing immense strain on them. This can lead to liver and kidney damage, diabetes, and difficulty breathing.

With all this added discomfort, it is perfectly understandable why your dog is reluctant to exercise! The problem is, with this reluctance, your dog is bound to gain even more weight. If not remedied quickly, it can cut your dog's lifespan down by up to two years.

Meal Planning

Correct food portions and meal planning is your first step to controlling weight gain. You can cut down a good number of pounds, which will ease the strain on your dog's body, allowing them to get back into an exercise routine comfortably.

Firstly, cut down on the treats that are full of sugars and fat, and stop giving your dog any human foods! Dogs aren't able to digest the same foods that we do.

Next, purchase food that suits your dog's needs. Metabolic and weight control foods are specially formulated for this issue. However, you can use normal senior dog foods if you learn to portion them correctly.

Good dog foods will come with a feeding chart that indicates the correct portion sizes for your dog's weight and activity level. For example, the chart may tell you that a 20-pound, low-activity dog should be fed 5 ounces a day. However, a 20-pound, high-activity dog should be fed 6 ounces. This is because high-activity dogs are burning off the calories much quicker.

If you know that your dog should be fed 6 ounces a day, split this into 2 portions and feed them 3 ounces for breakfast and 3 ounces for dinner.

Weight Loss Management

Speak to your veterinarian about what your dog's ideal weight should be. You can then work at gradually reducing their meal portions until they reach this weight. Graduality is key! Starving your dog is cruel and can lead to a whole new list of health issues.

If your dog weighs 20 pounds, feed them the recommended amount for a 19-pound dog. Once they get to 19 pounds, feed them the amount for an 18-pound dog. Continue feeding like this until your dog reaches their ideal weight.

There is no doubt that you will start to see improvement in their energy levels immediately. Be sure not to revert to old habits. Just because your dog is now at a stable weight does not mean that you can start giving them tons of treats and ice cream again.

Choosing Your Food

Your choice of food is going to depend greatly on the size of your dog, their breed, and what medical conditions they may be suffering from. It can be quite stressful to choose the right one, and it is always best to chat with your veterinarian if you need help. Senior dogs are more prone to sensitivities, so it is important to introduce new foods gradually and monitor them. If they show signs of allergy or digestive issues, you will need to rethink your food choice.

Adult vs. Senior Foods

Puppies need to do a great deal of growing in the first year or two of their lives. During this time, it is important to provide them with vitamins and minerals that promote healthy bone growth and digestive care. Puppy foods will have a higher fat and protein content to compensate for their active lifestyle.

Once your dog reaches adulthood, they should switch to a maintenance diet. These foods are generally lower in fat and carbohydrates, and the vitamin and mineral content will shift. Calcium and phosphorus content, which promote bone growth and health, will be considerably less in adult foods because your dog is no longer growing. Overall, this diet is designed to promote general health and maintain your dog's metabolism and immune system.

Senior dog diets contain much less fat. This is because old dogs' metabolisms slow down considerably, and they cannot process and expend the amount of energy they get from their food. Without this adjustment, old dogs are likely to gain weight and can suffer from constipation or diarrhea. The protein content in this food is much higher as it helps the body to maintain muscle mass.

Once again, the vitamin and mineral content will shift. Most senior foods will contain new supplements such as glucosamine for joint health and fish oils to combat allergies and skin conditions.

Breed-Specific Foods

Some pure breeds are more prone to genetic disorders and require specialized diets to keep them fit and healthy. This mainly includes small and toy breeds such as Yorkshire Terriers, Chihuahuas, and Pugs and giant breeds such as the Great Dane. However, specialized diets are also recommended for Labradors and German Shepherds who are prone to hip dysplasia.

Medical Foods

Let's face it, you will likely end up purchasing prescription food for your senior. These foods are specifically designed with a variety of nutrients and ingredients to combat specific medical conditions.

Mobility foods are great for dogs that are suffering from stiff joints and arthritis. They include Omega-3 fatty acids and antioxidants, which relieve inflammation. As well as glucosamine and chondroitin, which promote healthy joints.

Hypoallergenic food can be used for seniors that suffer from skin and food allergies. These avoid common allergens such as grains, soy, dairy, and artificial additives.

If your dog struggles with digestive issues, easily digestible metabolic foods are the best choice. These have a high fiber content and contain probiotics and flaxseed oils, which protect the stomach.

Weight control foods are ideal for obese seniors. They have a low fat, high fiber, high-protein content with an overall low-calorie count. This food has to be paired with regular exercise to work efficiently.

Each of these specialized foods comes in different sizes to suit small, medium, or large dogs. If your dog struggles to eat kibble, you can opt for the soft, canned options. If your dog suffers from two or more conditions, it is best to chat with your veterinarian. They will be able to direct you on which food is best and which ones you could potentially mix.

Clean Water

Keeping your dog's food and water bowls clean is absolutely vital. Your senior pup's immune system is not what it used to be, and bacteria build-up can have dire consequences. E. coli, yeast, mold, and salmonella can all grow in moist, dirty bowls. This is more common in plastic bowls, which may also release a variety of chemicals when left to decay. Stainless steel or glass bowls are best. They are easy to clean and reduce the risk of bacteria build-up.

Food bowls should be washed after every meal, and water bowls should be changed twice a day. Change the water again if it has been contaminated by debris, food, and, if you have a water lover, dirty paws. I like to have two sets of bowls and while one is in use, the other is in the dishwasher.

Helpful Vitamins and Supplements

Vitamins and supplements can make a considerable improvement to your senior dog's quality of life. However, it is important to use them correctly and not overload your dog's system.

All supplements will come with instructions that will direct you on how much to give your dog per day. Make sure to stick to these guidelines! Mixing up several different supplements can be quite dangerous. If you feel this is necessary, it is best to chat with your veterinarian first. They can help you decide what is best for your dog, which supplements are vital, and which ones you can ditch.

Multivitamins

Multivitamins are a great, all-around supplement that can be given to dogs of any age. These contain basic minerals, vitamins, and oils that promote overall body and mind health. Vitamins A, B, and E are added to support the brain, heart, and skin. While minerals such as calcium, iron, zinc, and copper support bone, blood, and organ health.

Geriatric Vitamins

These vitamins are created specifically for senior dogs. They contain vital minerals and vitamins that aren't usually found in standard multivitamins. Biotin and Omega oils promote skin and fur health and relieve general skin conditions. Vitamin C and E are natural antioxidants, and vitamin B improves the immune system. Most senior vitamins will also contain glucosamine, which reduces inflammation and relieves arthritis symptoms.

Medical Supplements

If your dog needs extra help with a specific condition, it is best to choose an appropriate medical supplement. These will contain specialized oils, vitamins, and minerals that are proven to combat the effects of certain conditions.

As with any supplement, the cheaper you go, the less effective they will be. Purchasing top-quality products will ensure that your dog's condition improves and reduce the chance of side effects.

Antioxidants

All of our bodies contain pesky little molecules called free radicals which directly damage the cells that form our organs, muscles, and tissues. They can form during periods of stress, illness, and dietary changes, but become more prominent when the body ages. Antioxidants such as vitamins A, C, and E, magnesium, and zinc fight off free radicals and support the immune system to prevent illness.

Joint Care

Joint supplements will greatly improve your dog's overall mobility. This supplement generally comes in a liquid form, which is easy to measure and pour onto your dog's breakfast. It contains glucosamine and chondroitin. Both of these ingredients are scientifically proven to increase the production of joint fluid. This fluid is responsible for the health of the cartilage that covers the joints. Most joint supplements will also contain Omega-3 oil, which reduces inflammation and pain.

Digestive Care

The stomach is full of good bacteria that help us to digest our food. As your dog ages or becomes ill, these bacteria are lost, and they will start to experience stomach upsets. Probiotics will reintroduce these bacteria and restore normal gut health. Digestive supplements are a little more advanced. They have a high fiber content and contain probiotics and digestive enzymes, which help the body to efficiently absorb nutrients.

Digestive supplements and probiotics are completely safe in the correct dosage and can be given to your dog for an extended period of time.

Allergy Care

Allergy supplements will generally contain probiotics and digestive enzymes to help with food-related allergies. Omega-3, 6, and 9 fatty acids and biotin help to keep the skin healthy and combat the effects of skin-related allergies. Good quality allergy supplements will contain quercetin and turmeric. These are natural antihistamines and anti-inflammatories, which will fight off the cause of the allergy.

Chapter 5:

Keeping Fit (Slowly)

Exercising your senior dog is just as important as exercising a puppy. Regular movement is vital for digestive health and without it, your dog can become prone to obesity and constipation. However, it is not only the body that ends up suffering. Anxiety and boredom-related behavioral problems are often linked directly to a lack of regular exercise and outdoor exposure.

It can be tricky and even a little scary trying to exercise a senior dog, especially ones that have existing medical conditions. The last thing you want to do is force them into a situation where they could get hurt. The key is choosing an exercise that suits your dog and their condition and then keeping the sessions short and sweet. Ten minutes of exercise a day is better than none! Let's take a look at some age-friendly exercises and how you can adapt them to suit your dog's needs.

Knowing When To Slow Down

Dogs live for the now, not for the future! If all your senior wants to do is eat and nap all day, they will. If they feel like sprinting around the house, they will. If it doesn't hurt right now, why would it later? They may not understand, but we certainly do, and it is our responsibility to protect and care for them. Even when it means stopping them from having fun.

Are You Listening To Your Dog?

It can be pretty confusing trying to communicate with your dog. They send out such mixed signals! It is concerning when your dog limps their way back to you after fetching the ball. Except, their tail is wagging, and they have a huge goofy grin on their face as they wait for you to throw it again. Maybe they are actually okay? Think of it this way, if your toddler throws up after eating too many sweets, but then continues to eat more, would you let them? Always focus on what their bodies are telling you.

Abnormal Behaviors

Your dog will display numerous abnormal behaviors, which should tell you that they need to stop. By ignoring these red flags, you are guaranteeing injury. The most obvious sign will be slowing down by themselves or reluctance to partake in any physical activities. This is not necessarily due to injury or pain. Your dog's body just can't keep up, and they are likely to tire out quicker.

Appetite changes and excessive drinking should always be taken seriously. This is commonly caused by illness, digestive problems, or dental pain.

Excessive panting and drooling are often signs of heat stroke, stress, and dehydration. Dehydration is not necessarily caused by a lack of available water or exposure to heat. It can be caused by illness or kidney disease.

Disorientation, bumping into objects and irritability can indicate several health conditions. If your dog is displaying any of the behaviors above, during or after exercising, you should stop your routine completely. Your veterinarian will be able to diagnose the cause and treat it if necessary. Once your pup has recovered, introduce exercise slowly.

Signs and Symptoms of Pain and Injury

If your dog begins to favor one leg over the other during exercise or play time, it is best to stop the activity immediately. This could just be from stiffness or a bit of weakness. However, if it continues the next day, it is likely a sprain or worse.

Whining and crying are obvious signs of pain. If you can't see any obvious injuries or limps, you can run your hands over their body and down their legs. If they whimper or pull back at any point, you have located the sore spot.

Dogs will often hack and cough when they have eaten or breathed in something that doesn't agree with them. Isolated hacking is normal. However, if your dog coughs or hacks routinely during exercise, you could be dealing with a more serious problem. This could be a sign of respiratory infection, heart conditions, and tracheal collapse.

Dogs That Never Stop!

Some dogs just don't stop. High-energy breeds such as border collies, greyhounds, and huskies are usually the guilty parties. They could have a broken leg, but sure enough, you will find them zooming around the house. If you have a dog like this, you are going to need to tighten the reins.

Household changes can make a big difference. While most dogs will stop trying to jump onto the bed when it begins to hurt, high-energy breeds will generally never give up. Start using ramps, and dog stairs in the house, whether your dog thinks they need them or not. If they still enjoy bounding down the stairs after a tumble or two, block the stairs off.

You cannot end their daily exercise routines without chaos ensuing, so it is important to replace activities with ones that are just as rewarding. Make sure to avoid their excitement triggers, or at least change their response to them. For example, if your pup bounds to the bottom of the yard the moment you pick up a ball thrower, you have two choices. You can either stop playing fetch completely, or you can throw the ball short distances with your arm until they realize that they are running too far to catch it. The right choice is easy!

Veterinary Check

Your veterinarian should be your first stop if you are planning out a new exercise routine for your senior pup. They will be able to conduct a full medical examination and give you the green light to exercise. If they feel it is necessary, they may take x-rays to check on the health of your old dog's bones and joints. If they do pick up any medical conditions, they will direct you on which exercises to avoid and which to focus on.

How to Slow Them Down

Whether you're trying to slow down a hyperactive greyhound or trying to get an elderly basset off their butt. The methods below are sure to keep your pup fit, healthy, and injury free.

Find a New Routine

Old dogs like routine. They are already going through changes that they don't quite understand. Introducing any further adjustments can disturb their lifestyle and add to unwanted stress. When switching to a new routine, it is important to taper off physically demanding activities slowly and provide new senior-friendly ones that are just as fun.

Shorter Walks

Walking is a fantastic low-impact, full-body workout. It stretches out muscles, ligaments, and joints, which keeps them flexible and strong. Improved blood flow helps to reduce pain and inflammation, which will provide immense relief from arthritis.

With all these benefits, you can see why your dog should still go on regular walks, even in their older age. However, it is time to go a lot slower. You may notice that they are becoming increasingly sensitive. Their tired little feet will feel the heat of asphalt and the cold of snow more intensely. They will dehydrate faster, and their muscles will tire out quicker.

Keep this in mind when choosing your walking route and avoid walking in extreme weather. Your walks need to be short but consistent, and don't forget to slow down your own pace! If you find your pup feels stiff in the morning, cut down the distance further.

Indoor Exercises

If you find that you are indoors more than out, switch up your games to make them house friendly. If your pup loves to play fetch, move the game indoors. You can purchase soft balls that are designed specifically for older dogs. They don't bounce, which saves your lamps! They are soft, which makes them easy to pick up, and when you throw them, they will travel a shorter distance.

Tug of war is a fun game that you can play indoors. It is a great workout for your dog's neck, shoulders, and jaws. Choose a soft fabric rope that will be kind to your dog's mouth. Make sure you play gently and if your dog starts to get too worked up, pause the game until they become calm.

For small to medium dogs, you can even take a lap around the house! Get creative and adapt your normal routine to suit your new lifestyle.

Swimming and Hydrotherapy

Swimming is a great way to keep your dog in shape. It's a full-body workout, but it is incredibly easy on the muscles and joints. Without your dog's full weight on their legs, their joints can stretch and work without strain.

This doesn't mean that you can just throw your pup into the pool. It's best to get into the pool with them and use a special harness to guide their movements and keep them above water. Inflatable devices can also be used to prevent your dog from drowning if they get too tired.

Hydrotherapy was developed for dogs that have suffered injuries such as broken bones, head trauma, and paralysis. There are plenty of specialized canine rehabilitation centers that offer this service. If you are interested in swimming your dog regularly, it is best to visit one of these centers first and ask them to guide you through it.

Physiotherapy

Physiotherapy is a fun way to improve your dog's physical health while bonding with them. Using the palm of your hand, you can rub down your dog's muscles in gentle, slow strokes. This will improve blood flow, which will loosen up knots and reduce inflammation.

After the massage, you can gently stretch out your dog's legs to loosen up their joints. Avoid stretching them when they are in a standing position, as they can lose balance and fall over! Keep the sessions short and sweet with a ten-minute time limit. If your dog pulls away from you or shows any signs of pain, stop for the day. Massaging and stretching your dog before and after walks can greatly improve their mobility and keep them active.

Combating Boredom

A shorter exercise routine is going to lead to boredom. Keep your dog busy throughout the day to stop any unwanted behaviors and prolonged naps. Mentally stimulating tasks will help to keep your dog's mind working, which will combat dementia and senility.

Stimulating Puzzles

Puzzle feeders are a great way to keep your senior's mind sharp. If you use treats with your puzzles, your dog may gain a lot of weight! Instead, use their daily meals in the puzzles to keep their weight stable. Your dog is likely to get bored if you use the same old puzzles. You can switch things up by putting their food deep inside a snuffle mat.

If your dog needs a bit more exercise, you can play hide and seek. Get them to sit and wait, or put them in another room. Hide their food or treats around the house and let them use their noses to find it. Don't hide too many treats as you may forget where they are and if your dog doesn't find them, you are in for an ant invasion.

New Tricks

Despite what they say, you can definitely teach an old dog new tricks. It may be a little harder for your senior to concentrate, but they are still perfectly capable of learning and enjoying training. Choose tricks and commands that are not too physically taxing. That means, no jumping through hoops of fire.

One of my favorite physical tricks that are light on your dog's knees is dancing. You can train your pup to walk in between and around your legs using hand signals and treats. Put this to a song, and it is a great three-minute exercise for both of you.

Whatever tricks you decide to teach, make sure you do it in moderation. As soon as your pup is getting tired or distracted, it is time to stop.

Play Dates

Your dog will never be too old for friends. Play dates are a great way to spice up your senior dog's routine, and it gives them a chance to just be a dog again. Play dates are mentally stimulating and super exciting. It is physically challenging enough to keep them fit without getting hurt.

This, of course, depends on the playmate. Stick to adult and old dogs that your pup is already familiar with. Introducing them to a young, boisterous puppy that likes to play rough is not going to end well. During the play dates, be mindful of your dog's behavior and if you notice that they get tired or start to feel grumpy, it is time to go home.

Fun In The Sun

Just being in a new place is stimulating enough. Take a trip to the beach or the lake. Have a picnic in the forest or visit a new dog park. You don't need to walk or hike when you get there. Settle down on a blanket and allow your dog to sniff and explore the new world around them.

Chapter 6:

Aging Doesn't Have To Be Scruffy!

Dogs aren't like cats, they don't spend hours grooming themselves with their tongues. Grooming occurs when they partake in everyday activities. As they run, their claws are filed down naturally. Chewing bones and food helps to dislodge any plaque build-up in their teeth. Even just running through bushes or rolling on the grass, is a normal way for your dog to groom their fur.

As your dog ages, their bodies begin to slow down and while they might still enjoy a good roll on the grass, they aren't able to keep up with their usual grooming routine. You may have noticed that your dog suddenly has bad breath, or trouble chewing. When they walk across the wooden floor, they leave behind a trail of scratches! Their once easy-to-brush fur is matted, and you find yourself wiping away gunk from their eyes every day. This is all incredibly uncomfortable and if you don't keep up with regular grooming, it can actually begin to impact their health.

Haircuts and Fur Maintenance

Common Problems

Whether your pup has short and thin fur or long and thick fur, you are likely to encounter some sort of issue as they age. Thankfully, these problems are pretty easy to fix with a regular grooming routine.

Dermatitis

Older dogs become sensitive to chemicals, foods, and plants as they age. These sensitivities can cause mild allergic reactions, which lead to very itchy skin. Dogs suffering from these allergies will lick and chew their skin until it becomes raw. You may notice that they have patches of bare skin and, in severe cases, wounds. While it is best to treat these medically, regular baths with specialized shampoos can soothe the skin and reduce the itch.

Matted Fur

Matted fur is uncomfortable at best, but it can also affect your dog's ability to regulate their body temperature. They use their fur as insulation and if it is matted, the cold will seep in, and they may start to shiver.

Sensitive Areas

Seniors that are prone to potty accidents, will often have matted fur around their sensitive areas. This is due to urine and faces collecting in the fur, which makes it tangle. It looks terrible, smells terrible, and it is extremely uncomfortable for your dog. If left, the bacteria build-up can cause skin and urinary tract infections.

Wounds

Just like people, your dog's skin will begin to thin and lose elasticity, making them more prone to cuts and sores. If your dog has long, thick fur, you may not even notice them until the fur becomes matted around it. Bacteria and dirt will stick to any discharge or blood and can infect the wound.

Grooming

Dogs will generally need to be fully groomed every four to six weeks. This would include a haircut, wash, dry, pedicure, and a face wash. However, these grooming sessions can take up to an hour, depending on the size of your dog and their fur type. Senior dogs can simply not stand that long. Even if they are laying down, the constant noise and rubbing are simply too exhausting.

Instead of one big groom, split it up into shorter, ten minute sessions over a day or even a week.

Regular Brushing

Regular brushing is the best way to keep your dog clean and free of knots. They are much more prone to matting, and you may find you need to brush them daily to keep up.

You will need to ditch the old brushes and invest in gentle ones that have soft bristles. Slicker brushes are great for seniors as they don't snag on tangles or scrape the skin. Small gentle brushes the size of a toothbrush work really well for facial grooming.

To Shave or Not to Shave?

This is quite a debated subject. Older dogs are more susceptible to the cold, so many owners like to keep their coats long. However, old dogs are also more susceptible to matted fur, skin conditions, and infections. Ultimately, the choice is going to depend on what conditions your dog is suffering from and if you can keep up regular grooms to keep their fur healthy.

While a full-body shave may not be the best option for your pup. There are definitely areas of the body that can greatly benefit. Ears, faces, paws, and butts should be regularly maintained, whether it is a full shave or a trim.

For fur in between their paw pads and inside their ears, I suggest using a cordless mini clipper. These are awkward areas to get into, and it is difficult to see where the skin is. The clippers are designed with a safety feature that prevents you from nicking the skin.

Long fur around your dog's face should be trimmed to a reasonable length. This will stop it from poking into their eyes, nose, and mouth and collecting bacteria and gunk. I prefer to use scissors to trim around my dog's eyes and nose.

Shaving or at least trimming your senior's sensitive areas will prevent any urine and feces from becoming matted in the fur. It will also make it much easier to clean them if they have had an accident.

If you want to do a full-body shave, grab yourself a large pair of corded clippers. The large size allows you to do a quicker cut. You can also change the blade, depending on how short you want the fur. Always shave with the grain, not against it.

I like to get my dogs into a comfortable laying down position first. I shave as much area as I can and then give them a short break. They need to stand for their tummy and leg shaves, so I try to get that done as quickly as possible and if needed, I give them another break in between.

Bathing

If you keep up with regular brushes and shaves, then bath time should be a quick affair. Grab your supplies and brush out any knots and matted fur. A mild natural shampoo works well, but you may need to use an antifungal or antibacterial one if your dog has a skin condition.

Using a non-slip mat and keeping them in a seated position will keep them from sliding around the tub. Make sure that the water is at body temperature, you don't want it too hot or cold. Wash them gently and be sure to rinse off all the soap before you take them out.

Don't worry about washing their faces at this point. This can be done later, it is more important to get their bodies dry.

Drying

Always dry your pup after a bath. Even if it is a hot day, you need to dry them! Seniors struggle to regulate their body temperature, and the drastic change from a warm water bath to a cold room will leave them a shivering mess. Use a towel to get the bulk of the water off their fur, but make sure to rub gently so that they don't lose balance.

Thereafter, you should use a hair dryer. Always use it on the lowest possible settings and never focus the dryer on one spot as it can burn their skin. Make sure that their chest, ears, and armpits are completely dry.

Dental Care and Cleanings

Common Dental Problems

Around 80% of dogs will suffer from dental infections at some point in their lives. The pain and discomfort will affect their appetite, and they will begin to lose weight.

Periodontal Disease and Gingivitis

These diseases are caused by a build-up of plaque and bacteria. Senior dogs are more susceptible due to their lowered immune system and change in diet. Dogs that are suffering from gum disease will often have terrible breath, and you may notice frequent bleeding in their mouth.

Grab a flashlight and open their mouths to check for infection. Their gums will be red, swollen, and tender to the touch. If your pup winces when you lift their lips, you are already in for trouble. A build-up of plaque is quite noticeable and can stain the teeth brown if left for long enough. If the infection is not treated, the bacteria can enter the bloodstream and impact vital organs such as the heart, kidney, and liver.

Broken or Filed Teeth

Your dog's teeth will naturally file down with age. There is no reason to be concerned when this happens, and the worst thing that can happen is that your dog won't be able to shred through whole foods.

Broken teeth are common in seniors, as their teeth become brittle after so much wear and tear. This usually occurs when they bite down on something hard or if they sustain an injury. Broken teeth are incredibly painful and will quickly become infected if not treated.

Teeth Cleaning

Brushing your dog's teeth should become part of your weekly grooming routine as they enter their senior years. Preventing gum disease and tooth decay is much easier and cheaper than dealing with infections and tooth extractions.

Chewing and Food

Your dog will naturally clean their teeth when chewing on bones and hard, bulky foods. These are likely no longer options for your senior, but there are some other tricks that can help.

Soft rubber chew toys with bumps and spikes on them work wonders to loosen up any food and plaque that could be trapped in their teeth.

You can also buy dental chews, which are tasty treats that contain ingredients that break down plaque and bacteria.

If your senior dog can still chew kibble, it is worth adding in a few to their meals!

Toothbrushes and Pastes

Doggy toothpaste is not the same as human toothpaste. Most human toothpastes will contain high levels of sodium and xylitol, which can cause serious illness. Pet-friendly toothpastes are completely natural and only contain ingredients that are safe for your pooch to swallow.

While you can technically use a human toothbrush for your dog, you risk them swallowing the bristles if they break. Some brushes are also too hard and can hurt the gums. Dog toothbrushes will usually have soft plastic bristles on the end. You can buy ones that look similar to human ones but are much longer and have a slight curve which allows you to get right to the back of their mouth.

Your other option is a toothbrush that slips over your finger. This makes it a little easier for you to navigate their mouth, but should only be used if you trust them not to nip you!

How To

The hardest part about brushing your dog's teeth is getting them to let you do it. Ideally, you want to train your dog from a young age, but most seniors are pretty good at learning new grooming routines. Start off by getting them used to you touching their mouth. Speak to them gently and give them pats and a couple of treats when they are calm. You can then move on to getting them used to the toothbrush and the taste of the toothpaste. Once they are comfortable and intrigued, you can go in for the clean!

Grab your brush and put a drop of toothpaste on the bristles. Start at the front of your dog's mouth and brush gently in a circular pattern.

Add more toothpaste if needed and slowly work your way to the back of their mouth.

Veterinary Dental Cleanings

Brushing your dog's teeth once a week is a good way to maintain dental health. However, it is still recommended that your dog gets a full dental cleaning at least once a year. During the cleaning, your veterinarian will also be able to take x-rays and check for any decay and broken teeth. If they need to, they will extract any dead teeth.

This process can be a little stressful for owners as your dog will need to be put under anesthetic. Don't worry too much, the veterinary team knows exactly what they are doing! Your dog will undergo a medical examination and at this point, you will need to disclose any strange behavior, medications they may be on, and if they have any allergies to medications. If your veterinarian is happy with their health, they will continue with the cleaning.

Claw Health and Trimmings

There are two parts to a dog's claw. The quick, which supplies blood to the claw, and the end tip and casing known as the shell. The quick is full of nerves, and cutting into it can cause extreme pain and bleeding. This is the fastest way to ensure that your dog never lets you cut their claws ever again.

The quick is a light pink color, which is easy to see if your dog has light-colored claws. If your dog has black claws, you will need to do some guesswork and be cautious not to cut it during trims. If your pup has not had regular trims, the quick is likely to be quite long. However, with regular manicures, it will recede.

Common Problems

There is no way around it, long claws are guaranteed to cause health problems. Senior dogs are more susceptible to these, as their joints and muscles are already taking on a lot of strain.

Broken Claws

Stubbing your toe sucks. Breaking your toenail during that stub warrants the use of every forbidden word in the book. Dogs that have long claws are more likely to get them snagged on furniture, fabric, and paving. While we can treat our broken claws quickly, your dog has to wait for you to notice. Broken claws will often need to be treated by a veterinarian. In severe cases, they may need to surgically remove the entire claw.

Arthritis and Injury

Long claws reduce your dog's traction, which makes it more likely for them to slip and injure themselves, but that's not the worst issue. If the claw hits the ground, it pushes back into the toe and places pressure on the foot and leg.

That pressure can cause tendon injuries, early arthritis, and in severe cases, deformed feet. All of these are incredibly painful, and dogs will typically shift their weight to their hind legs to compensate, which can cause backache.

Claw Clipping

You want your dog's claws to be long enough for them to use, but short enough to avoid any discomfort. If your dog's claws touch the floor when they are standing, they are too long. If you can hear them walking toward you, they are too long!

Before you get started, make sure that you have everything you need. This includes your clipper or grinder, cotton pads, and plenty of treats. I recommend buying a product like Kwik Stop, which helps to stop any bleeding if you accidentally cut the quick.

Clippers and Grinders

There are three types of tools that you can use to cut your dog's claws.

Standard nail clippers work in the same way that human nail clippers do, but they have a curved edge to suit the shape of a dog's claw. You can buy different sizes and strengths to suit your dog breeds.

Guillotine trimmers have a hole at the end of the tool. You put your dog's claw through this hole and then squeeze. This is a great tool for large dogs that have thick claws, as you don't have to squeeze as hard.

Grinders are essentially dremels that have been modified for pooches! You can buy cordless ones that work well for small dogs or larger corded ones that pack more power for thick claws. I love these as you are less likely to cut into the quick of the claw, and you can smooth the edge of the claw. The only downside of using a grinder is the sound it makes.

How To

Get your dog into a comfortable position and hold their paw firmly. You want your thumb on the toe pad and your finger on top. Placing pressure on the pad will push your dog's claw out. You want to clip the tip of the claw straight across. Give your dog a treat before and after every cut to reward them for their good behavior.

If you are using a grinder, you will need to get your dog acclimatized to the sound first. Leave it on and give them a couple of treats. Use it on the tip of a claw and then treat them again. When they are calm, you can grind away! Filing the claws will cause a lot of dust, so be sure to do this in an open area.

The dewclaw is located on the inside of the front leg. Not all dogs have them, but those that do, usually don't use them enough for them to file down naturally. It's important to keep these clipped too as they snag easily.

For indoor pets, it is best to trim the claws every three to four weeks. If your senior still enjoys a stroll, you may be able to push it to five weeks.

When to Worry

If your dog's claws are embedded in their skin, you need professional help. A groomer will have enough experience to file down the claws without causing any further injury. Keep an eye on those paws, though. Open wounds need to be treated and kept clean.

Eyes, Ears, and Nose

Common Problems

Your eyes, ears, and nose are all vital sense organs and any disruption to their normal function can be incredibly frustrating. Without proper grooming, you may find that your dog struggles to see and hear. If left untreated for long periods of time, infections and complete sense loss can occur.

Gunky and Weeping Eyes

Weeping or gunky eyes are not unusual and are not always a cause for concern. Dogs' eyes naturally expel any dust and dirt that has become trapped. You will likely notice this first thing in the morning when they wake up. The discharge should be a normal white to a gray color with a watery consistency.

If the fur around your dog's eye is thick, this discharge may become trapped and collect dirt, which causes tear stains. Again, this is not necessarily a problem as long as there are no other symptoms.

Your dog's eyes should be bright and clear, and the white of the eye should be just that, white! If you notice that the eye has a film over it or the white of the eye is red, this is likely a sign of conjunctivitis. This is a very itchy condition! Dogs that have conjunctivitis will often paw at their eyes and blink excessively.

Ear Infections and Blockages

Dogs that are suffering from ear infections and blockages will typically paw and scratch behind and inside their ears excessively. It can get to the point where they actually scratch their skin open, leaving bare patches and wounds. It can be caused by a dirt build-up, injury, and moisture in the ear that can't dry out.

Dogs that have long fur around the ears are more likely to experience a dirt build-up and infection. It's important to keep the furs around the ear cut short to prevent this. Some dogs are also just gross. They love to roll in anything disgusting and on many occasions, I have had to sit and clean out some nasty substances in and around my dog's ear.

Runny and Dry Noses

Runny and dry noses are not always a cause for concern. Dry noses are commonly a sign of sunburn and, in extreme cases, dehydration. Runny noses are usually caused by mild allergies and any irritants they may have sniffed up. There are a few simple treatments and cleans that you can do at home to provide immediate relief.

Eye Cleaning

It is relatively easy to clean your dog's eyes, and it is one of the grooming activities that most dogs don't seem to mind. You should clean them every time you bathe them, but pups that are prone to eye discharge and tear stains require a wipe down every day or two.

How To

Using a damp cotton cloth, gently wipe your dog's eye. Start in the middle of the eyelid and wipe to the outer or inner edge to push any gunk out. Rinse out the cotton cloth often to ensure that you aren't wiping any gunk back into the eye. If you notice that there is a lot of debris, you can use a saline eye wash to flush it out.

For thick tear stains, you can hold the damp warm cotton cloth over the hair to loosen it. Then brush the debris out with a comb. If the discharge has gone hard, you need to repeat this step throughout the day. Do not tug the fur as it will pull the soft skin around the eye and cause pain.

Once their eyes are clean, you will need to trim the fur around their face. Focus on any longer hairs that may poke into their eyes. Any thick fur under the eyes should also be trimmed to a reasonable length, as these hairs can collect dirt.

When to Worry

If you notice that the discharge has changed to a greeny-yellow color or become thicker, your dog may be suffering from an eye infection. Bloodshot and excessively watery eyes are also symptoms of eye infections and conjunctivitis.

The only thing you can really do is rinse their eyes out with saline solution to remove any debris that may be stuck. This will help relieve the itch. In most cases, conjunctivitis and any other infections will need to be treated with a topical antibiotic ointment, which can be purchased from your veterinarian.

Ear Cleaning

It's best to check your dog's ears after every bath to ensure that they are clean and looking healthy. Most dogs don't require regular deep cleaning, and all you need to do is remove any visible dirt.

How To

After their bath, lift their ears and check for any dirt, parasites, and wounds. If it looks clear, you can dip a cotton pad in mineral oil and gently wipe the outer ear to remove any bits of dirt. Do not use a wet cotton pad that could drip water into the ear canal, as this can cause a yeast infection and earache!

If your dog requires a deeper ear clean, you can purchase a specialized ear wash. Be sure to check the ingredients. Good washes have antibacterial and antifungal properties, which can prevent infections. You don't want products that contain hydrogen peroxide or alcohol, as they are too harsh and will dry out the skin and ear canal.

Hold your dog's ear up and pour the ear wash in until the canal is full. Keep your dog's ear up and gently massage the base to break up any wax or dirt that may be stuck. Let go of the ear and allow your dog to shake it all out. This is the messiest part of the process, so take a few steps back. Once it is all out, use a cotton cloth to wipe away any excess wash and gunk.

Only use cotton wool and cloths to clean the ear and avoid Q Tips as these can push debris further into the ear canal or even puncture the eardrum. Use the first knuckle on your index finger as a guide to how deep you can go into the ear canal. Any further and you risk causing injury.

When to Worry

If your dog experiences pain at any point, stop immediately! They could be struggling with an inner ear infection and further cleaning will be extremely painful. If you spot any blood, inflammation, blockages, or parasites, you should take your pup to your veterinarian for treatment.

Nose Cleaning

A dog's nose is its guide to navigating the world. We know that they should be moist, but what is the reason behind that? The moisture of the nose holds and absorbs scents from their surroundings, which is part of why their sense of smell is so great. When they lick their noses, they taste the scent, which provides them with even more information. Pretty weird, right? This is why keeping their noses clean and functioning is vital.

How To

If your pup has a dry nose, it could be due to something as simple as dirt. Wipe the nose with a warm moist cloth to remove any gunk and wait for an hour to two.

If it doesn't moisten, and you notice the skin is peeling, it could be due to sunburn. You can purchase a specialized sunburn balm that will rehydrate the skin. Remember, dogs lick their noses repeatedly, so you need to ensure that you find a dog-safe balm that can be ingested. This also means that you are going to have to reapply the balm every hour or so.

Runny and blocked noses are a little more difficult to treat, especially if your dog is unruly during grooming. First off, you will need to clean any debris and muck around the nose. You can do this with a warm cloth and a mild soap. If you opt for soap, make sure to rinse it off completely!

Next, clean up around the nose and mouth. If your dog has long hairs that point up into the nostrils, you will need to cut these short. The same goes for any long hairs that trap discharge and dirt underneath. Scissors can be used to cut the hairs, but mini clippers can get the job done quickly without the risk of snipping the skin. This is a great option if your dog is a wiggler.

With the dirt-trapping hairs gone, take your pup into the bathroom and turn the hot tap on in the shower to create steam. The steam will help to loosen up any mucus in the nose. You can also hold a warm cloth at the top of the nose and gently massage it.

This should relieve some irritation and blockage. Your dog's nose is likely to run, so you will need to ensure that you wipe away the discharge often.

When to Worry

Dry noses are also a symptom of dehydration and illness. If you find that their nose is dry for an extended period, it is time to worry.

If you can't get your dog's nose unblocked, and it has started to affect their breathing, you will need to schedule a check-up to find out what is going on! Your veterinarian may use a sinus rinse to clear the nose, which will provide immediate relief. If the discharge is a yellow-green color, or you notice blood in it, your dog may have a respiratory infection.

Chapter 7:

Senior Dog Life Hacks

Adapting to senior life can be tricky. Your dog can no longer do the things they love without feeling discomfort or getting hurt. The loss of these abilities is frustrating and confusing, and they often feel left behind and scared.

While some senior dogs slow down by themselves, others haven't quite figured out that they aren't spring chickens anymore. You have likely already made changes to your environment and lifestyle to accommodate them. However, depending on your dog's personality, not all of these changes will work when put into practice. Adapting these changes slightly can make a significant difference in your dog's quality of life.

If there is something specific you are struggling with, chances are, somebody has already dealt with it and solved it before! Below are some outstanding dog-approved life hacks that I first learned during Sam's senior years.

Bumpy Car Rides

If you have a small, senior dog that likes to look out of the window while you drive, then this hack is for you! During the summer months, we would often travel to the lake, which is three hours away. Ordinarily, it was just Sam and I and he would sit in the front seat next to me. One of his favorite things to do was look out the window and enjoy all the new sights, sounds, and smells.

However, as he aged, he began to lose his balance and would frequently fall. If I had to use the brakes, no matter how softly, he would fall against the dash and onto the floor. He would desperately scramble back up onto the seat, scared to miss anything exciting, but the moment I started to drive again, he would slip between the seat and the door!

These once tranquil trips quickly turned into a nightmare. One day, while we were packing up and getting ready to head home, I got an idea! I packed my laundry bag, pillows, and blankets on the floor until it was level with the passenger seat. Every time I had to brake or accelerate, Sam would have a soft space to land if he lost his balance.

As time went on, I noticed that he was only able to stand for a few minutes to look out the window before getting tired. I stacked up the pillows a little higher so that he could lie down comfortably and watch the world go by. The only negative thing about this hack is that I wish I had thought of it sooner.

Wait, Don't Jump!

Elderly dogs, regardless of their size, need to be helped in and out of the car. Even if they look like they can make it, don't let them do it. I once made the mistake of allowing Sam to jump out by himself. The next thing I knew, he was lying on the driveway screaming.

I immediately panicked and picked him up to console him, and he began yelping every time I touched his front leg. We hopped straight back into the car and sped off to the veterinarian for an x-ray. Thankfully, it was just a sprain and the only treatment needed was love and rest. I wrapped his little leg up with some flexible bandage tape, and he was able to put his weight on it with minimal limping. After a few days, he was back to his normal self.

I got lucky that day, and the injury he sustained could have been much, much worse. Sam was a smaller dog, and it was easy enough to pick him up to put him in and out of the car. For my larger dogs, I use a sling. This helps me to pick them up without breaking my back! Ramps work especially well for giant dogs, and they are easy to move and store.

The Floor is Like Ice!

If you have hardwood floors or tiles, there is no doubt you have watched your dog skid across the room. Sam would bolt down the carpeted stairs and as soon as he hit the wood floor, he would go sliding like a hockey puck and slam into the furniture.

While this was absolutely hilarious to us when he was a young pup, it became dangerous as he aged, and it was only a matter of time before he hurt himself. Even while standing still, his four little paws would slide. It was as if he were standing on ice, and he would constantly shuffle his paws to try to keep his balance.

There is a surprisingly simple fix to this problem. Using a mini clipper, I would remove all the fur I could from in between his paw pads. I would regularly trim his claws to keep them short. This helped tremendously with the sliding.

I Can't Get To Bed

Does your little dog sleep in your bed? Well, then you have probably noticed that they are having trouble mastering the jumps they were once capable of. As they age, their joints become stiff and they develop arthritis. They simply aren't as limber as they once were, and this is unlikely to change.

If they are having to make a second or third attempt to jump onto the bed or sofa, it is time to make a change before they hurt themselves! The good news is, there is an easy fix to the issue. Buy a set (or two, or three) of pet stairs to put next to your bed or sofa. Your furry little friend will now be able to access the snuggles they rightly deserve.

The Stairs Are Too High!

While pet stairs are easy enough to navigate, your senior dog is likely to struggle with taller staircases. These could include porch stairs, deck stairs, and the most troublesome, staircases within the home.

You may have noticed that they struggle to climb the stairs, or they sit and cry, asking for you to help them. If you have deck stairs, your pup will probably choose to potty on the deck rather than use the stairs to access the yard. In the worst-case scenario, they begin to tumble down them, which can cause serious injury.

If you have a small or medium size dog, it is time to start picking them up and carrying them up and down the stairs. For larger dogs, I suggest you build a doggie ramp on shorter staircases, such as porch stairs. If they are struggling up your home stairs, you can use a sling lift to assist them.

If your dog has unsupervised access to your home, I recommend installing a baby gate at the bottom of the stairs to ensure that they can't use the stairs without you. This will reduce the risk of injury and keep your furry friend safe.

I Feel Scared

Living in a multi-dog household, I have had to navigate many personalities, and accommodate my dog's likes and dislikes accordingly. Some of my dogs love the crate, so I have always had one set up in my living room. When not in use, I leave the door open so that they can use it when they please. Sam, on the other hand, hated being closed up in it, which is why it was such a shock to find him curled up in it!

As he aged, his hearing and eyesight deteriorated and his awareness and alertness dwindled. The crate had become a safe haven for him and when he wanted to nap, he was able to curl up inside of it. This sense of security is vital for an aging dog, and it gives them a chance to get some peace and quiet away from the other pets.

If you have other pets, and you don't own a crate, this is a good time to invest in one.

What is Growing on Me?

As Sam aged, he began to develop these little moles all over his body. Some of which grew to the size of a pea! Of course, I was worried, so we went to the veterinarian for a check-up. She explained that they were benign lipomas and there was nothing to worry about. Due to his age, it would be harder for him to go through removing them than it would be to just live with them.

However, they quickly become too gross to handle! They would ooze and bleed, which would then dry in his fur and smell. This made him uncomfortable, so I decided to keep his fur shaved short and bathe him every week to soothe his skin. While he was more comfortable, the cold hit him a lot harder and my other dog began to clean the exposed wound. Other than being disgusting, it also caused Sam more pain as the lipomas were constantly opened.

To solve both problems, I bought Sam an entirely new wardrobe. He had T-shirts for warm days and sweatshirts and sweaters for colder days. These kept him warm and stopped my other dog from licking them. The lipomas were no longer exposed to dirt and bacteria and when they oozed or bled, I could easily change his soiled shirt and treat them.

I Don't Want a Haircut

Sam never really enjoyed being groomed, but it has always been a necessity, especially once the lipomas developed. As he got older, the groomers were no longer able to work with him as he could not stand for long periods of time. It couldn't be that hard to groom him, I thought. So, I set out to purchase a large corded pet clipper and a battery-operated mini one.

They were easy enough to use, but Sam was not having any of it. He refused to stay on the kitchen floor, he would try to bite the clippers and every time he got the chance, he would run away from me. I tried to use a leash, as the groomers did, but every time his heart would race, and he would begin to shake. I couldn't stand it anymore, so I decided to switch it up.

One sunny spring day, I grabbed some towels, training treats, and the clippers. I covered a patio chair with towels so that it was comfortable, and I placed him onto the chair. Sam's favorite thing in the entire world was food, and using treats was the best way to get him to do anything.

I sat in front of him and offered him a treat. I turned the clippers on and gave him another treat. He was still relaxed, so I began to shave him slowly, giving him treats now and then and a bunch of "good boys." I shaved as much of his body as I could while he was laying down and when I got him to stand, I would give him little breaks in between sections.

As we repeated these grooming sessions, he became more and more comfortable, and I was able to use the mini clippers to trim the fur around his ears, snout, and eyes. I still can't believe how much a change of scenery and a bit of comfort changed his mindset!

For larger dogs, you can purchase grooming stands and pillows which can keep them comfortable during the process.

I'm So Cold!

As your dog ages, they begin to have difficulties regulating their body temperature. You may notice that they have started to shiver, even when it feels warm to you! It's important to take this seriously, as they can develop hypothermia if they don't warm up.

Make sure your dog has a sweater for indoors and a warm coat for outdoors. If they sleep at the foot of your bed, get them a warm blanket to snuggle up in. During the winter months, you can place their bed near a heater vent, or fireplace. There are tons of electric heating pads and blankets on the market, and these are a great option for those summer months when you don't want to turn the heater on.

When Did Eating Become Difficult?

As a child, I was taught that dogs only needed to eat once a day. As I got older and adopted my first dog, I realized that dogs are healthier, better behaved, and sleep better at night if they have two meals a day. I realized that Sam wasn't able to stand long enough to actually finish his food. I began feeding him three to four times a day, and noticed an immediate improvement!

Some senior dogs have trouble standing or balancing on tiled or hardwood floors while eating. Placing a rug under their bowls and feeding area can help with their traction, making it easier to stand. Raised food bowls are a great option to solve balancing issues as they reduce the strain on your dog's body.

Their immune system can become compromised, so it is vital to keep their food and water dishes clean!

I Can't Hold it in!

Are you finding yourself cleaning the carpets more often now that your dog has gotten older? Does your furry friend look directly at you while they squat in the middle of your living room? Do you find yourself standing in wet spots when you walk sleepily down the hallway in the morning?

If you do, then you are probably ready to tear your hair out. This is an incredibly frustrating problem to deal with, and you are likely to find yourself angry with your pet, even though you know it is not their fault.

I struggled with this issue for years, and waking up in the middle of the night to let Sam out was not working out well for me. I finally discovered my carpet-saving rescue, doggy diapers! This may sound a little strange, but you can purchase specialized diapers in different sizes for both male and female dogs. Boy diapers are simple wraps that wrap around the belly. Girl diapers look more traditional, and they wrap between their legs and over their rumps.

If you aren't able to frequently change their diapers, you can look at using indoor potty pads. These should only be used on tiled or wooden floors, but placing a towel underneath them can provide extra protection for carpets. It is easy to train your dog to use them, and they work especially well for owners that are at work for most of the day.

I Can't See You!

It's just a matter of time before your furry friend's eyesight begins to deteriorate, and you may notice that their eyes look cloudy or milky. There are a couple of reasons why this may happen, and it is best to get it checked out by your veterinarian. They will be able to find the cause and assess the extent of the eyesight loss. This will give you a better idea of what you are dealing with and what to expect if it were to get worse.

With eyesight loss comes fear, and your dog will have trouble identifying who is coming through the door. To reduce this stress, have your family and friends extend their hands down so that your dog can give them a good sniff. If your dog knows them well and can recognize their voices, you can also ask them to announce themselves before walking in.

This will help keep your dog calm.

I Can't Hear You!

The days of loud, scary thunderstorms are over and the sound of the garbage truck no longer causes a barking frenzy! While this seems like a blessing, there are more cons than pros to hearing loss. During Sam's senior years, I would let him out into the yard to do his business, but when I would call him back, he would stare off into the distance as if he did not hear me.

Calling him for dinner no longer worked, and I found myself shouting his name out, which was not pleasant for anyone. Then one day I smacked my hand against the door and the loud thump caused him to look at me. Eureka!

From then on, I would smack the table or door, or clap my hands until he turned to look at me. I could then motion for him to come, and he happily walked towards me.

Chapter 8:

Life-Changing Products and Tools

I knew that my life would change as Sam reached his senior years, but I never expected how creative I would become! Every time Sam encountered a problem, I found myself heading to the store and grabbing supplies to build some sort of DIY contraption that, I prayed, would help him. Some of it worked, some of it, not so much, but those failures helped me to make something even better. It was a great bonding experience, and I often remember Sam giving me some odd looks when I would whip out the DIY pet sling.

Thankfully, there are a bunch of people out there that are much more creative than I am and have the right tools to build some incredible things. With the pet market booming, there is no end to the remarkable new contraptions that are quickly becoming lifesavers. The great part about the products and tools listed below is that they come in different sizes to suit your dog's breed. Not to mention how much time you will save!

If only these products had been available then, I am confident that Sam would have been a little happier to not have been the test dummy.

Easy Transport Products

Losing mobility doesn't mean that your dog has to miss out on adventures. There are some fantastic products that ensure your pup enjoys some fun in the sun without any discomfort.

Car Crate

If you find that your dog is struggling to balance and often falls during car rides, it is time to look at getting a car crate. These are a little different from the standard household crates. They are smaller, which restricts your dog's movements, which helps to keep them from falling over. You can purchase them in different materials. Metal mesh crates have a lot of airflow, but they can become uncomfortable if your dog lays against the sides.

Soft mesh crates are much more comfortable and work well for small dogs. Plastic crates are easy to carry and block out the hot sun. Whichever one you prefer, make sure to purchase the right size for your pup!

Car Ramp

Car ramps are an absolute must-have for larger dogs. While jumping up into a car is not ideal, jumping down out of a car is downright dangerous. As your dog lands, they put immense strain on their joints and spinal column, which can cause serious injury. If you have a truck or SUV, it is definitely time to invest in a ramp.

Ramps are foldable, which makes them easy to store and transport. They are coated with non-slip materials, which provide your dog with traction and prevent slipping!

Car Seat Covers

These covers not only protect your seats, but they also protect your dog from falling too! They come in a box shape and clip to the back of your front seats. This prevents your pup from trying to jump into the front seat, and it stops them from falling down onto the floorboard. Seat covers will usually cover the entire back seat, but you can purchase boxed ones for smaller dogs. These follow the same concept but fit snugly on one seat.

If your small dog enjoys looking out the window, you can go one step further and purchase a platformed box seat for them.

Car Seat Extender

These are great for larger dogs that need a little extra room to lay down. It is easy to put them together and pull them apart, which makes it convenient to store them in your trunk. The rectangular shape fits into the floorboards of the back seat, and they have strips that will clip onto your front seats for extra support. This creates a platformed area that essentially extends your back seat into a larger space.

Wagon

Wagons are a great transportation tool for dogs that suffer from mobility issues. They are easy to pull and can be purchased in different sizes to suit all dog breeds. If your dog is recovering from an injury, a wagon is the best way to stick to your normal exercise routine. Even if they are unable to partake in the walk, they can still enjoy the view!

I, personally, enjoy having a wagon with me during longer walks. If my senior pup starts to get tired, they can hop in and take a break without me having to cut the walk early.

Pet Stroller

Pet strollers are the wagon equivalent for small and toy dogs. Strollers do have some advantages over wagons. They can be zipped up, which can prevent your dog from making a run for it. This feature is also ideal for keeping your pup out of the direct sun during those hot days. They are easy to fold, which automatically makes them easy to store and transport. My personal favorite part of having a stroller is being able to toss my water bottle and bag into it.

Bike Trailer

If you and your dog enjoy cycling, it is time to get a bike trailer. These durable mesh trailers run on two or three wheels, depending on size. They clip easily onto the back of your bicycle and are light and balanced, which ensures that you don't fall.

They are designed with mesh tops that can be folded back so that your dog can enjoy the breeze through their very own sunroof. Hardy, rugged ones have been designed for owners and dogs that enjoy camping and forest cycling.

Bike trailers aren't limited to old dog use. They are perfect for any dog that needs a break from an outdoorsy adventure.

Medical Products

Potty Pads

If your pup has been struggling to hold it in, it is time to pick up some indoor potty pads. Disposable pads come in different sizes to cater to all dog breeds, and a lot of them are scented if you are concerned about the smell. They are thick and absorb urine well. However, I recommend using a double layer or purchasing larger ones to avoid any leaks. This is especially helpful for when you are away or asleep, as your pup may need to go more than once.

You can purchase washable potty pads which can be reused. These are a little difficult to use for large dogs but are perfect for small and toy dogs.

If you live in an apartment or your dog is struggling to cope with your porch stairs, you can use a grass potty pad. These are usually made of artificial grass which is placed on top of a tray. It is easy to wash and there is no need to deal with urine smells indoors.

Dog Diapers

Doggy diapers can be used for seniors that have frequent accidents, even while asleep. They come in different sizes and can be purchased for males or females. While the design is different, the structure is identical to baby diapers. This means the cheaper you go, the less effective they are. Mid-range diapers soak in the urine and turn it into gel to avoid any leaks. It is important to remember that doggy diapers are not made for poop, so they cannot be worn all day. Using these in conjunction with potty pads is a great way to avoid accidents.

Slings and Harnesses

While similar to normal harnesses, slings will typically wrap under your dog's belly, close to their hind legs. They are mainly used to assist dogs that are recovering from spinal or limb injuries. However, new slings and harnesses have been developed especially for aging dogs. The sling has a handle that allows you to lift your dog off the floor without breaking your back.

The best part about using slings is that your dog is still able to walk, climb stairs and even perform small jumps. The only difference is that you are keeping the bulk of their weight off the ground, which takes the strain off their joints. Some of the new slings that have been developed can be worn all day, which allows you to assist your pup when they struggle to get out of bed.

Hip Support Braces

If your dog is struggling with hip mobility, you can look into buying support braces. These wrap around the hips and top of the hind legs and then connect to a standard harness. They hold your dog's hips in a secured position, which allows them to walk freely without discomfort.

These can be purchased for dogs of any size, but it is best to get them correctly fitted by a veterinarian or rehabilitation assistant. If they don't fit well, they can cause more harm than good.

Braces should be used to support senior dogs with lower back pain, arthritis or early symptoms of hip dysplasia. If your dog is suffering from a more serious condition, you should consider a doggy wheelchair.

Doggy Wheelchairs

You can buy two types of wheelchairs, one with two rear wheels and one with four. Which one you choose will depend on what kind of support your pup needs. They are generally used for dogs that have suffered from an injury or paralysis. However, they are incredibly helpful for senior dogs with severe arthritis or leg weakness.

They are fully adjustable and can be purchased for dogs of all sizes. No need to cancel that camping trip! You can even change the wheels to suit different types of terrain.

Grooming Support Pillows and Stands

Grooming stands and pillows were developed to keep unruly dogs still during grooming sessions. However, they double up as great support devices for senior dogs. They fit under your dog's belly and keep them in a standing position. The tops are padded to keep your dog comfortable and stop any chaffing. This position makes it easy for you to access all areas of their body, making grooming much, much quicker.

You can purchase them in different sizes, and most are adjustable. For seniors, getting the height right is vital, as this will help keep the bulk of their body weight off their joints! Just be sure to monitor your pup throughout the whole process and give them a break if needed.

Homeopathic Balms

There are tons of fantastic natural balms and ointments that can prevent and treat skin conditions. Doggy sunscreen is a must-have if you have a light-skinned dog. Most of these come in spray form and are quick-drying so that your dog doesn't get a chance to lick it off.

If your pup does end up getting sunburned, you can use a snout soother. This soothes and softens dry, peeling, and burnt noses. Just make sure to check that all the ingredients are edible before applying them.

Your pup's little paw pads will become more sensitive as they age. Walking on snow, hot asphalt, stones, and the rough ground will likely chaff or injure them. You can buy a specialized paw wax that can be used before and after walks. These generally contain antibacterial and antifungal elements. This means the wax will soothe the skin while protecting it from infections.

Tools For A Comfortable Home

Getting old is uncomfortable enough. Adding flat, uncomfortable beds, slippery floors, and couches that are too high to jump on makes getting old an absolute misery. Keep your dog comfortable and cozy with these fantastic products.

Crate

Crates and indoor kennels are great comfort tools for senior dogs. You don't have to purchase the conventional metal one. In fact, using a wooden enclosed one is sometimes better. These crates help to muffle noise and block out light. It also keeps your dog safe from other household pets that enjoy pushing their muzzles through the metal to get a quick sniff.

Orthopedic Beds

If you have a large and heavy dog, these are VITAL. Most dog beds start off nice and fluffy, but after a few washes they are flat, and your dog ends up sleeping on the hard floor. Orthopedic beds have thick memory foam mattresses that keep their shape and keep your dog's hips intact. You can buy ones that lay flat on the floor or elevated ones. Elevated ones are great as they add a little extra protection from the cold floor in winter.

When buying a bed, it is important to make sure that it is actually big enough for your dog. You don't want their heads falling off the side. If your pup does enjoy stretching out, you can purchase ones that have L or U-shaped pillows, which will stop them from rolling off.

Heated Dog Pads

Heat pads are a great source of warmth and comfort for pets of any age. Senior dogs that struggle to keep warm or suffer from stiff joints and arthritis benefit the most from these. The heat is soothing and promotes blood flow, which eases digestive pain and reduces inflammation. You can purchase them in different sizes to suit your breed, and they fit snugly under your dog's bed or blanket.

They usually have three different settings which allow you to adjust the temperature, which means you can use it in warm weather too!

Pet Stairs and Ramps

We already know that pet stairs are great. They are light and easy to set up next to your bed or couch. Your pup can now get up and down without taking any strain on their joints. Mini ramps are very useful, especially if you have a toy dog that may struggle with the pet stairs. You can purchase the ramps in different sizes and heights, which allows you to use them on short staircases and porch stairs.

It's important to not go for the cheaper options if you are buying a ramp for long-term or outdoor use. You want one that is covered with non-slip materials to provide traction for your pup.

Traction Rugs and Mats

Using textured rugs and mats is a fantastic and cheap way to stop your dog from ice skating over hardwood and tiled floors. You don't even need to purchase expensive ones, yoga mats work just as well. As an added bonus, these mats can be used to create pathways through the house to help blind dogs navigate their surroundings.

Raised Dog Bowls

You can purchase raised bowls and stands at different heights to accommodate all sized dogs. Some of them are even adjustable. Lifting food and water bowls off the floor can help alleviate neck and joint strain, as your pet won't need to stay in a bent over position to eat. Simply getting your dog out of that hunched position will promote overall digestive health. Combining these bowls with traction mats is ideal for dogs that are prone to slipping on the floor or losing their balance.

Dog Clothes and Shoes

Fashion and function! By now, you know how important it is to get your dog a warm sweater for those cold days, but there are so many more accessories that will change your senior's life. Waterproof coats are the perfect accessory to keep your dog dry, and you will be able to continue your exercise routine while it is raining. Booties are great for keeping your dog's paws warm during snowy days, and you can purchase light ones that protect their paws from cold floors.

You can now buy upgraded dog shoes that come with non-slip pads underneath. These prevent your dog from slipping across smooth floors and protect their paws on hot asphalt.

If your dog doesn't like wearing booties, you can buy toe grips. Yes, that is a thing! These little rubberized grips fit over your dog's claws. While the grips won't be able to support your dog's ankles, they do help with traction.

Chapter 9:

Knowing When To Say Goodbye

Honestly, this is the absolute worst part of owning a dog. The heartbreak and pain you experience are enough to make you give up on the idea of ever adopting another one. We sadly only get a limited amount of time to spend with our dogs and, unfortunately, we inevitably need to say goodbye. Saying goodbye is not easy, and it is easy for us to get wrapped up in veterinarian visits and treatments to find any way possible to extend their lives for just a few more years. However, we need to remember that this is not just our lives, it is theirs too and when it is time for them to go, we have to let them go. Your duty as an owner is to provide them with the best possible life you can, and this includes a peaceful death.

As we have discussed already, each breed has an estimated lifespan, and some of you may have to say goodbye sooner than others. However, this is just that, an estimate. Each pup is different, and you will need to understand their medical condition and personalities to understand the signs and symptoms.

Signs Your Dog May be Ready to Pass

Just because your dog is displaying these symptoms, does not mean that they are days from passing. Your pup could have weeks or months left. Don't let the panic take over! These symptoms are common for a variety of illnesses, and they can be difficult to differentiate. However, if your dog is very old and these symptoms seem to have no cause, you need to get prepared to say your goodbyes.

Appetite

A loss of appetite is a common symptom of stress, illness, and underlying medical conditions. However, through all this, it is likely that your pup will still try to stomach their favorite treats. More often than not, dogs that are ready to pass will completely lose their appetite, including a refusal to eat their favorite foods. This could be accompanied by a refusal to drink water as well.

Lethargy and Disinterest

As we now know, lethargy could be a symptom of several medical conditions. However, when this becomes extreme and there are no medical reasons behind why, you need to prepare yourself. Your dog will likely sleep for long periods of the day, battling to get up and refusing to play or exercise.

Attention-Seeking or Emotional Detachment

Depending on your dog, they will react in one of two ways. A normally loving and cuddly dog may begin to detach itself from you completely. At the same time, a usually independent dog may begin to seek constant attention and comfort. Both are completely normal, and this is just a way for your dog to cope with the inevitable. While emotional detachment is devastating, it is important to remember that this is about your dog, not you. You should provide them with a safe haven and give them their space when they ask for it.

Confusion and Lack of Coordination

Aging can take its toll on the muscles and mind. As the muscles deteriorate and arthritis kicks in, your dog may lose their ability to coordinate their bodies. They may walk into furniture, wobble while they walk, or fall for no reason. This can cause confusion and frustration. Their minds will also deteriorate over time, and they may forget what they were doing, and where they are and even lose their sense of direction.

To keep your dog calm and comfortable, you should reduce the need for them to walk long distances to access food, water, and potty areas. Move their bowls and potty pads into the room where they sleep. Make sure to monitor and assist them if need be when they go outdoors.

Dull Eyes

In the end, there is something distinctly different about your dog's eyes. Almost as if the sparkle that was once there is gone. It's a difficult symptom to describe, but it is unforgettable when you see it. I like to believe that at this point, they had already begun their trot across the rainbow bridge, but decided to turn around and hang on just a little longer to spend those last minutes with you.

Consult Your Veterinarian

There are symptoms that you can manage at home, and there are some that need medical attention. If you notice that your dog is experiencing any of the following signs, seek guidance from your veterinarian.

Illness

Very old dogs are fragile and with their lowered immune system, they are often unable to fight even the simplest of illnesses anymore. Medical conditions are also likely to get much worse at this point. Treating the symptoms will provide your dog with comfort, but if you think that your dog is suffering in any way, get them the help that they require.

Pain

Pain is the worst symptom you could hope for. There is nothing more distressing than watching your dog suffer. If they are experiencing pain, crying out, or whimpering, you will need to take them for a check-up. Depending on the severity, your veterinarian will give you pain medication which will make them more comfortable. Worst-case scenario, your veterinarian may speak to you about euthanasia.

Breathing Difficulties

A change in breathing is a completely natural sign that your dog may be nearing their last hours of life. If your pup is comfortable and happy, let them be. Put a light blanket over their body to keep them warm and be sure to stay by their side. However, if you can see that they are in pain, gasping, or becoming increasingly panicked, call your veterinarian straight away.

Total Incontinence

Total incontinence occurs when their muscles have become so weak that they are unable to hold it in for minutes at a time. This could also mean that a number of their organs are failing. This is a scary thought, but it is not necessarily painful. Regardless, it can become uncomfortable and even embarrassing for your dog. If they are hiding from you and whimpering when it happens, speak to your veterinarian.

Saying Goodbye

Saying goodbye is overwhelming at best. You will likely be full of strong emotions. Sadness, love, guilt, and even anger can take over. Regardless of how you feel, you will need to remain calm. Speak to them, stroke them gently, and display only love. Dogs can pick up on emotions and body language quickly, and if you are in distress, they may mimic your feelings or try to respond to them.

Getting Them Comfortable At Home

Try to continue your normal daily routines. This will depend heavily on your dog's health, of course. Long walks may not be possible anymore, but keeping up feeding, playing and cuddling routines is still important. A sudden and drastic change in routine and daily activities can lead your dog to feel confused and isolated.

Limit their pain. Use pain management medication and homeopathic remedies to reduce pain and inflammation. This will greatly improve their quality of life and allow them to enjoy their last few weeks. Stronger medications may be needed toward the end.

A warm, comfortable, and quiet spot for them to relax is the top priority. You do not want your dog to suffer in any way. Eliminate the cold, the pain, and the noise, and you will see an immediate improvement in their behavior.

Sometimes this is unavoidable, but if you can, don't let your dog go alone. Being able to have that last cuddle is a great comfort for them, and they can go with ease. This is also a critical part of the grieving process for you. If you are unable to be home at all times, ask a friend or family member to dog-sit them for you. It is not the same as being there yourself, but at least you can rest assured that they weren't alone and received love until the very end.

Medical Intervention

Medical intervention is generally only needed for dogs that have been struggling with chronic conditions and illnesses. This is the most difficult way to say goodbye, and many owners find themselves riddled with guilt afterward. Your responsibility has always been to your dog, keeping them healthy, happy, and full of love. You will need to take this into account for their death as well. A quick, peaceful goodbye is better than your dog spending their last days in pain and discomfort.

What Is Euthanasia?

Your veterinarian will not take the decision to euthanize lightly, and they will ensure that there is nothing more that they can do before they recommend it. If the decision is final, your dog will be taken to a quiet room and made comfortable. You will be given time to say your goodbyes, and you will have the option of being with your dog during the procedure.

Your veterinarian will then inject your dog with an overdose of anesthetic. This is completely painless, and your dog will fall asleep before the injection is even finished. They will then pass peacefully within a matter of minutes.

Should I Stay With My Dog?

A veterinary practice is a strange and sometimes scary place. Being in this environment can be quite distressing to your dog, and they aren't able to understand what is happening or why they are there. During any other veterinary visit, you are there to comfort them and hold their paw during the check-ups. Suddenly being alone in there is just too confusing for them.

While the veterinarian and assistants are well-trained and will treat your dog with nothing but love and empathy, it is not quite the same. This will be the last time you can hold them, comfort them, and assure them that they were completely and utterly adored. What more could a dog ask for?

While I always recommend that you stay with your dog, it is completely understandable if you are unable to. If this is something that you know you just can't cope with, it is still important to say your goodbyes before they go. You don't want your dog to go alone and be confused, especially if you were distressed during your final goodbye. Ask a friend or family member that your dog knows and loves to take your place during the procedure.

In some cases, your veterinarian will actually be able to come to your house. This is ideal as your dog can pass in a comfortable space they know and love.

Choosing a Resting Place

Choosing the right resting place for your companion is a critical part of the grieving process. A few years ago, burial was generally considered the only option. It is a great way to say your final goodbyes and have a memorial service. This also provides closure for family members that were not with your pup when they passed. However, if you do not own your property or intend to move to a new city or country, this option is definitely not for you.

If your pup has been put to sleep, you may not be able to take them home to bury them. Cremation is a great option in this case and is often the preferred one overall. This is done by a specialized pet crematorium which will offer a range of memorabilia. Ornate urns are a great option if you want to keep your dog close. Or, opt for a simple box if you intend to spread or bury your pup's ashes. Your veterinarian or the crematorium can even take a paw and nose prints for you. These can be set in stone or printed on paper.

Chapter 10:

Coping With Loss

Each one of us is different. We all process loss in different ways. For some, it may only take a few days to come to grips with the loss of a beloved pet. For others, it can take years. This doesn't make us any stronger or weaker than one another, and it is important to never doubt yourself through this trying period. The loss of a pet is hard enough, you don't need to worsen it for yourself.

Our pets give us a sense of purpose. On our darkest days, they give us a reason to get out of bed. They are a continuous reminder of how beautiful life can be. Yes, they can be a little annoying every so often. You may trip over them or want to scream when you are cleaning up the third pee puddle of the day. Yet, the moment they are gone, you find yourself missing the little things you didn't even realize they did.

It's Okay To Cry!

Experiencing any kind of loss is overwhelming, yet the loss of a pet hits differently. You are allowed to cry. You are allowed to scream! Don't feel ashamed of your feelings, and never try to bottle them up and forget them. It is so important to accept these emotions, and expressing them can relieve some of the pain you are feeling. Grieving is a long, exhausting, and difficult process and is often harder than being with your dog when they pass. Finding a strong, empathic support system is the only way to get through it.

Be Kind to Yourself

Don't pressure yourself into moving on. There is no allotted time for grief, and the idea that you "should just get over it" is more damaging than mourning for a bit longer. Our pets provide us with so much more love and support than we realize. We set up routines in our lives to care for them and spend time with them. We come home to their excitement each day. Their permanent presence in our home means that there is never a time when we are actually alone. Losing a pet is not just losing a partner. It's losing their love, support, and your daily routine, and purpose. It is no surprise that it is so difficult to accept it.

The unexpected death of a pet can be particularly hard. The guilt of not being there when it happened and feeling as though you could have prevented it can be overwhelming. The constant "what ifs" are not healthy, but as hard as it is, you need to let go of that guilt.

If you feel this way, you shouldn't try to take it on alone. If you have the opportunity to, speak to your veterinarian. They will be able to provide you with insight into what could and couldn't have been done. Which is sometimes all you need to have some closure. Having a healthy support system in which you can express your feelings of guilt without fear of judgment is vital.

Mourn Together

If you have a family or a partner, it is important to remember that they are grieving too. Children are especially affected by the loss of the pet, as most are unable to fully comprehend the concept of death. Take the time to talk it through with them and show them that it is okay to feel sad and express their emotions. Share your favorite stories and remember all the good times you had together. Sometimes, being the support system for others can help you to mourn too.

Believe it or not, dogs can mourn too. Their best friend has disappeared, and they don't understand why. Grieving dogs will often become less active, and you may find that they wander around the house whining or whimpering. This can be worsened as they pick up on what you are feeling. Take the opportunity to mourn together. Spend time together, give them love and attention, and partake in fun activities that will make you both smile.

Join a Support Group

When you grieve, it is only natural to reach out to somebody in hopes of receiving compassion and support. However, some people have never owned a dog, and they have absolutely no idea how the loss of one can impact you. You are unlikely going to get the support that you need from them and in some cases, you may actually feel worse. This isn't their fault. They aren't trying to deliberately hurt you, they just genuinely don't understand how it feels. Support groups may be a much better option for you if you don't have any close friends or family that understand what you are going through.

Joining a group doesn't necessarily mean you have to meet in person, which, let's face it, can be quite scary. Online support groups are a great way to meet people who are going through or have gone through the same loss. These platforms allow people to express their sadness, guilt, and anger without embarrassment or shame. Being able to read about other people's experiences and how they have coped with loss is a great way to get some perspective on your situation and learn new methods of how to cope with loss.

Moving On

You are not betraying your dog by moving on. Don't ever feel guilty about it. The thought of forgetting about them completely is terrifying, but I can assure you that is simply not possible. Dogs have such a big impact on us and while we may forget small details here and there, we can never ever forget their presence. There are tons of ways to document the times you spent together and if you ever feel like their memory is slipping, you can go back and remind yourself.

Memorials

Funerals are a wonderful way to get closure. Once your dog has passed, you will likely realize that there is so much more that you wanted to say or do for them, but just never had the chance. This allows you to say your final goodbyes and let them know how much you loved them. This closure is not just for you. Friends, family members, and especially children that were close to your dog will have the opportunity to say goodbye as well.

Being able to share this moment with the people you love is so important. Each of you should share your favorite story, remembering the best and funniest times you had together. Prepare for laughs and tears.

Create a memorial box to bury with your pet. You can include their favorite toys, collar, and blankets. Writing out your feelings and your most inner thoughts that you may not want to express in front of others can be healing. You can bury your letter with your box.

Mark their burial spot so that you will always be able to come back to it when you are feeling down and want to talk to them. You can do this with a cross or a stone, but I really love to plant flowers or a beautiful tree. If you and your dog had a favorite spot at the doggy park, consider donating a bench with a plaque to remember them.

Scrap Books

Scraps books are another great way to keep your dog close to you at all times. Put in their photos, especially ones of the two of you together. Under each photo, write down a story or a letter to them to ensure the memory lasts a lifetime. You can tape in a piece of their favorite blanket or a scrap of their favorite plush toy as well.

Make sure that you take photos before it is too late! If you don't have any, you can hire a professional photographer and have a doggy photoshoot.

Create a New Routine

This is non-negotiable. You likely have a bunch of extra time on your hands and if you aren't using it properly, you can fall into a deep pit of depression. Find a way to fill this void! Regular exercise is a great way to burn off excess energy and frustration. We have just learned how beneficial it is for the mind, so do not give it up. Meditative and calming routines such as yoga classes can help to increase your mental well-being. Visiting friends and keeping social will bring back some joy in your life. Don't feel guilty about laughing.

Give Back

If you feel that you are ready to be around dogs again, I suggest volunteering at an animal shelter. It may be sad at first, but these are dogs that are desperate for love, attention, and stability. The work you will do there is incredibly important, and you can honor your dog's memory by helping them.

Who knows, you may even meet a pup that needs you as much as you need them.

Sometimes It's Better to Forget

We all grieve in different ways and for some of us, the grief is simply too overwhelming. Being around your dog's things, seeing photographs, meeting other pets, or just hearing their names can send you into hysterics. In times like this, it may be best to forget. It is not possible to forget them completely, but clearing out your home of their memory may help. Donate their things to an animal shelter that would be able to put them to good use. I suggest that you box and store your photographs of them, just in case you want to revisit your time together at a later stage.

It's best to avoid other dogs at this point, but you won't need to do this forever! Most importantly, don't feel guilty. If this is how you are able to cope with loss, then put yourself first and do it.

Adopting a New Dog

Most people that have never owned dogs before will tell you to just get another one. This is not something that should be rushed! Bringing a new dog into a turbulent household is not healthy. You need to make sure that you are in an emotionally stable state before you make this decision. You cannot rely on a dog to fix you.

Replacing a dog is also just not possible. Each pup is so unique and their personalities and traits are wildly different. Trying to replace your dog can lead you to resent your new one when they don't behave the same way. You need to adjust your expectations and be prepared to invite a new, special, and unique animal into your life.

However, that being said, you should not close yourself off from the idea of adopting a new dog. Once you are ready and in the right headspace, your new pup can help you to get back on track. Volunteering at an animal shelter is a great way to test how you feel and if you are actually ready to take this new step. It is also the best way to bond with new dogs, learn their personalities, and find out if you are compatible. Love cannot be forced, and the two of you need to choose each other.

Conclusion

I know that we have ended on a sad note, but it is time to wipe away those tears and focus on the now. Your dog may be in their senior years, but you still have plenty of time left with them. If you put some of these methods into practice, you will likely end up with more time than expected.

Hopefully, at this point, you are feeling a bit calmer and more confident in your parenting skills. You now know how to groom your dog at home, adjust their diets to provide them with tons of energy, and continue a healthy slow exercise routine to keep them fit. If you have been concerned about your dogs' health, I hope that these medical chapters have given you the power to identify their illnesses and seek treatment where necessary. Never forget that prevention is the best form of cure, and your vigilance can save your dog's life.

Caring for your senior dog correctly will not only improve their quality of life but yours too. By letting go of that stress and anxiety, you have opened up space for love and joy. Which is all your dog really wants for you! This kind of energy is healing within itself, and the happier you are, the happier your dog will be.

While things will definitely improve, let's not pretend that there won't be difficult times. There will be ups and downs and laughs and tears. Depending on your dog's condition, you may not be able to do it all alone. Find a support system and seek guidance from your veterinarian and rehabilitation assistants. Use the platforms given to you to further your knowledge and better understand what your dog is going through. Social media support groups are a fantastic place to learn new techniques and life hacks and chat with people who are dealing with similar issues as you. You will find that even these dark days will pass. Stay positive, keep smiling, and enjoy every moment that you have left.

Dogs are such a beautiful gift and while we may become frustrated at times, the love, and joy they bring into our lives are insurmountable.

We are given such a short time together, and it is our responsibility to ensure that their lives are completely fulfilled.

Incorporate all the things that your dog loves to do! If they want to sleep on your bed, let them. If you have never celebrated their birthday, bake them a dog-friendly cake. Have you always wanted to visit that special lake with them? If they are well enough, make the trip. It's time to stop focusing on the destination, and start enjoying the journey.

If you have enjoyed this book, please leave a review on Amazon!

Other Publications:

Adult Dog Training Through Positive Reinforcement: Learn the Essential Skills Needed to Shape an Obedient and Well-behaved Dog

About the Author

A Lifetime of Learning and Loving Dogs

My lifelong love for dogs has been a constant in my life. I've always had a special place in my heart for those who need a helping paw, especially those who've faced adversity. For over 30 years, I've dedicated myself to helping dogs and their owners build strong, positive relationships.

Through years of learning about canine health, nutrition, behavior, obedience, and training, I've gained a comprehensive understanding of our furry friends. I'm confident that the knowledge and insights I share can benefit you and your pup.

My gentle, positive approach to training focuses on building trust, understanding, and effective communication. I believe that a well-trained dog is a happy dog, and I'm passionate about empowering others to achieve their training goals.

My books offer practical advice and proven methods to create a harmonious bond with your furry friend. Whether you're a seasoned dog owner or a first-time pet parent, my goal is to help you transform lives, one dog at a time.

By understanding the challenges of dog ownership, I offer expert advice on care and simple, effective training techniques based on respect and love, not fear. Together, we can create a fulfilling life for both you and your dog.

Let's embark on this journey together and create a lifetime of happy memories with your canine companion.

-Hope Chambers

References

References: Book 1

Agadoni, L. (2022, March 18). *How to help a scared dog overcome their fears.* Care. https://www.care.com/c/how-to-help-your-scared-dog-overcome-his-fear/

AKC Staff. (2019a, July 15). *Your Complete Guide to First-Year Puppy Vaccinations.* American Kennel Club. https://www.akc.org/expert-advice/health/puppy-shots-complete-guide/

AKC Staff. (2019b, September 26). *AKC Groups: Sporting, Hound, Working, Terrier, Toy, Non-Sporting, Herding.* American Kennel Club. https://www.akc.org/expert-advice/lifestyle/7-akc-dog-breed-groups-explained/

AKC Staff. (2020, March 3). *Proper Puppy Nutrition Nourishes Rapid Growth & Development.* American Kennel Club. https://www.akc.org/expert-advice/health/proper-puppy-nutrition-nourishes-rapid-growth/

AKC Staff. (2021, September 28). *How to Stop Puppy Biting.* American Kennel Club. https://www.akc.org/expert-advice/training/stop-puppy-biting/

AKC Staff. (2022a, January 1). *Puppy Schedule: Daily Routine for New Puppies.* American Kennel Club. https://www.akc.org/expert-advice/training/setting-schedules-and-developing-a-routine-for-your-new-puppy/#:~:text=Keep%20to%20a%20regular%20routine

AKC Staff. (2022b, December 13). *A Survival Guide for Dog Diarrhea.* American Kennel Club. https://www.akc.org/expert-advice/health/doggie-diarrhea/#:~:text=Withholding%20food%20for%2012%20to

Alvarez, L. (2022, November 16). *How Much Should You Feed Your Puppy? A Complete Puppy Feeding Chart.* The Honest Kitchen. https://www.thehonestkitchen.com/blogs/pet-wellness/puppy-feeding-chart

Annerike. (2021, March 7). *Raising and caring for puppies: 20 clever tips.* Prins Petfoods. https://www.prinspetfoods.com/advice-info/raising-and-caring-for-puppies

Ansorge, R. (2021, May 8). *Nutritional Needs of Puppies.* Fetch. https://pets.webmd.com/dogs/feeding-puppy

Aquanta. (n.d.). *A General Guide to Puppy Safety.* Dog Health. https://www.doghealth.com/care/safety/2329-a-general-guide-to-puppy-safety

Ardente, A. (2023, January 17). *How To Choose the Right Food for Your Puppy.* PetMD. https://www.petmd.com/dog/nutrition/best-puppy-food

Arford, K. (2020, October 20). *10 Science-Based Benefits of Having a Dog.* American Kennel Club. https://www.akc.org/expert-advice/lifestyle/10-science-based-benefits-dog/

Arford, K. (2021a, September 1). *Dog First-Aid Kit Essentials: What To Include For Injuries And Emergencies.* American Kennel Club. https://www.akc.org/expert-advice/health/dog-first-aid-kit-essentials/

Arford, K. (2021b, September 2). *The Best and Worst Toys for A Teething Puppy.* American Kennel Club. https://www.akc.org/expert-advice/health/best-puppy-toys/

Arnold, B. (2020, September 14). *How to Train Your Kids (To Be Exceptional Dog Owners).* The Dogington Post. https://www.dogingtonpost.com/train-your-kids-dogs/

Asher, M. (2020, February 20). *Dog Training Methods And 5 Essential Dog Obedience Commands.* Pets Best. https://www.petsbest.com/blog/dog-training-basic-commands/

Ashley, S. A. (2020, April 6). *Dog Body Language: 45 Ways Your Dog Is Secretly Communicating with You.* PureWow. https://www.purewow.com/family/dog-body-language

ASPCA. (n.d.). *Mouthing, Nipping and Biting in Puppies.* ASPCA. https://www.aspca.org/pet-care/dog-care/common-dog-behavior-issues/mouthing-nipping-and-biting-puppies#:~:text=Either%20ignore%20him%20for%2010

ASPCA. (2014, September 25). *House Training Your Dog or Puppy.* ASPCA. https://www.aspca.org/news/house-training-your-dog-or-puppy

ASPCA. (2015a). *Food Guarding.* ASPCA. https://www.aspca.org/pet-care/dog-care/common-dog-behavior-issues/food-guarding

ASPCA. (2015b). *People Foods to Avoid Feeding Your Pets.* ASPCA. https://www.aspca.org/pet-care/animal-poison-control/people-foods-avoid-feeding-your-pets

ASPCA. (2022). *Pet Statistics.* ASPCA. https://www.aspca.org/helping-people-pets/shelter-intake-and-surrender/pet-statistics

Australia, B. P. (n.d.). *Tired of yapping? How to stop nuisance dog barking.* Buddy Pet Australia. https://buddypet.co/blogs/learn/tired-of-yapping-how-to-stop-nuisance-dog-barking

Australian Veterinary Association. (2019, October 9). *What to do if your pet vomits or has diarrhoea.* Vet Voice. https://www.vetvoice.com.au/articles/what-to-do-if-your-pet-vomits-or-has-diarrhoea/

BatterSea. (2016, October 4). *Toxic food for dogs.* Batter Sea. https://www.battersea.org.uk/pet-advice/dog-care-advice/toxic-food-dogs

Battersea. (2020a, February 21). *How to teach your dog not to jump up.* Battersea. https://www.battersea.org.uk/pet-advice/dog-advice/how-teach-your-dog-not-jump

Battersea. (2020b, October 14). *How to stop my puppy mouthing.* Battersea. https://www.battersea.org.uk/pet-advice/dog-advice/how-stop-my-puppy-mouthing

Battersea. (2021, March 15). *How to Stop Your Dog Barking.* Battersea. https://www.battersea.org.uk/pet-advice/dog-advice/how-stop-your-dog-barking#:~:text=Stay%20silent%20and%20don

Bauhaus, J. M. (2021, August 19). *How to Clean Dog Ears.* Hill's Pet Nutrition. https://www.hillspet.com/dog-care/routine-care/how-to-clean-dog-ears#:~:text=Use%20a%20cotton%20ball%20or

Becker, M. (2022, September 21). *Dog Training 101: Essential Tools You'll Need.* Vetstreet. https://www.vetstreet.com/our-pet-experts/dog-training-101-essential-tools-youll-need

Bell, J. S. (2017, September 25). *Ten Most Common Hereditary Diseases in Dogs.* World Small Animal Veterinary Association Congress Proceedings, 2017. World Small Animal Veterinary Association Congress Proceedings. https://www.vin.com/doc/?id=8506247

Bergel, H. (2021, February 12). *How to Teach a Puppy to Walk on Leash.* Daily Paws. https://www.dailypaws.com/dogs-puppies/dog-training/basic/how-to-teach-a-puppy-to-walk-on-leash

Best Behaviour Dog Training. (2022, April 29). *Dogs are a big commitment - do you have time?* Best Behaviour Dog Training. https://www.bestbehaviourdogtraining.co.uk/blog-post/Time-for-a-dog/

Beverly Hills Vet. (2018, October 30). *Scaredy-Dog: Common Dog Fears.* Beverly Hills Veterinary Associates. https://www.beverlyhillsvets.com/blog/scaredy-dog-common-dog-fears/

Blue Valley Animal Hospital. (2022, June 9). *The Importance of Dog Vaccines.* Blue Valley Animal Hospital. https://www.bluevalleyanimalhospital.net/blog/the-importance-of-dog-vaccines/

Blyth, T. (n.d.). *What is the socialisation Period?* KC College. https://www.tarynblyth.co.za/what-is-the-socialisation-period

Boecker, A. (2019, February 4). *Puppy School: Yes or No? (How useful is it really?).* Hundeo: Dog Training. https://www.hundeo.com/en/training/puppy-training/puppy-school/

Brown, A. (2022, November 11). *What dog owners need to know about the four training quadrants.* Koru K9 Dog Training. https://www.koruk9.com/tips-and-tricks/what-dog-owners-need-to-know-about-the-four-training-quadrants/#:~:text=The%20four%20quadrants%20are%20Positive

Burke, A. (2018, July 3). *Common Fears and Phobias in Dogs and How to Help Treat Them.* American Kennel Club. https://www.akc.org/expert-advice/training/common-fears-and-phobias-in-dogs/

Burke, A. (2021, June 21). *Dog Coughing: Causes and Treatment Options.* American Kennel Club. https://www.akc.org/expert-advice/health/dog-coughing-causes-treatment/

Callahan, K. (2022, March 22). *No Need for Force | How to Get Dog to Stop Pulling on Leash.* Whole Dog Journal. https://www.whole-dog-journal.com/training/how-to-stop-your-dog-from-pulling-on-the-leash/

Carr, E. C. J., Wallace, J. E., Pater, R., & Gross, D. P. (2019). Evaluating the Relationship between Well-Being and Living with a Dog for People with Chronic Low Back Pain: A Feasibility Study. *International Journal of Environmental Research and Public Health,* 16(8), 1472. https://doi.org/10.3390/ijerph16081472

Cesar's Way. (2016, March 22). *Ultimate Raising A Puppy Guide.* Cesar's Way. https://www.cesarsway.com/puppy-101-the-ultimate-guide-to-raising-a-puppy/

Chewy Editorial. (2018, July 2). *5 Common Congenital Dog Diseases.* BeChewy. https://be.chewy.com/5-common-genetic-diseases-of-dogs/

Chewy Editorial. (2023, March 22). *Puppy Feeding Guide: How Much to Feed a Puppy & More.* BeChewy. https://be.chewy.com/puppy-feeding-guide/

Clancy, M. (2020, March 31). *13 Essential Items To Have In Your Dog's First-Aid Kit.* Dogtime. https://dogtime.com/dog-health/general/21573-things-in-dog-first-aid-kit

Clark, M. (2019, January 10). *7 Most Popular Dog Training Methods.* Dogtime. https://dogtime.com/reference/dog-training/50743-7-popular-dog-training-methods

Clason, D. (2022, November 15). *Steps you can take to stop the bad behavior of leash pulling.* PawTracks. https://www.pawtracks.com/dogs/leash-pulling-training/

Clur, K.-B. (2022, June 8). *10 Best Vitamins and Supplements for Puppies in 2023.* Pet Keen. https://petkeen.com/best-vitamins-supplements-for-puppies/

Companion Animal Psychology. (2021, May 26). *Top Tips on Puppy Raising from the Experts (Guide).* Companion Animal Psychology. https://www.companionanimalpsychology.com/2021/05/top-tips-on-puppy-raising-from-experts.html

Comstock, J. (2022, June 23). *How to Socialize a Puppy & Why It's So Important.* Daily Paws. https://www.dailypaws.com/dogs-puppies/dog-training/basic/how-to-socialize-a-puppy

Crittenden, C. (2021, October 25). *5 Basic Commands Every Dog Should Know (And How to Teach Them).* Petful. https://www.petful.com/behaviors/basic-commands-your-dog-should-know/

The Dog Blog. (2023, March 13). *Monitoring a Healthy Weight for Your Puppy*. Bil-Jac. https://www.bil-jac.com/the-dog-blog/posts/monitoring-a-healthy-weight-for-your-puppy/

Dog Sense. (2020, March 30). *21 (Super Easy) Ways To Mentally Stimulate Your Dog*. Dog Sense. https://dogsense.co.nz/mental-stimulation-for-dogs/

Dog Trust. (n.d.-a). *How to stop your dog pulling on the lead*. Dog Trust. https://www.dogstrust.org.uk/dog-advice/training/outdoors/walking-nicely-training

Dog Trust. (n.d.-b). *How to stop your dog resource guarding food and toys*. Dog Trust. https://www.dogstrust.org.uk/dog-advice/training/unwanted-behaviours/resource-guarding-food-and-toys

Dog Zen. (2016, December 8). *Choosing the best puppy from a litter*. Dog Zen. https://dogzen.com/choosing-a-puppy/

Doggy Treat Box Blog. (2021, September 30). *Puppy essentials, What equipment you need for your new puppy*. Doggy Treat Box. https://doggytreatbox.com/puppy-essentials-what-equipment-you-need-for-your-new-puppy/

Donovan, L. (2019a, July 30). *Leash Train Your Puppy In 5 Easy Steps*. American Kennel Club. https://www.akc.org/expert-advice/training/teach-puppy-walk-leash/

Donovan, L. (2019b, October 31). *Puppy Socialization: How to Socialize a Puppy*. American Kennel Club. https://www.akc.org/expert-advice/training/puppy-socialization/

Donovan, L. (2022, November 8). *What Dog Is Right For Me? How to Choose The Perfect Breed*. American Kennel Club. https://www.akc.org/expert-advice/dog-breeds/what-dog-is-right-for-me/

Drake, A. (n.d.). *How to Introduce a New Puppy to Your Older Dog*. The Dog People. https://www.rover.com/blog/introduce-new-puppy-older-dog/

Elliott, G. (2022, October 4). *Kids and Pets: What You Need to Know For Safe Interactions.* The Dog People. https://www.rover.com/blog/introducing-a-dog-to-your-children/

Elliott, P. (2018, June 13). *A First Time Owner's Guide to Caring for a New Puppy.* Petfeed. https://petcube.com/blog/puppy-guide/

Embark. (2018, April 13). *How to Introduce Your Puppy to Outdoor Activities.* Embark Pets. https://embarkpets.com/blogs/news/how-to-introduce-your-puppy-to-the-outdoors#:~:text=Some%20essential%20training%20skills%20your

Fantegrossi, D. (2018, September 24). *10 Of The Most Common Fears And Phobias In Dogs.* IHeartDogs. https://iheartdogs.com/common-fears-phobias-dogs/

Farricelli, A. (2023, February 26). *10 Impulse Control Games for Dogs.* PetHelpful. https://pethelpful.com/dogs/Impulse-Control-Games-for-Dogs

Fetch Masters. (n.d.). *Dog Socialization Problems.* FetchMasters. https://fetchmasters.com/dog-socialization-problems/

Fi Team. (2021, March 23). *10 Reasons Why You Should Get a Puppy.* Fi. https://blog.tryfi.com/10-reasons-why-you-should-get-a-puppy/

Firth, P. (2021, March 3). *The Ideal Daily Puppy Routine.* Zigzag Puppy Training. https://zigzag.dog/blog/new-puppy/getting-your-puppy/ideal-puppy-training-routine/

Flaim, D. (2012, April 16). *Teaching Kids to Love Dogs from an Early Age.* Whole Dog Journal. https://www.whole-dog-journal.com/care/dogs-kids/teaching-kids-to-love-dogs-from-an-early-age/

Flaim, D. (2016, March 11). *The Importance of Trimming Dog Nails*. Whole Dog Journal. https://www.whole-dog-journal.com/care/nail-clipping/the-importance-of-clipping-dogs-nails/

Flaim, D. (2019, September 9). *Teaching Young Children to Respect Dogs*. American Kennel Club. https://www.akc.org/expert-advice/training/teaching-young-children-respect-dogs/

Flowers, A. (2021, July 7). *Socializing a New Puppy*. Fetch. https://pets.webmd.com/dogs/guide/socializing-new-puppy

Four Paws. (2020, October 11). *Does a Dog Fit My Lifestyle?* Four Paws. https://www.four-paws.org/our-stories/publications-guides/does-a-dog-fit-my-lifestyle

Four Paws. (2022, May 27). *Fear, Anxiety and Phobias in Our Pets*. Four Paws. https://www.four-paws.org/campaigns-topics/topics/companion-animals/fear-anxiety-and-phobias-in-our-pets

Fulcher, S. (2014, January 2). *Ten Reasons Your Dog May Develop Behavior Problems*. Clicker Training. https://www.clickertraining.com/ten-reasons-your-dog-may-develop-behavior-problems

Gantt, E. (2021, May 7). *How to Set a Daily Routine for Your New Puppy*. Wagwalking. https://wagwalking.com/wellness/how-to-set-a-daily-routine-for-your-new-puppy

Geier, E. (2023, March 2). *We Review the Best Dog Harnesses for Every Kind of Dog*. Rover Reviews. https://www.rover.com/blog/reviews/review-best-dog-harnesses/

Gerrity, S. (2021, April 27). *How to Create a Pet First Aid Kit, According to a Vet*. Daily Paws. https://www.dailypaws.com/dogs-puppies/health-care/dog-first-aid-emergency/pet-first-aid-kit

Gibeault, S. (2018, April 30). *Positive Rewards Dog Training Tips*. American Kennel Club. https://www.akc.org/expert-advice/training/training-rewards/

Gibeault, S. (2020a, November 19). *Impulse Control for Dogs.* American Kennel Club. https://www.akc.org/expert-advice/training/teaching-your-pup-self-control/

Gibeault, S. (2020b, December 23). *How to Stop Your Dog from Jumping up on People.* American Kennel Club. https://www.akc.org/expert-advice/training/how-to-stop-your-dog-from-jumping-up-on-people/

Gibeault, S. (2021, June 23). *How to Make Vet Visits Stress-Free & Pleasant for Your Dog.* American Kennel Club. https://www.akc.org/expert-advice/training/make-vet-visits-stress-free/

Gibeault, S. (2022, February 25). *How to Raise a Confident Puppy.* American Kennel Club. https://www.akc.org/expert-advice/training/how-do-you-raise-a-confident-puppy/

Grayson, A. (2019, May 5). *Not every dog is a social butterfly.* Augusta Grayson. https://www.caninetraining.co.nz/blog/dog-dog-sociability

Greyhound World. (2020, December 27). *How Fast Is A Greyhound?* Greyhound World. https://greyhound.world/how-fast-is-a-greyhound/

Haley. (2019, October 18). *Adopt OR Shop: Just Do It Responsibly.* Paws and Reflect. https://pawsandreflect.blog/adopt-or-shop-just-do-it-responsibly/

Harleman, J. (n.d.). *5 Common Dog Fears and How to Help.* The Dog People. https://www.rover.com/blog/common-dog-fears/

Hartz. (2015, March 13). *How to Treat Your Dog for Intestinal Parasites.* Hartz. https://www.hartz.com/how-to-treat-your-dog-for-intestinal-parasites/#:~:text=Roundworms%20and%20hookworms%20can%20be

Hastings Staff. (2018, September 21). *8 Ways to Prepare Your Home for a New Dog's Arrival.* Hastings Veterinary Hospital.

https://hastingsvet.com/8-ways-to-prepare-your-home-for-a-new-dogs-arrival/

Henderson, R. (2023, February 25). *Top 5 Tips for Adopting a New Dog.* PetHelpful. https://pethelpful.com/dogs/Top-5-Tips-for-Adopting-a-New-Dog

Horowitz, A. (2022, November 11). *9 Best Dog Training Tools & Products Professional Trainers Swear By.* Pupford. https://pupford.com/best-dog-training-products/

Horwitz, D. (n.d.). *Overcoming Fears with Desensitization and Counterconditioning.* VCA Animal Hospitals. https://vcahospitals.com/know-your-pet/overcoming-fears-with-desensitization-and-counterconditioning#:~:text=Desensitization%20is%20a%20technique%20of

How to Train a Dream Dog. (2019, May 23). *10 Tips to Keep Your Puppy Safe.* How to Train a Dream Dog. https://www.howtotrainadreamdog.com/10-tips-to-keep-your-puppy-safe/

The Humane Society of the United States. (n.d.-a). *Positive reinforcement training.* The Humane Society of the United States. https://www.humanesociety.org/resources/positive-reinforcement-training

The Humane Society of the United States. (n.d.-b). *Stop your dog from jumping up.* The Humane Society of the United States. https://www.humanesociety.org/resources/stop-your-dog-jumping#:~:text=Teach%20your%20dog%20that%20they

Jaclyn, F. (2021, April 16). *15 Things Every New Puppy Parent Must Have.* DogTime. https://dogtime.com/lifestyle/21800-things-puppy-parent-must-have

Johnson, M. (2022, June 23). *Try These Easy Tricks To Stop A Puppy From Barking.* PawTracks. https://www.pawtracks.com/getting-started/how-to-stop-puppies-from-barking/

Jones, E. (2019, November 22). *Impulse Control Games for Dogs: Teaching Self-Control!* K9 of Mine. https://www.k9ofmine.com/impulse-control-games-for-dogs/

Jones, J. (2019, December 1). *Training A Puppy For Grooming.* Small Dog Place. https://www.smalldogplace.com/training-a-puppy-for-grooming.html

Jones, N. (2020, November 18). *How to take your puppy outside.* PetPlan. https://www.petplan.co.uk/pet-information/puppy/advice/first-steps-outside/

Karnes, M. (2016, September 14). *More Harm than Good: 3 Reasons Why I Never Socialize my Puppies.* The Collared Scholar. https://www.collared-scholar.com/more-harm-than-good-3-reasons-why-i-never-socialize-my-puppies/

Kearl, M. (2020, March 26). *Introducing New Puppies To Homes With Senior Dogs.* American Kennel Club. https://www.akc.org/expert-advice/puppy-information/introducing-puppies-to-senior-dogs/

Kelley, T. L. (2022, November 22). *When Can Puppies Go Outside? What a Vet Wants You to Know.* Daily Paws. https://www.dailypaws.com/dogs-puppies/health-care/puppy-care/when-can-puppies-go-outside

The Kennel Club. (n.d.-a). *Finding the right dog.* The Kennel Club. https://www.thekennelclub.org.uk/getting-a-dog/are-you-ready/finding-the-right-dog/

The Kennel Club. (n.d.-b). *How do I stop my puppy biting?* The Kennel Club. https://www.thekennelclub.org.uk/dog-training/getting-started-in-dog-training/dog-training-and-games/how-do-i-stop-my-puppy-mouthing/?gclid=Cj0KCQjwocShBhCOARIsAFVYq0i0e4eo-eRwyrrPpSB9Tte8CQKiLz41tb6gw5JagrViTslVD2XRx2saAjkjEALw_wcB

The Kennel Club. (n.d.-c). *What is puppy socialisation?* The Kennel Club. https://www.thekennelclub.org.uk/getting-a-dog/caring-for-your-new-puppy/what-is-puppy-socialisation/

Kilstein, H. (2021, December 29). *7 Steps to Raising a Dog that Enjoys Being Groomed.* Dogington Post. https://www.dogingtonpost.com/7-steps-to-raising-a-dog-that-enjoys-being-groomed/

Kristen. (2014, September 7). *Types of Rewards - Miami Dog Training.* Crown Dog Training. https://crowndogtraining.com/2014/09/07/types-of-rewards/

Landsberg, G. (2022, October). *Behavior Modification in Dogs.* Veterinary Manual. https://www.msdvetmanual.com/dog-owners/behavior-of-dogs/behavior-modification-in-dogs

Larese, S. (n.d.). *How to Prepare and What to Expect When Adopting a Dog.* HGTV. https://www.hgtv.com/lifestyle/family/pets/top-tips-for-adopting-a-dog

Lauren, T. (2022, March 16). *Can My Puppy Eat Adult Dog Food?* The Dodo. https://www.thedodo.com/dodowell/can-puppies-eat-adult-dog-food

Leaks, P. (2015, November 24). *5 Methods That Will Help Reduce Resource Guarding.* Puppy Leaks. https://www.puppyleaks.com/reduce-resource-guarding/

Lee, L. (2021, August 17). *Why Is My Dog Coughing, and When Should I Go to the Vet?* Good Health. https://www.goodrx.com/pet-health/dog/dog-coughing

Leicht, K. (2022, October 13). *13 Ways to Teach Kids How to Interact with Dogs Safely!* K9 of Mine. https://www.k9ofmine.com/teaching-kids-interact-with-dogs/

Leonhardt, C. (2020, April 5). *Dog Training Tools To Avoid.* Busy Dog. https://www.busydogcolorado.com/post/training-tools-to-avoid

Llera, R., & Buzhardt, L. (n.d.). *Choosing the Right Puppy from a Litter.* VCA Hosptals. https://vcahospitals.com/know-your-pet/choosing-the-right-puppy-from-a-litter

Long, B. (2017, August 24). *Basic Obedience Training for Puppies: Where to Start.* American Kennel Club. https://www.akc.org/expert-advice/training/basic-obedience-training-for-your-dog/

Lowrey, S. (2021, September 18). *Puppy's First Vet Visit: How to Reduce Vet Anxiety.* American Kennel Club. https://www.akc.org/expert-advice/puppy-information/puppy-first-vet-visit-success/

Lunchick, P. (2018, September 25). *Teach Your Puppy These 5 Basic Commands.* American Kennel Club. https://www.akc.org/expert-advice/training/teach-your-puppy-these-5-basic-commands/

Madison, J. (2013, May 6). *The Advantages and Disadvantages of Having a Dog.* PetHelpful. https://pethelpful.com/dogs/The-Advantages-and-Disadvantages-of-Having-a-Dog

Madson, C. (2023, January 5). *When and How to Start Socializing Your Puppy.* Preventive Vet. https://www.preventivevet.com/dogs/when-to-start-socializing-your-new-puppy

Mansourian, E. (2016, June 16). *Puppy Feeding Fundamentals.* American Kennel Club. https://www.akc.org/expert-advice/health/puppy-feeding-fundamentals/

Martin, N. (2020, March 6). *How to Choose the Right Dog Crate: Your Complete Guide.* The Dog People. https://www.rover.com/blog/how-to-choose-right-dog-crate-complete-guide/

Mauran, C. (2022, May 8). *A guide to teaching children how to pet dogs.* Mashable. https://mashable.com/article/parents-teach-children-how-to-pet-dogs

Meyers, H. (2023, March 24). *Puppy-Proofing Tips for Your Home And Yard.* American Kennel Club. https://www.akc.org/expert-advice/puppy-information/puppy-proofing-tips-for-your-home-and-yard/#:~:text=Keep%20doors%20and%20windows%20closed

Michaels, L. (2014, August 12). *Pet Parenting Positively.* Dog Psychologist. https://www.dogpsychologistoncall.com/positive-pet-parenting/

Miller, P. (2021, October 28). *Dog Impulse Control Training.* Whole Dog Journal. https://www.whole-dog-journal.com/training/dog-impulse-control-training/

Nicholas, J. (2021, May 2). *Everything You Need to Know About Crate Training Your Puppy or Adult Dog.* Preventive Vet. https://www.preventivevet.com/dogs/everything-you-need-to-know-about-crate-training-your-puppy-or-adult-dog

Nicholas, J. (2023, March 1). *10 Point Checklist for Puppy Proofing Your Home.* Preventive Vet. https://www.preventivevet.com/dogs/checklist-for-puppy-proofing-your-home

O, A. (2018, July 5). *A Minimalist Perspective, Pros And Cons Of Getting A Dog.* Break the Twitch. https://www.breakthetwitch.com/getting-a-dog/

Pachel, C. (2021, June 3). *How to Introduce a Puppy or Adult Dog to Your Children.* Preventive Vet. https://www.preventivevet.com/dogs/how-to-introduce-a-puppy-or-adult-dog-to-your-children

Parrish, C. (2022, November 17). *Buying Guide: How to Choose the Best Dog Crate for Your Pet.* BeChewy. https://be.chewy.com/dog-crate-buying-guide/

PDSA. (n.d.-a). *How to calm an anxious dog.* PDSA. https://www.pdsa.org.uk/pet-help-and-advice/looking-after-your-pet/puppies-dogs/dogs-and-phobias

PDSA. (n.d.-b). *New puppy checklist.* PDSA. https://www.pdsa.org.uk/pet-help-and-advice/looking-after-your-pet/puppies-dogs/new-puppy-checklist

Perfectly Rawsome. (2018, December 17). *NRC Nutritional Requirements for Puppies, Puppy Nutrition, Raw Feeding.* Perfectly Rawsome. https://perfectlyrawsome.com/raw-feeding-knowledgebase/nutritional-requirements-for-puppies/

Perry, S. (2023, March 22). *9 Things You Need Before Bringing Home a Puppy.* Be Chewy. https://be.chewy.com/new-puppy-checklist-9-things-you-need-before-bringing-home-a-new-puppy/

Pet Help. (2018, January 22). *Fears & Phobias in Dogs.* Animal Rescue League. https://www.arl-iowa.org/news/pet-help/fears--phobias-in-dogs/?gclid=Cj0KCQjwocShBhCOARIsAFVYq0j5NMABSRfcHig9sWEvdTosS2TuthE-6fJy5x1MJ1xYkjX2K5M_x-IaAvuREALw_wcB

Petfeed Team. (2020, April 29). *22 Ways to Play with and Exercise Your Dog Indoors.* Petfeed. https://petcube.com/blog/indoor-dog-exercise/

PetMD Editorial. (2019, July 25). *Why Is My Dog Scared of Everything?* PetMD. https://www.petmd.com/dog/behavior/why-my-dog-scared-everything

Pets in Peace. (n.d.). *Adopt or Shop A Pet: The Pros and Cons.* Pets in Peace. https://www.petsinpeace.com.au/adopt-or-shop-a-pet-the-pros-and-cons/

The PetPlate Team. (2022, June 6). *10 Things to Prepare for a New Puppy.* PetPlate. https://www.petplate.com/blog/new-puppy-checklist/

Pocket Suite. (2021, July 7). *9 Most Popular Dog Training Methods.* PocketSuite. https://pocketsuite.io/post/9-most-popular-dog-training-methods/

Pro Plan. (n.d.). *Puppy nutrition.* The Kennel Club. https://www.thekennelclub.org.uk/health-and-dog-care/health/health-and-care/a-z-of-health-and-care-issues/puppy-nutrition/

Pryor, K. (2019, April 30). *Don't Socialize the Dog!* Clicker Training. https://www.clickertraining.com/dont-socialize-the-dog

Pup Life. (n.d.). *Getting A Puppy? Prepare For The Commitment!* PupLife Dog Supplies. https://www.puplife.com/pages/getting-a-puppy-prepare-for-the-commitment#:~:text=You%20can

Pupford. (2023, April 5). *How to Exercise Your Dog Indoors: 21 Games, Ideas and Exercises.* Pupford. https://pupford.com/how-to-exercise-dog-indoors/

Puppy Academy. (2022, March 14). *Create a Daily Puppy Schedule!* The Puppy Academy. https://www.thepuppyacademy.com/blog/2020/2/3/create-a-daily-schedule-for-your-puppy

Puppy Academy. (2022, April 11). *Why Puppies Bark and How to Stop it!* The Puppy Academy. https://www.thepuppyacademy.com/blog/2022/4/11/why-puppies-bark-and-how-to-stop-it

Puppy Leaks. (2018, December 21). *10 Ways to Give Your Dog More Mental Stimulation.* Puppy Leaks. https://www.puppyleaks.com/more-mental-stimulation/

Purina. (n.d.). *Preparing for a Puppy: 10 Things You Need to Know.* Purina. https://www.purina.co.uk/articles/dogs/puppy/welcoming/preparing-for-your-new-puppy

Randall, S. (2015, August 30). *Adopting A Dog That Fits Your Lifestyle.* Top Dog Tips. https://topdogtips.com/adopting-a-dog-that-fits-your-lifestyle/

Rea, F. (2021, March 23). *22 things I wish I had when I brought my new puppy home.* Insider. https://www.insider.com/guides/pets/puppy-supplies

Reisen, J. R. (2020, July 26). *Preparing for a New Puppy*. American Kennel Club. https://www.akc.org/expert-advice/home-living/preparing-new-puppy/

Rosling, E. (2022, April). *7 fun brain games for dogs mental stimulation*. Barc London. https://www.barclondon.com/blogs/dog-training-behaviour/brain-games-for-dogs

Royal Canin. (n.d.-a). *How To Feed A Puppy*. Royal Canin. https://www.royalcanin.com/za/dogs/puppy/puppy-feeding-and-nutrition#feeding

Royal Canin. (n.d.-b). *Preparing for your puppy's arrival*. Royal Canin. https://www.royalcanin.com/za/dogs/puppy/preparing-for-your-puppys-arrival

Royal Canin. (n.d.-c). *Puppy Health & Wellbeing*. Royal Canin. https://www.royalcanin.com/za/dogs/puppy?&utm_campaign=2021-rc-za-consideration-birthGrowth-idcp19332655335&utm_source=googlesearch&utm_medium=brand-searchPaid-test2&gclid=Cj0KCQjwuLShBhC_ARIsAFod4fJxEOUBOsVGm2LXCNEDxso8cnr4YvIhJwDwx7wLQ-3I7k1cUPP2o7QaAmM-EALw_wcB&gclsrc=aw.ds

Royal Canin. (n.d.-d). *Puppy Socialisation - Puppy Behaviour*. Royal Canin. https://www.royalcanin.com/za/dogs/puppy/how-to-socialise-a-puppy

RSPCA. (n.d.). *What you need to know about puppy vaccinations*. RSPCA. https://www.rspca.org.uk/adviceandwelfare/pets/dogs/health/vaccinations

RSPCA. (2019, September 19). *How do I introduce a new dog or puppy to children?* RSPCA. https://kb.rspca.org.au/knowledge-base/how-do-i-introduce-a-new-dog-or-puppy-to-children/#:~:text=When%20it%20is%20time%20for

Sachdev, P. (2018). *Foods Your Dog Should Never Eat*. Fetch. https://pets.webmd.com/dogs/ss/slideshow-foods-your-dog-should-never-eat

Schmidt, E. (2022, October 19). *This Pet Parenting Style Makes Your Dog The Happiest And Most Social*. The Dodo. https://www.thedodo.com/dodowell/want-secure-resilient-dog-parent-way-study-says

Seymour, K. S. (2022, June 21). *The 10 Best Toys for Puppies, According to a Vet*. Daily Paws. https://www.dailypaws.com/gear-apparel/dog-supplies/dog-toys/best-toys-for-puppies

Sharpe, S. (2021, November 5). *How to Crate Train Your Dog in 9 Easy Steps*. American Kennel Club. https://www.akc.org/expert-advice/training/how-to-crate-train-your-dog-in-9-easy-steps/

Shojai, A. (2011). *Introducing a New Puppy to an Older Dog*. The Spruce Pets. https://www.thesprucepets.com/introducing-dogs-and-puppies-2805078

Shojai, A. (2020, July 10). *10 Ways to Help Stop a Puppy Dog From Barking*. The Spruce Pets. https://www.thesprucepets.com/puppy-barking-2804577

Shojai, A. (2021a, January 9). *How to Establish a New "Puppy Routine."* The Spruce Pets. https://www.thesprucepets.com/building-a-routine-with-new-puppy-2804667

Shojai, A. (2021b, August 24). *10 Expert Tips to Ground Jumping Jack Puppies*. The Spruce Pets. https://www.thesprucepets.com/puppy-jumping-and-biting-2805079

Shojai, A. (2021c, December 26). *An Insider Shares Grooming Tips Your Puppy Wants You to Know*. The Spruce Pets. https://www.thesprucepets.com/how-to-groom-a-puppy-2804810

Shojai, A. (2022, January 13). *5 Reasons Puppies Are Good for Us*. The Spruce Pets. https://www.thesprucepets.com/health-benefits-of-puppies-2804874

Small Door Veterinary. (n.d.). *Exercise Needs for Puppies, Adults and Senior Dogs*. Small Door Veterinary. https://www.smalldoorvet.com/learning-center/wellness/exercise-needs-dog-lifestages

Stregowski, J. (2020, April 23). *Adopting a Dog? Here's How to Prepare for Bringing Home a New Friend*. The Spruce Pets. https://www.thesprucepets.com/after-adopting-a-dog-1117330

Stregowski, J. (2021, December 16). *5 Ways to Get Your Dog to Be Happy About Going to the Vet*. The Spruce Pets. https://www.thesprucepets.com/get-dog-to-love-the-vet-1118672#:~:text=Ask%20your%20vet%20clinic%20when

Sweeney, E. (2021, February 8). *Everything You Need to Know About Dog Supplements, According to Veterinarians*. Good Housekeeping. https://www.goodhousekeeping.com/life/pets/g35432790/best-supplements-for-dogs/

Thompson, M. (2022, November 2). *5 Reasons To Send Your Dog To Obedience School*. Pawp. https://pawp.com/5-reasons-to-send-your-dog-to-obedience-school/#:~:text=A%20good%20obedience%20school%20does

Truzy, T. (2022, April 12). *8 Steps to Prepare You For Your New Rescue Dog*. PetHelpful. https://pethelpful.com/dogs/8-Steps-to-Prepare-you-for-Your-New-Rescue-Dog

Vet West. (2016, March 10). *20 Tips to Puppy Proof Your Home*. Vetwest Animal Hospitals. https://www.vetwest.com.au/pet-library/20-tips-to-puppy-proof-your-home

Walden, L. (2020, August 18). *Understanding common dog fears.* Pet Professional. https://www.petprofessional.com.au/info-centre/understanding-common-dog-fears/

Ward, H. (2022, October 12). *Toys to Keep Dogs Busy.* Trusted Housesitters. https://www.trustedhousesitters.com/blog/pets/toys-to-keep-dogs-busy/?gclid=Cj0KCQjw_r6hBhDdARIsAMIDhV9heU21ALCuVjMDnd-Iz3Zxhj85Efp0-GaK--1Ag8zzqeLSBvxuhC4aAgLcEALw_wcB

Ward, H. (2023, January 18). *How to Train a Dog to Walk on a Leash.* Trusted Housesitters. https://www.trustedhousesitters.com/blog/owners/how-to-train-a-dog-to-walk-on-a-leash/?gclid=Cj0KCQjw_r6hBhDdARIsAMIDhV-FsxkUA8FbvbNiP3HbIE8eQ1Kzv8ZGVYJKglg1XPt8w-6Bo2pojP8aAiOfEALw_wcB

Weir, M., & Panning, A. (n.d.). *Instructions for Ear Cleaning in Dogs.* VCA Animal Hospitals. https://vcahospitals.com/know-your-pet/instructions-for-ear-cleaning-in-dogs

Weiss, E., Gramann, S., Spain, V., & Slater, M. (2015). Goodbye to a Good Friend: An Exploration of the Re-Homing of Cats and Dogs in the U.S. *Open Journal of Animal Sciences*, 05(04), 435–456. https://doi.org/10.4236/ojas.2015.54046

Welton, M. (2000). *Should You Get a Dog? Pros and Cons of Owning a Dog.* Your Pure Bred Puppy. https://www.yourpurebredpuppy.com/buying/articles/should-you-get-a-dog.html

Whelan, C. K. (2022, March 18). *8 tips for raising the perfect puppy.* Care. https://www.care.com/c/8-tips-for-raising-the-perfect-puppy/

Wiginton, K. (2021, July 15). *Prepare Your Home and Family for a Dog.* Fetch. https://pets.webmd.com/dogs/adoption-21/dog-prep-family-home

Williams, G. (2023, April 5). *10 Most Common Fears Your Dog Might Be Experiencing and How You Can Help.* P.L.A.Y. https://www.petplay.com/blogs/tips/10-most-common-fears-your-dog-might-be-experiencing-and-how-you-can-help

Williams, K., & Downing, R. (n.d.). *Feeding Growing Puppies.* VCA Animal Hospitals. https://vcahospitals.com/know-your-pet/feeding-growing-puppies

Woodnutt, J. (2022, January 31). *How to stop puppy food aggression: Six tips from a vet.* Pets Radar. https://www.petsradar.com/advice/puppy-food-aggression-five-tips-to-stop-it

WVS. (n.d.). *10 Reasons Why You Should Adopt, Don't Shop!* Worldwide Veterinary Services. https://wvs.org.uk/news/10-reasons-why-you-should-adopt-dont-shop

Yates, J. T. (2021, July 15). *9 things to know before getting a pet.* RACV. https://www.racv.com.au/royalauto/lifestyle-home/pets/how-to-prepare-home-for-pet.html

Image References: Book 1

Freepik. (n.d.-a). *Beautiful English Toy Spaniel Dog* [Image]. Freepik. www.freepik.com/free-photo/beautiful-english-toy-spaniel-dog-pet-portrait_19866300.htm#&position=0&from_view=collections

Freepik. (n.d.-b). *Beautiful pet portrait, small dog with cage* [Image]. Freepik. www.freepik.com/free-photo/beautiful-pet-portrait-small-dog-with-cage_21249119.htm#&position=0&from_view=collections

Freepik. (n.d.-c). *Dog Begging for Treats* [Image]. Freepik. www.freepik.com/free-photo/adorable-chihuahua-dog-with-female-owner_33790736.htm#&position=19&from_view=collections

Freepik. (n.d.-d). *Dog destroying pillow* [Image]. Freepik. www.freepik.com/free-photo/smiley-dog-making-mess-floor_29652613.htm#&position=38&from_view=collections

gpointstudio. (n.d.). *Gray puppy at the vet* [Image]. Freepik. www.freepik.com/free-photo/gray-puppy-vet_12428663.htm#&position=13&from_view=collections

Helmuth, J. (2022). *Puppies playing on grass* [Image]. Pexels. https://www.pexels.com/photo/close-up-shot-of-a-puppies-playing-on-grass-12538680/

Kittle, B. (2021). *Puppy pulling leash* [Image]. Unsplash. https://unsplash.com/photos/4_0wkzDL8fE

Rachyt73. (2020). *Muddy Puppy* [Image]. Pixabay. https://pixabay.com/photos/puppy-muddy-puppy-puppy-playing-5413165/

Rawpixel. (n.d.). *Group portrait of five adorable puppies* [Image]. Freepik. www.freepik.com/free-photo/group-portrait-five-adorable-puppies_3532486.htm#&position=21&from_view=collections

Wirestock. (n.d.). *Hungry Dog* [Image]. Freepik. www.freepik.com/free-photo/hungry-white-brown-dog-with-big-ears-brown-eyes-ready-eat-bowl-full-food_28741516.htm#&position=21&from_view=collections

References: Book 2

AKC Staff. (2019, September 26). AKC groups: Sporting, hound, working, terrier, toy, non-sporting, Herding. *American Kennel Club*. https://www.akc.org/expert-advice/lifestyle/7-akc-dog-breed-groups-explained/

All Dogs Unleashed. (2019, August 1). Teaching a hunting dog not to chase - The challenges of training hounds with strong instincts.

All Dogs Unleashed Dallas. https://www.alldogsunleashed.com/blog/training-hounds-with-strong-instincts/

Anderson, E. (2021, January 20). Punishment vs. interruption: Properly managing your dog's behavior. *Whole Dog Journal.* https://www.whole-dog-journal.com/behavior/punishment-vs-interruption-properly-managing-your-dogs-behavior/

Asher, M. (2020, February 20). Dog training methods and 5 essential dog obedience commands. *Pets Best.* https://www.petsbest.com/blog/dog-training-basic-commands/

Ashley, S. A. (2020, April 6). Dog body language: 45 ways your dog is secretly communicating with you. *PureWow.* https://www.purewow.com/family/dog-body-language

ASPCA. (n.d.). Behavioral help for your pet. *ASPCA.* https://www.aspca.org/pet-care/general-pet-care/behavioral-help-your-pet

ASPCA. (2014, September 25). House training your dog or puppy. *ASPCA.* https://www.aspca.org/news/house-training-your-dog-or-puppy

ASPCA. (2015). Common dog behavior issues. *ASPCA.* https://www.aspca.org/pet-care/dog-care/common-dog-behavior-issues

Australia, B. P. (n.d.). Tired of yapping? How to stop nuisance dog barking. *Buddy Pet Australia.* https://buddypet.co/blogs/learn/tired-of-yapping-how-to-stop-nuisance-dog-barking

Battersea. (2020, February 21). How to teach your dog not to jump up. *Battersea.* https://www.battersea.org.uk/pet-advice/dog-advice/how-teach-your-dog-not-jump

Becker, M. (2022, September 21). Dog training 101: Essential tools you'll need. *Vetstreet.* https://www.vetstreet.com/our-pet-experts/dog-training-101-essential-tools-youll-need

Bender, A. (2020, May 6). Training small dogs: What you need to know. *The Spruce Pets.* https://www.thesprucepets.com/tips-for-training-small-dog-breeds-1118254

Bender, A. (2021a, February 5). Teach an old dog new tricks: 5 training tips. *The Spruce Pets.* https://www.thesprucepets.com/training-tips-for-adult-dogs-1118253

Bender, A. (2021b, February 13). Top 10 basic dog training commands. *The Spruce Pets.* https://www.thesprucepets.com/basic-dog-training-commands-1117311

Bennink, B. (n.d.). There is no such thing as a bad dog - Only untrained dogs. *Good Doggy.* https://www.gooddoggysaratoga.com/blog/2017/8/8/there-is-no-such-thing-as-a-bad-dogs-only-untrained-dogs

Blake, M. (2019, June 11). Guide to sporting dog breeds and characteristics. *LoveToKnow.* https://www.lovetoknowpets.com/dogs/sporting-dogs

Callahan, K. (2022, March 22). No need for force: How to stop your dog from pulling on leash and more. *Whole Dog Journal.* https://www.whole-dog-journal.com/training/how-to-stop-your-dog-from-pulling-on-the-leash/

Camps, T., Amat, M., & Manteca, X. (2019). A review of medical conditions and behavioral problems in dogs and cats. *Animals, 9(12), 1133.* https://doi.org/10.3390/ani9121133

Canine Scholars. (n.d.). Dog & puppy systematic desensitization training. *Canine Scholars Dog Training.* https://www.caninescholars.com/dog-training-methods/systematic-desensitization/

Chewy Editorial. (2016, December 20). 4 outdated dog training techniques to avoid. *BeChewy.* https://be.chewy.com/training-training-tips-5-outdated-dog-training-techniques-to-avoid/

Chewy Editorial. (2019, November 15). How to socialize an older dog: Expert trainer tips. *BeChewy.* https://be.chewy.com/socializing-an-older-dog/

Chewy Editorial. (2020, January 12). How to potty train an older dog. *BeChewy.* https://be.chewy.com/how-to-potty-train-an-older-dog/

Clason, D. (2022a, August 12). Follow these steps to successfully crate train your older dog. *PawTracks.* https://www.pawtracks.com/dogs/crate-train-older-dog/

Clason, D. (2022b, November 15). Steps you can take to stop the bad behavior of leash pulling. *PawTracks.* https://www.pawtracks.com/dogs/leash-pulling-training/

Crittenden, C. (2021, October 25). 5 basic commands every dog should know (and how to teach them). *Petful.* https://www.petful.com/behaviors/basic-commands-your-dog-should-know/

Culp, C. (2018, December 2). DOG PSYCHOLOGY Part 1: What is dog psychology? *Thriving Canine.* https://www.thrivingcanine.com/blog/2018/12/02/dog-psychology-part-1-what-dog-psychology

DeSantis, D. (2022, May 1). 21 dog training commands - basic to advanced for a well-behaved dog. *Puppy in Training.* https://puppyintraining.com/dog-training-commands/

Dog Academy. (2022, March 12). How to train a herding dog. *Dog Academy.* https://dogacademy.org/blog/herding-dog-training/

Dog Psychology 101. (2018, January 24). Dog psychology vs human psychology, dog psychology 101. *Dog Psychology 101.* https://dogpsychology101.com/human-psychology-vs-dog-psychology/

Dog Trust. (n.d.). How to stop your dog pulling on the lead. *Dog Trust.* https://www.dogstrust.org.uk/dog-advice/training/outdoors/walking-nicely-training

Dogtopia. (2019, February 11). How to socialize an older dog. *Dogtopia.* https://www.dogtopia.com/blog/how-to-socialize-an-older-dog/

Dugatkin, L. A. (2014). *Principles of Animal Behavior.* W.W. Norton & Company.

Dwilson, S. (2020, March 4). Is it too late to train my older dog? *K&H Pet Products.* https://khpet.com/blogs/dogs/how-late-is-too-late-to-train-an-older-dog

Eckstein, S. (2021, May 8). Understanding why dogs bark. *Fetch.* https://pets.webmd.com/dogs/guide/understanding-why-dogs-bark

Elliot, P. (2021, January 8). How to obedience train an older dog. *Wag Walking.* https://wagwalking.com/training/obedience-train-an-older-dog

Elliott, G. (2022, October 4). Kids and pets: What you need to know for safe interactions. *The Dog People.* https://www.rover.com/blog/introducing-a-dog-to-your-children/

Erb, H. (2020, December 1). How to potty train an older dog: Housetraining adult dogs. *American Kennel Club.* https://www.akc.org/expert-advice/training/how-to-housetrain-an-adult-dog/#:~:text=Take%20her%20out%20first%20thing

Farricelli, A. (2022, April 20). Can you really train a hound? *PetHelpful.* https://pethelpful.com/dogs/-Can-You-Really-Train-a-Hound

Fetch Masters. (n.d.). *Dog socialization problems. FetchMasters.* https://fetchmasters.com/dog-socialization-problems/

Feyrecilde, M., Horwitz, D., & Landsberg, G. (n.d.). Controlling pulling on walks. *VCA Animal Hospitals.* https://vcahospitals.com/know-your-pet/controlling-pulling-on-walks

Flowers, A. (2021, July 19). Dog behavioral problems - barking, chewing, and more. *Fetch.* https://pets.webmd.com/dogs/ss/slideshow-behaviorial-problems-in-dogs

Fulcher, S. (2014, January 2). Ten reasons your dog may develop behavior problems. *Clicker Training.* https://www.clickertraining.com/ten-reasons-your-dog-may-develop-behavior-problems

Gibeault, S. (2018, April 30). Positive rewards dog training tips. *American Kennel Club.* https://www.akc.org/expert-advice/training/training-rewards/

Gibeault, S. (2020a, January 27). Understanding dog body language: Decipher dogs' signs & signals. *American Kennel Club.* https://www.akc.org/expert-advice/advice/how-to-read-dog-body-language/#:~:text=Dogs%20with%20their%20tails%20pointing

Gibeault, S. (2020b, November 2). Changing your dog's behavior with desensitization & counterconditioning. *American Kennel Club.* https://www.akc.org/expert-advice/training/changing-your-dogs-behavior-with-desensitization-and-counter-conditioning/

Gibeault, S. (2020c, December 17). How to teach your dog to drop it. *American Kennel Club.* https://www.akc.org/expert-advice/training/teaching-your-dog-to-drop-it/#:~:text=Place%20a%20high%2Dvalue%20treat

Gibeault, S. (2020d, December 23). How to stop your dog from jumping up on people. *American Kennel Club.* https://www.akc.org/expert-advice/training/how-to-stop-your-dog-from-jumping-up-on-people/

Gibeault, S. (2021a, January 3). How to teach your dog to stay. *American Kennel Club.* https://www.akc.org/expert-advice/training/dont-move-fido-teach-your-dog-to-stay/

Gibeault, S. (2021b, February 3). How to teach your dog to sit. *American Kennel Club.* https://www.akc.org/expert-advice/training/how-to-teach-your-dog-to-sit/

Grayson, A. (2019, May 5). Not every dog is a social butterfly. *Augusta Grayson.* https://www.caninetraining.co.nz/blog/dog-dog-sociability

Green, S. (n.d.). Consequences that can come from a poorly trained dog. *Mummy Matters.* https://deepinmummymatters.com/consequences-can-come-poorly-trained-dog/

Hastings Staff. (2018, September 21). 8 ways to prepare your home for a new dog's arrival. *Hastings Veterinary Hospital.* https://hastingsvet.com/8-ways-to-prepare-your-home-for-a-new-dogs-arrival/

Hinds, J. (2016, December 14). 10 reasons why dogs pull. *Jo Hinds.* https://johinds.com/2016/12/14/8-reasons-why-your-dog-may-pull-on-the-lead/

Horowitz, A. (2022, November 11). 9 best dog training tools & products professional trainers swear By. *Pupford.* https://pupford.com/best-dog-training-products/

Horwitz, D. (n.d.-a). Dog behavior problems - greeting behavior - jumping up. *VCA.* https://vcahospitals.com/know-your-pet/dog-behavior-problems-greeting-behavior-jumping-up#:~:text=Usually%20the%20motivation%20for%20the

Horwitz, D. (n.d.-b). Overcoming fears with desensitization and counterconditioning. *VCA Animal Hospitals.* https://vcahospitals.com/know-your-pet/overcoming-fears-with-desensitization-and-counterconditioning#:~:text=Desensitization%20is%20a%20te chnique%20of

Hospital, L. V. V. (2020, November 13). Undoing the damage: untraining bad habits in dogs. *Leon Valley Veterinary Hospital*. https://www.leonvalleyvet.com/blog/undoing-damage-untraining-bad-habits-dogs/

Ingersoll, C. (n.d.). Is it ever too late to train a dog? *Alpha-Dog*. https://alphadogpets.com/blog/41578/is-it-ever-too-late-to-train-a-dog

Jones, J. (2022, November 28). Small dog training: How, where, when and why. *Small Dog Place*. https://www.smalldogplace.com/small-dog-training.html

Jones, O. (2021, October 15). Why do dogs jump on you? 3 reasons (and how to stop it). *Pet Keen*. https://petkeen.com/reasons-why-dogs-jump-on-people/

Kasinger, C. (2019, January 10). 8 tips to socialise your dog with other dogs and humans. *The Dog People*. https://www.rover.com/uk/blog/8-tips-to-socialise-your-dog-with-other-dogs-and-humans/

Kerns, N. (2011, March 1). (Proper greetings #3) Stop your dog from jumping on people. *Whole Dog Journal*. https://www.whole-dog-journal.com/tips/proper-greetings-3-stop-your-dog-from-jumping-on-people/

Kokocińska-Kusiak, A., Woszczyło, M., Zybala, M., Maciocha, J., Barłowska, K., & Dzięcioł, M. (2021). Canine olfaction: physiology, behavior, and possibilities for practical applications. *Animals, 11(8), 2463*. https://doi.org/10.3390/ani11082463

Kristen. (2014, September 7). Types of rewards - Miami dog training. *Crown Dog Training*. https://crowndogtraining.com/2014/09/07/types-of-rewards/

Landsberg, G. (2019). Behavioral problems of dogs. *Veterinary Manual; MSD Veterinary Manual*.

https://www.msdvetmanual.com/behavior/normal-social-behavior-and-behavioral-problems-of-domestic-animals/behavioral-problems-of-dogs

Lange, K. E. (2022, June 10). From trauma to trust. *The Humane Society of the United States*. https://www.humanesociety.org/trauma-trust

Lawlor, V. (2021, December 17). How to potty train an older dog who's set in their ways. *PawTracks*. https://www.pawtracks.com/dogs/potty-training-an-older-dog/

Leonhardt, C. (2020, April 5). Dog training tools to avoid. *Busy Dog*. https://www.busydogcolorado.com/post/training-tools-to-avoid

Lesser, J. (2022, November 1). The 7 types of dog breeds. *The Spruce Pets*. https://www.thesprucepets.com/types-of-dog-breeds-4688776

London, K. B. (2022, May 16). A guide to dog-to-dog greetings. *The Wildest*. https://www.thewildest.com/dog-behavior/guide-dog-dog-greetings#:~:text=John%20Bradshaw%2C%20PhD%2C%20males%20typically

Long, E. (2022, October 31). How you "parent" your dog matters, actually. *Lifehacker*. https://lifehacker.com/how-you-parent-your-dog-matters-actually-1849721051

Lounge, H. (2021, June 28). How to socialize an adult dog and why it's never too late. *Hounds Lounge*. https://www.houndslounge.com/blog/how-to-socialize-an-adult-dog-and-why-its-never-too-late/#:~:text=It

Lowrey, S. (2022, March 11). Excessive dog barking: Reasons & and how to stop it. *American Kennel Club*. https://www.akc.org/expert-advice/training/excessive-dog-barking-causes-stop/

Lumontod, P. (2020, July 30). 25 most common dog behavior problems. *Top Dog Tips*. https://topdogtips.com/most-common-dog-behavior-problems/

Lunchick, P. (2018, September 25). Teach your puppy these 5 basic commands. *American Kennel Club*. https://www.akc.org/expert-advice/training/teach-your-puppy-these-5-basic-commands/

Madson, C. (2019a, January 29). Dog training aversives: What are they and why should you avoid them? *Preventive Vet*. https://www.preventivevet.com/dogs/dog-training-aversives

Madson, C. (2019b, February 27). How to help a dog that's missed early socialization. *Preventive Vet*. https://www.preventivevet.com/dogs/how-to-help-adult-dog-with-socialization

Madson, C. (2019c, March 26). How to stop your dog from door dashing. *Preventive Vet*. https://www.preventivevet.com/dogs/how-to-stop-your-dog-from-door-dashing

Madson, C. (2020a, August 25). Teaching your dog to stop jumping. *Preventive Vet*. https://www.preventivevet.com/dogs/stop-your-dog-from-jumping

Madson, C. (2020b, September 26). How to potty train an adult dog. *Preventive Vet*. https://www.preventivevet.com/dogs/how-to-potty-train-an-adult-dog

Madson, C. (2021, March 1). Does ignoring your dog's bad behavior work? *Preventive Vet*. https://www.preventivevet.com/dogs/ignoring-bad-behavior-in-dogs

Maev. (2020, July 7). How changing your dog's food can correct their behavioral issues. *Medium*. https://medium.com/@Maev/how-changing-your-dogs-food-can-correct-their-behavioral-issues-954831450326

Marrs, M. (2022, October 18). 8 essential dog training equipment items for 2022! *K9 of Mine*. https://www.k9ofmine.com/dog-training-equipment/

Martin, N. (2020, March 6). *How to Choose the Right Dog Crate: Your Complete Guide. The Dog People.* https://www.rover.com/blog/how-to-choose-right-dog-crate-complete-guide/

McCann Dog Training. (2019a). Are you accidentally being a BAD leader for your dog? [Video]. *YouTube*. https://www.youtube.com/watch?v=QntS570VFZ0&list=PL7BBgLulhernWIrrSY_UWNauNDBssvmTi

McCann Dog Training. (2019b). The unpopular truth about socializing your dog [Video]. *YouTube*. https://www.youtube.com/watch?v=YVvd8RrRjRA

McCann Dog Training. (2021a). The 3 steps for teaching your dog to greet people nicely [Video]. *YouTube*. https://www.youtube.com/watch?v=BTlrYgOVbzY

McCann Dog Training. (2021b). Leash walking training for dogs that are ALWAYS pulling! [Video]. *YouTube*. https://www.youtube.com/watch?v=y2yj2xtCo-k

McCann Dog Training. (2021c). The BIG mistake people make when teaching a dog to drop something [Video]. *YouTube*. https://www.youtube.com/watch?v=IhHpc3MziLI/

McCann Dog Training. (2021d). STOP dog jumping IMMEDIATELY with a DIFFERENT approach! [Video]. *YouTube*. https://www.youtube.com/watch?v=zGNSSh7LOKc

McCann Dog Training. (2022a). STOP your dog from pulling on leash with this STRANGE game [Video]. *YouTube*. https://www.youtube.com/watch?v=PYcKKBWcg1o

McCann Dog Training. (2022b). Stop your dog from whining in their crate [Video]. *YouTube*. https://www.youtube.com/watch?v=wQq7PfXyQvY&t=533s

McMillan, B. (2022, October 26). Brandon McMillan's 10 essential dog training tools. *MasterClass.* https://www.masterclass.com/articles/brandon-mcmillans-essential-dog-training-tools

Meyers, H. (2021, January 11). Correcting dog behavior: How to stop bad dog behavior. *American Kennel Club.* https://www.akc.org/expert-advice/training/how-to-curb-unwanted-dog-behaviors/

Michaels, L. (2014, August 12). Pet parenting positively. *Dog Psychologist on Call.* https://www.dogpsychologistoncall.com/positive-pet-parenting/

Millan, C. (2015, June 18). How to crate train an adult dog. *Cesar's Way.* https://www.cesarsway.com/how-to-crate-train-an-adult-dog/

Millan, C. (2019a, September 25). How to socialize an adult dog. *Cesar's Way.* https://www.cesarsway.com/how-to-socialize-an-adult-dog/

Millan, C. (2019b, October 31). 5 essential commands you can teach your dog. *Cesar's Way.* https://www.cesarsway.com/5-essential-commands-you-can-teach-your-dog/

Nicholas, J. (2021, May 2). Everything you need to know about crate training your puppy or adult dog. *Preventive Vet.* https://www.preventivevet.com/dogs/everything-you-need-to-know-about-crate-training-your-puppy-or-adult-dog

Pachel, C. (2021, June 3). How to introduce a puppy or adult dog to your children. *Preventive Vet.* https://www.preventivevet.com/dogs/how-to-introduce-a-puppy-or-adult-dog-to-your-children

Palika, L. (2017, August 9). Dog behavior: My dog pulls on the leash. *Fear Free Happy Homes.* https://www.fearfreehappyhomes.com/dog-behavior-my-dog-pulls-on-the-leash/

Paretts, S. (2021, November 12). What to look for when choosing a dog crate. *American Kennel Club*. https://www.akc.org/expert-advice/training/what-to-look-for-when-choosing-a-dog-crate/#:~:text=Size%20is%20the%20most%20important

Parrish, C. (2022, November 17). Buying guide: How to choose the best dog crate for your pet. *BeChewy*. https://be.chewy.com/dog-crate-buying-guide/

PAWS. (n.d.). Re-housetraining your adult dog. *PAWS*. https://www.paws.org/resources/re-housetraining-your-adult-dog/

Paws Abilities. (2017, February 16). Understanding dog-dog sociability. *Paws Abilities*. https://paws4udogs.wordpress.com/2017/02/16/understanding-dog-dog-sociability/

Pet Backer. (2022, October). Are dogs social animals? *Pet Backer*. https://www.petbacker.com/blog/facts/are-dogs-social-animals

Pet Finder. (n.d.). Tips for the first 30 days of dog adoption. *Petfinder*. https://www.petfinder.com/dogs/bringing-a-dog-home/tips-for-first-30-days-dog/

Petmate Academy. (2020, November 12). 10 basic commands to teach your dog. *Petmate*. https://www.petmate.com/10-basic-commands-to-teach-your-dog/article/a90090

PetMD Editorial. (2014, June 13). How your dog's food affects his mood. *PetMD*. https://www.petmd.com/dog/centers/nutrition/evr_multi_how_your_dogs_food_affects_his_mood

PetMD Editorial. (2017, September 29). 5 reasons your dog won't stop barking. *PetMD*. https://www.petmd.com/dog/behavior/5-reasons-your-dog-wont-stop-barking

PetMD Editorial. (2018, February 6). How to heal an emotionally traumatized pet. *PetMD*.

https://www.petmd.com/dog/behavior/how-heal-emotionally-traumatized-pet

Phenix, A. P. (2017, August 3). 5 training tips for your working dog breed. *Dogster.* https://www.dogster.com/dog-training/training-tips-for-your-working-dog-breed

Pryor, K. (2012, September 5). The eight ways of changing behavior. *Clicker Training.* https://www.clickertraining.com/node/290

Pryor, K. (2018). Don't shoot the dog! The new art of teaching and training. Ringpress Books Ltd.

Pyror, K. (2013, February 1). Don't socialize the dog! *Clicker Training.* https://www.clickertraining.com/dont-socialize-the-dog

Ramos, B. (2015, September 24). If your dog has these bad behaviors, you need to take them to obedience training. *SheKnows.* https://www.sheknows.com/living/articles/1094999/signs-your-dog-needs-obedience-training/

Randall, B. (2022, April 3). How to stop a dog pulling on the lead and start walking to heel. *Country Life.* https://www.countrylife.co.uk/out-and-about/dogs/how-to-stop-a-dog-pulling-on-the-lead-and-start-walking-to-heel-six-tips-from-top-dog-trainer-ben-randall-241134

Richmond, M. (2018, October 17). Five steps to stopping unwanted behavior. *Whole Dog Journal.* https://www.whole-dog-journal.com/training/five-steps-to-stopping-unwanted-behavior/

Robert Cabral. (2019). Teach your dog not to jump out of the CAR - Car safety - Dog training video [Video]. *YouTube.* https://www.youtube.com/watch?v=0uYZGPz03Fo

Rodriguez, J. (2012). Sporting group dogs | Common dog training and behavior problems. *Do Behave.* http://www.do-behave.com/ct-dog-trainer/sporting-group-dogs.html

RSPCA. (n.d.-a). How to stop your dog barking too much. *RSCPA*. https://www.rspca.org.uk/adviceandwelfare/pets/dogs/behaviour/barking

RSPCA. (n.d.-b). Train your dog to stop pulling on the lead. *RSPCA*. https://www.rspca.org.uk/adviceandwelfare/pets/dogs/training/walknicely

RSPCA. (2019, September 19). How do I introduce a new dog or puppy to children? *RSPCA*. https://kb.rspca.org.au/knowledge-base/how-do-i-introduce-a-new-dog-or-puppy-to-children/#:~:text=When%20it%20is%20time%20for

Schade, V. (2021, August 9). How to crate train a dog: Step-by-step ionstructions. *BeChewy*. https://be.chewy.com/how-to-crate-train-a-puppy-a-step-by-step-guide-from-an-expert/

Schmidt, E. (2022, October 19). This pet parenting style makes your dog the happiest and most social. *The Dodo*. https://www.thedodo.com/dodowell/want-secure-resilient-dog-parent-way-study-says

Schoniger, S. (2018, December 11). The impact of nutrition on your dog's moods and behavior. *Dog Is Good*. https://www.dogisgood.com/the-impact-of-nutrition-on-your-dogs-moods-and-behavior/#:~:text=If%20your%20dog%20isn

Scott, J. P., & Fuller, J. L. (2012). *Genetics and the social behavior of the dog*. The University of Chicago Press.

Sharpe, S. (2021, November 5). How to crate train your dog in 9 easy steps. *American Kennel Club*. https://www.akc.org/expert-advice/training/how-to-crate-train-your-dog-in-9-easy-steps/

Small Door Veterinary. (n.d.). Everything you need to know about caring for your new dog. *Small Door Veterinary*. https://assets.ctfassets.net/82d3r48zq721/22nWe0saMAC9LY

TCfAGdHZ/74d38778d3eb51128bb52734be5339ff/Small-Door-Veterinary-Dog-Parenting-101.pdf

Stregowski, J. (2020, April 23). Adopting a dog? Here's how to prepare for bringing home a new friend. *The Spruce Pets*. https://www.thesprucepets.com/after-adopting-a-dog-1117330

Terrier Rescue. (n.d.). Ten top tips to terriers. *Terrier Rescue*. https://www.terrierrescue.co.uk/ten-top-tips-to-terriers/

The Humane Society Of The United States. (n.d.). How to get your dog to stop barking. *The Humane Society of the United States*. https://www.humanesociety.org/resources/how-get-your-dog-stop-barking#:~:text=Ignore%20the%20barking&text=Regular%20exercise%20and%20the%20use

The Humane Society of the United States. (n.d.). Positive reinforcement training. *The Humane Society of the United States*. https://www.humanesociety.org/resources/positive-reinforcement-training

The Humane Society of the United States. (2018). Crate training 101. *The Humane Society of the United States*. https://www.humanesociety.org/resources/crate-training-101

Todd, Z. (2021, April 14). 13 common dog training mistakes and how to avoid them. *Companion Animal Psychology*. https://www.companionanimalpsychology.com/2021/04/13-common-dog-training-mistakes-and-how.html

Trot, S. (2021, June 4). Helping a rescue dog to overcome trauma: How to build trust. *Now Fresh*. https://nowfresh.com/en/helping-a-rescue-dog-to-overcome-trauma

Trott, S. (2021, May 21). How to train a herding dog. *SpiritDog Training*. https://spiritdogtraining.com/how-to-train-a-herding-dog/

True, C. (2020, June 23). Adopting a rescued dog? Know the signs of trauma. *Healthy Paws*.

https://blog.healthypawspetinsurance.com/adopting-a-rescued-pet-watch-for-signs-of-trauma-and-be-patient#:~:text=Dogs%20who%20have%20suffered%20abuse

Truzy, T. (2022, April 12). 8 steps to prepare you for your new rescue dog. *PetHelpful.* https://pethelpful.com/dogs/8-Steps-to-Prepare-you-for-Your-New-Rescue-Dog

Tupler, T. (2020, July 30). How to use a crate for potty training an older dog. *PetMD.* https://www.petmd.com/dog/training/ins-and-outs-potty-training-older-dogs-0

Turner, J. F. (2022, February 6). Tips to train a bull terrier. *Animal Wised.* https://www.animalwised.com/tips-to-train-a-bull-terrier-945.html

Wag Walking. (n.d.). Behavioral problems in dogs - symptoms, causes, diagnosis, treatment, recovery, management, cost. *Wag Walking.* https://wagwalking.com/condition/behavioral-problems

Wiginton, K. (2021, July 15). Prepare your home and family for a dog. *Fetch.* https://pets.webmd.com/dogs/adoption-21/dog-prep-family-home

Wild Earth. (n.d.). Got a yappy dog? How to stop a dog from barking. *Wild Earth.* https://wildearth.com/blogs/dog-knowledge/how-to-stop-a-dog-from-barking

Will Atherton Canine Training. (2021). How to stop your dog PULLING on the leash [Video]. *YouTube.* https://www.youtube.com/watch?v=DU1Kz7NWrWc

Withrow, D. (2018). Why do dogs try to jump on you. *WagWalking.* https://wagwalking.com/behavior/why-do-dogs-try-to-jump-on-you

Yates, J. T. (2021, July 15). 9 things to know before getting a pet. *RACV.* https://www.racv.com.au/royalauto/lifestyle-home/pets/how-to-prepare-home-for-pet.html

Yes, Dog! (n.d.). Force free. *Yes, Dog!* https://yesdog.ca/force-free/

Zak George's Dog Training Revolution. (2015). *How to STOP your dog from running out of the front door! Stay while distracted* [Video]. *YouTube.* https://www.youtube.com/watch?v=6yw_l3Ci_Q0

Zoom Room. (n.d.). How to stop a dog from jumping up in 5 easy steps. *Zoom Room Dog Training.* https://zoomroom.com/admin/stop-dog-jumping/

Image References: Book 2

825545. (2015, March 16). Walking on lead [Image]. *Pixabay.* https://pixabay.com/photos/dachshund-dog-school-dog-training-672780/

Collingwood, C. C. (2022, May 12). Dog barking [Image]. *Unsplash.* https://unsplash.com/photos/b0nRWZ2P8Tw

Coulton, M. (2020, September 22). Dog playing with toys [Image]. *Pexels.* https://www.pexels.com/photo/a-dog-lying-on-the-floor-4445461/

Gabe. (2022, January 2). Two dogs playing [Image]. *Pexels.* https://www.pexels.com/photo/close-up-shot-of-dogs-playing-together-10705801/

Handa, M. (2017, July 11). Pug jumping [Image]. *Pixabay.* https://pixabay.com/photos/pug-tongue-jumping-dog-2494575/

Hunter, M. (2016, February 27). Sad dog on carpet [Image]. *Unsplash.* https://unsplash.com/photos/iS0Aq3QPsJ4

Street, J. (2018, September 3). Dog reading book [Image]. *Unsplash.* https://unsplash.com/photos/MoDcnVRN5JU

Toshima Style. (2022, December 27). Dog running on grass [Image]. *Pexels.* https://www.pexels.com/photo/a-brown-dog-running-on-brown-grass-14866443/

Verschueren, A. (2021, September 21). Dog in crate [Image]. *Unsplash.* https://unsplash.com/photos/qvbG3-tZnyc

Warrington, B. (2019, May 3). Four dogs sitting together [Image]. *Unsplash.* https://unsplash.com/photos/WSAOGHKEqFc

References: Book 3

Abraham, M. (n.d.). *Senior dogs | Dog health.* The Kennel Club. https://www.thekennelclub.org.uk/health-and-dog-care/health/health-and-care/a-z-of-health-and-care-issues/senior-dogs/

Advanced Care Veterinary Hospital. (2021, February 2). *Why is it Important to Trim Your Pet's Nails?* Advanced Care Veterinary Hospital. https://advancedpetvet.com/2021/02/02/why-is-it-important-to-trim-your-pets-nails/#:~:text=However%2C%20long%20nails%20create%20potential

AKC Staff. (2015, March 23). *How to Clean Dogs Ears & Eyes.* American Kennel Club. https://www.akc.org/expert-advice/health/eyes-and-ears-of-good-grooming/#:~:text=Healthy%20eyes%20are%20bright%20and

AKC Staff. (2019, November 20). *Your Dog's Age In Human Years: A Conversion Chart.* American Kennel Club. https://www.akc.org/expert-advice/health/how-to-calculate-dog-years-to-human-years/

AKC Staff. (2022a, May 3). *Nutrition and Supplement Tips for Senior Dogs.* American Kennel Club. https://www.akc.org/expert-advice/nutrition/nutrition-and-supplements-for-senior-dogs/

AKC Staff. (2022b, December 13). *A Survival Guide for Dog Diarrhea.* American Kennel Club. https://www.akc.org/expert-

advice/health/doggie-
diarrhea/#:~:text=Withholding%20food%20for%2012%20to

Alusin, M. (2017, July 4). *5 signs it's time to say goodbye to your dog.* Dog's Best Life. https://dogsbestlife.com/dog-health/5-signs-its-time-to-say-goodbye-to-your-dog/?cn-reloaded=1

Amatenstein, S. (2021, December 14). *How to Cope with The Loss of A Pet.* Psycom. https://www.psycom.net/loss-of-a-pet

America Holistic Veterinary Medical Association. (n.d.). *What is Holistic Veterinary Medicine?* American Holistic Veterinary Medical Association. https://www.ahvma.org/what-is-holistic-veterinary-medicine/

Anastasio, A. (2019, August 6). *Grieving a Pet: How to Cope With the Loss of a Dog.* American Kennel Club. https://www.akc.org/expert-advice/lifestyle/grieving-a-pet/

Animal Hospital of Clemmons. (n.d.). *What can I give my dog for a urinary tract infection?* Animal Hospital of Clemmons. https://www.animalhospitalofclemmons.com/site/veterinary-pet-care-blog/2020/12/18/urinary-tract-infection-in-dogs

Arford, K. (2021, September 1). *Dog First-Aid Kit Essentials: What To Include For Injuries And Emergencies.* American Kennel Club. https://www.akc.org/expert-advice/health/dog-first-aid-kit-essentials/

ASPCA. (2015). *Common Dog Diseases.* ASPCA. https://www.aspca.org/pet-care/dog-care/common-dog-diseases

Australian Veterinary Association. (2019, October 9). *What to do if your pet vomits or has diarrhoea.* Vet Voice. https://www.vetvoice.com.au/articles/what-to-do-if-your-pet-vomits-or-has-diarrhoea/

Bates, A. (2021, March 30). *The Consequences of Dog Inbreeding: Problems & Risks.* Pet Keen. https://petkeen.com/dog-inbreeding-consequences/

Bauhaus, J. M. (2021, August 19). *How to Clean Dog Ears*. Hill's Pet Nutrition. https://www.hillspet.com/dog-care/routine-care/how-to-clean-dog-ears#:~:text=Use%20a%20cotton%20ball%20or

Bednarik, K. (2018, July 9). *The 5 Most Common Chronic Conditions in Cats and Dogs*. Embrace Pet Insurance. https://www.embracepetinsurance.com/waterbowl/article/common-chronic-conditions-in-cats-and-dogs

Bell, J. S. (2017, September 25). Ten Most Common Hereditary Diseases in Dogs. *World Small Animal Veterinary Association Congress Proceedings, 2017*. https://www.vin.com/doc/?id=8506247

Blue Buffalo. (n.d.). *Gently Guide Your Dog through His Golden Years*. Blue Buffalo. https://bluebuffalo.com/articles/dog/gently-guide-your-dog-through-his-golden-years/

Blue Cross. (n.d.). *Time to say goodbye to your dog*. Blue Cross. https://www.bluecross.org.uk/advice/dog/time-to-say-goodbye-to-your-dog#:~:text=Persistent%20and%20incurable%20inability%20to

Bovsun, M. (2020, December 21). *Dog Constipation: Home Remedies and When to Call the Vet*. American Kennel Club. https://www.akc.org/expert-advice/health/dog-constipation/

Bubbly Paws. (2022, May 31). *Is Grooming Safe for Senior Dogs With Health Conditions?* Bubbly Paws. https://www.bubblypaws.com/barkblog/is-grooming-safe-for-senior-dogs-with-health-conditions#:~:text=With%20senior%20dogs%2C%20it%20is

Buddy Blog. (2019, July 18). *How much exercise should an old dog get?* Buddy Rest. https://buddyrest.com/blogs/buddyblog/how-much-exercise-should-an-old-dog-get

Burke, A. (2021, June 21). *Dog Coughing: Causes and Treatment Options.* American Kennel Club. https://www.akc.org/expert-advice/health/dog-coughing-causes-treatment/

Buzby, J. (2015, August 16). *9 Helpful Products for Aging Dogs.* The Grey Muzzle Organization. https://www.greymuzzle.org/grey-matters/health-and-well-being-common-health-issues-care-mobility/9-helpful-products-aging-dogs

Chewy Editorial. (2015, March 30). *Dog Grooming Tips For Senior Dogs.* BeChewy. https://be.chewy.com/dog-grooming-tips-for-senior-dogs/

Chewy Editorial. (2018, July 2). *5 Common Congenital Dog Diseases.* BeChewy. https://be.chewy.com/5-common-genetic-diseases-of-dogs/

CitiVet. (n.d.). *Your Senior Dog.* CitiVet. https://citivetgardens.co.za/dog-old-age/#:~:text=Besides%20the%20usual%20complete%20physical

Clancy, M. (2020, March 31). *13 Essential Items To Have In Your Dog's First-Aid Kit.* Dogtime. https://dogtime.com/dog-health/general/21573-things-in-dog-first-aid-kit

Clark, M. (2021a, April 9). *Gold Souls, Gray Faces: 6 Indoor Exercises For Senior Dogs.* DogTime. https://dogtime.com/dog-health/fitness/62279-indoor-exercises-senior-dogs

Clark, M. (2021b, August 5). *Gold Souls, Gray Faces: 6 Tips For Cleaning Your Senior Dog's Teeth.* DogTime. https://dogtime.com/dog-health/dog-dental-care/64355-cleaning-senior-dogs-teeth#4

Cohen, M. A. (2016, December 4). *The 6 Most Common Genetic Disorders in Dogs.* PetMD. https://www.petmd.com/dog/slideshows/6-most-common-genetic-disorders-dogs

Coile, C. (2020, February 26). *Eating Well Into Old Age: Health And Nutritional Needs For Senior Dogs.* American Kennel Club.

https://www.akc.org/expert-advice/nutrition/nutritional-needs-for-senior-dogs/

Cooper, S. (2021, December 26). *Try These Nutrition And Supplement Tips To Keep Your Older Dog Healthy*. PawTracks. https://www.pawtracks.com/dogs/vitamins-for-old-dog/

Cosgrove, N. (2020, December 1). *10 Best Senior Dog Vitamins & Supplements*. Hepper. https://www.hepper.com/best-senior-dog-vitamins-supplements/

Coston, Z. (2022, January 12). *How To Treat Your Dog's Constipation At Home*. Dutch. https://www.dutch.com/blogs/dogs/dog-constipation-home-remedies#

Crow, A., & Winnie. (n.d.). *The Importance Of Exercising Older Dogs*. Senior Tail Waggers. https://seniortailwaggers.com/exercising-older-dogs/

Dog Aging Project. (2020, November 25). *Understanding Behavioral Changes in Senior Dogs*. Dog Aging Project. https://dogagingproject.org/understanding-behavioral-changes-in-senior-dogs/#:~:text=Disorientation%20(staring%20blankly%20at%20walls

Dog Quality. (2020, March 5). *The Do's and Don'ts of Exercising Your Senior Dog*. Dog Quality. https://www.dogquality.co.uk/blogs/news/the-do-s-and-donts-of-exercising-your-senior-dog#:~:text=When%20exercising%20your%20senior%20dog

Donnelly, C., & Evans, J. (2022, December 9). *Discover 7 Natural Remedies to Soothe Your Dog's Itchy Skin*. The Spruce Pets. https://www.thesprucepets.com/home-remedies-for-itchy-dogs-4177184

Driver, K. (2022, December 7). *Is it Time to Say Goodbye? 21 Signs a Dog May Be Dying*. Care Credit. https://www.carecredit.com/well-u/pet-care/signs-a-dog-is-dying/

Farricelli, A. (2022, April 18). *Is My Dog Too Old for a Dental Cleaning?* PetHelpful. https://pethelpful.com/dogs/Is-My-Dog-Too-Old-for-a-Dental-Cleaning

Finlay, K. (2020, May 8). *How to Exercise Your Senior Dog.* American Kennel Club. https://www.akc.org/expert-advice/health/provide-senior-dog-proper-exercise/

Flaim, D. (2016, March 11). *The Importance of Trimming Dog Nails.* Whole Dog Journal. https://www.whole-dog-journal.com/care/nail-clipping/the-importance-of-clipping-dogs-nails/

Flowers, A. (2020, December 1). *Remedies to Relieve Dog Constipation.* Fetch. https://pets.webmd.com/dogs/remedies-dog-constipation

Flowers, A. (2022, November 20). *Hypothyroidism in Dogs.* Fetch. https://pets.webmd.com/dogs/hypothyroidism-in-dogs

Frosek, R. (n.d.). *14 Ways To Improve Your Older Dog's Life.* Modern Dog Magazine. https://moderndogmagazine.com/articles/14-ways-improve-your-older-dogs-life/103806

Gerkensmeyer, R. (2022, December 19). *How to Clean a Dog's Runny Nose.* WagWalking. https://wagwalking.com/grooming/clean-a-dogs-runny-nose

Gerrity, S. (2021, April 27). *How to Create a Pet First Aid Kit, According to a Vet.* Daily Paws. https://www.dailypaws.com/dogs-puppies/health-care/dog-first-aid-emergency/pet-first-aid-kit

Giorgio, K. M. (2021, May 10). *5 Common Senior Dog Health Issues to Watch For.* Daily Paws. https://www.dailypaws.com/dogs-puppies/health-care/senior-dog-health/common-senior-dog-health-issues

Goldstein, L. (2020, December 19). *When to Take Your Dog to the Emergency Vet.* Preventive Vet. https://www.preventivevet.com/dogs/when-to-take-your-dog-to-the-emergency-vet

Grzyb, K. (2018, November 26). *How to Manage Chronic Dog Illnesses Without Getting Overwhelmed.* PetMD. https://www.petmd.com/dog/care/how-manage-chronic-dog-illnesses-without-getting-overwhelmed

Hammers, M. (2017, November 15). *10 Ways to Heal After Losing a Pet.* EverydayHealth. https://www.everydayhealth.com/emotional-health/10-ways-heal-after-losing-pet/

Hartz. (2015, March 13). *How to Treat Your Dog for Intestinal Parasites.* Hartz. https://www.hartz.com/how-to-treat-your-dog-for-intestinal-parasites/#:~:text=Roundworms%20and%20hookworms%20can%20be

Hayes, C. (2020, July 29). *15 things that can make life easier for elderly dogs.* USA Today. https://www.usatoday.com/story/tech/reviewedcom/2020/07/29/15-things-can-make-life-easier-elderly-dogs/5538827002/

Healthy Paws. (n.d.). *Chronic Conditions in Dogs and Cat.* Healthy Paws Pet Insurance. https://www.healthypawspetinsurance.com/chronic-condition-coverage-for-pets#:~:text=Common%20Chronic%20Conditions&text=Diabetes

Heimbuch, J. (n.d.). *7 Things Your Senior Dog Would Like to Tell You.* Old Dog Haven. https://olddoghaven.org/7-things-your-senior-dog-would-like-to-tell-you/

Hitchcock, K. (2020, July 21). *15 Signs Your Dog is Dying: How to Know When Your Dog is Ready to Go.* K9ofmine. https://www.k9ofmine.com/signs-your-dog-is-dying/

The Humane Society Of The United States. (n.d.). *Coping with the death of your pet.* The Humane Society of the United States. https://www.humanesociety.org/resources/coping-death-your-pet

Johnson, M. (2022, March 21). *5 signs of inbreeding in dogs.* PawTracks. https://www.pawtracks.com/dogs/signs-of-inbred-dogs/

Kane, G. (2015, September 25). *Watch for Signs of Health Problems in Older Dogs.* American Kennel Club. https://www.akc.org/expert-advice/health/health-problems-older-dogs-senior-old-age/#:~:text=An%20older%20dog%20is%20more

The Kennel Club. (n.d.). *Inbreeding calculators (COIs).* The Kennel Club. https://www.thekennelclub.org.uk/health-and-dog-care/health/getting-started-with-health-testing-and-screening/inbreeding-calculators/

Khalsa, D. (2012, November 1). *12 Homeopathic Remedies For Dogs.* Dogs Naturally Magazine. https://www.dogsnaturallymagazine.com/12-homeopathic-remedies/

Klein, J. (2021, October 27). *Dog Euthanasia: When is it Time to Say Goodbye?* American Kennel Club. https://www.akc.org/expert-advice/health/knowing-time-say-goodbye-pet-euthanasia/

Klinger, C. (2018, December 5). *Treating Your Dog's Dry Nose.* Hill's Pet Nutrition. https://www.hillspet.com/dog-care/healthcare/dry-dog-nose-treatments

Kos-Barber, H. (2022, March 2). *Abscesses in Dogs.* PetMD. https://www.petmd.com/dog/conditions/skin/c_dg_abscessation

LakeCross Veterinary. (n.d.). *Signs & How to Treat Bladder Infections in Dogs.* LakeCross Veterinary. https://www.lakecross.com/site/blog-huntersville-vet/2021/09/30/bladder-infection-dog#:~:text=Antibiotics%20are%20the%20number%20one

Lee, C. (2019, January 20). *15 DDR Life Hacks for Deaf Dog Families.* Deaf Dogs Rock. https://deafdogsrock.com/15-ddr-life-hacks-for-deaf-dog-families

Lee, L. (2021, August 17). *Why Is My Dog Coughing, and When Should I Go to the Vet?* GoodRx Health. https://www.goodrx.com/pet-health/dog/dog-coughing

Lin, S. J. (2022, September 27). *My 15-year-old dog has mobility limitations, but these products have dramatically increased his quality of life.* Insider. https://www.insider.com/guides/pets/senior-dog-mobility-products#a-portable-wagon-with-a-tailgate-3

Marsden, S., Messonnier, S., & Yuill, C. (n.d.). *Veterinary Homeopathy.* VCA Hospitals. https://vcahospitals.com/know-your-pet/veterinary-homeopathy

Mayer, B. (2022, November 9). *Here's what to do if you notice your senior dog coughing and gagging.* PawTracks. https://www.pawtracks.com/dogs/old-dog-coughing-and-gagging/

Meyers, H. (2021, April 6). *Preventing Obesity in Senior Dogs.* American Kennel Club. https://www.akc.org/expert-advice/health/preventing-obesity-in-senior-dogs/

Meyers, H. (2022a, April 26). *Why Do Small Dogs Live Longer Than Large Dogs?* American Kennel Club. https://www.akc.org/expert-advice/health/why-do-small-dogs-live-longer/

Meyers, H. (2022b, August 2). *Why Is My Dog So Itchy? Possible Causes & Treatment.* American Kennel Club. https://www.akc.org/expert-advice/health/why-is-my-dog-so-itchy/

Miller, J. (2016, August 22). *Homeopathic Remedies for Your Dog.* American Kennel Club. https://www.akc.org/expert-advice/health/homeopathic-remedies-for-your-dog/

Nom Nom. (n.d.). *Senior Dog Food Guide for Older Dogs.* Nom Nom Now. https://www.nomnomnow.com/learn/article/senior-dog-food-guide

Oberbauer, A. M., Belanger, J. M., Bellumori, T., Bannasch, D. L., & Famula, T. R. (2015). Ten inherited disorders in purebred dogs by functional breed groupings. *Canine Genetics and Epidemiology*, *2*(1). https://doi.org/10.1186/s40575-015-0021-x

Palika, L. (2018, January 12). *7 Ways to Add Joy to Your Old Dog's Life.* The Honest Kitchen. https://www.thehonestkitchen.com/blogs/pet-obsessed/7-ways-to-add-joy-to-your-old-dogs-life

Paul, M. (2015a, June 7). *A Senior Dog Checkup: What to Expect.* Pet Health Network. https://www.pethealthnetwork.com/dog-health/dog-checkups-preventive-care/a-senior-dog-checkup-what-expect

Paul, M. (2015b, August 14). *6 Simple Tips for Exercising Your Senior Dog.* Pet Health Network. https://www.pethealthnetwork.com/dog-health/dog-checkups-preventive-care/6-simple-tips-exercising-your-senior-dog

Pennisi, E. (2017, January 11). *Why large dogs live fast—and die young.* Science. https://www.science.org/content/article/why-large-dogs-live-fast-and-die-young

Pet Basics. (n.d.). *Senior Dog Care: 6 Ways to Promote Healthy Aging.* Pet Basics. https://petbasics.elanco.com/us/health-and-care/senior-dog-care-supplements

Pet Mobility Solutions. (2022, December 27). *5 Things You Must Know Before Buying a Dog Wheelchair.* Handicapped Pets. https://www.handicappedpets.com/blog/5-need-to-know-dog-wheelchair-tips/

Pet Place Veterinarians. (2015, June 8). *14 Common Disorders of Senior Dogs.* Pet Place. https://www.petplace.com/article/dogs/pet-care/14-common-disorders-of-senior-dogs/

Pet Resort. (2017, June 14). *The Most Common Dog Illnesses: Symptoms and Treatment.* Hillrose Pet Resort. https://www.petresort.com/medical/most-common-dog-illnesses-symptoms-

treatment/#:~:text=Oral%20infections%20are%20actually%2
0the

Peters, A. (2022, September 1). *Dog Eye Gunk: What Is It, How to Clean It, and When to Worry.* The Dog People. https://www.rover.com/blog/reviews/dog-eye-gunk/

PetMD Editorial. (2009, March 6). *9 Natural Home Remedies for Your Dog.* PetMD. https://www.petmd.com/dog/wellness/evr_dg_home_remedi es

PetMD Editorial. (2011, April 26). *Holistic Medicine and How it Can Help Your Pet.* PetMD. https://www.petmd.com/cat/wellness/evr_ct_hollistic_medici ne_and_how_it_can_help_your_pet

Primm, K. (2015, September 30). *From The Vet: 5 Simple Hacks To Make Life Easier For Senior Dogs.* I Heart Dogs. https://iheartdogs.com/simple-life-hacks-to-make-it-easier-for-senior-dogs/

Pulley, K. (2019, March 18). *Home Treatment for a Dog Abscess.* Dogster. https://www.dogster.com/dog-health-care/treat-a-dog-abscess-at-home

Puotinen, C. J. (2017, January 24). *10 Weight Loss Tips for Senior Dogs.* Whole Dog Journal. https://www.whole-dog-journal.com/health/weight_control/10-weight-loss-tips-for-senior-dogs/

Puppy Leaks. (2018, July 5). *10 Tips For Exercising a Senior Dog.* Puppy Leaks. https://www.puppyleaks.com/senior-dog-exercise/

Queen's Park Pet Hospital. (2021, July 20). *Does Your Pet Have an Abscess?* Queen's Park Pet Hospital. https://www.queensparkpethospital.ca/does-your-pet-have-an-abscess/#:~:text=If%20the%20abscess%20hasn

Racine, E. (2019, September 2). *Dog Ear Infections: Symptoms, Causes, Treatment, and Prevention.* American Kennel Club.

https://www.akc.org/expert-advice/health/dog-ear-infections/#:~:text=How%20are%20Dog%20Ear%20Infectio ns

Randall, S. (2022, June 6). *10 Essential Home Remedies for Dogs to Have at Home.* Top Dog Tips. https://topdogtips.com/home-remedies-for-dogs/

Reisen, J. (2022, October 4). *Physical and Mental Signs that Your Dog is Aging.* American Kennel Club. https://www.akc.org/expert-advice/health/physical-mental-signs-dog-aging/

Robinson, L., Segal, J., & Segal, R. (2019). *Coping with Losing a Pet.* Help Guide. https://www.helpguide.org/articles/grief/coping-with-losing-a-pet.htm

Royal Veterinary College. (n.d.). *Dry eye in dogs.* Royal Veterinary College. https://www.rvc.ac.uk/small-animal-vet/teaching-and-research/fact-files/keratoconjuncitivitis-sicca-dry-eye#:~:text=Dry%20eye%20is%20usually%20treated

Rubin, J. L. (n.d.). *If Your Pet Is Officially Part Of The Senior Community, You Should Check Out These 21 Products.* BuzzFeed. https://www.buzzfeed.com/julialynnrubin/helpful-products-for-senior-pets

Simon, L. (2021, October 28). *Natural Cough Remedies in Dogs - Conditions Treated, Procedure, Efficacy, Recovery, Cost, Considerations, Prevention.* Wag Walking. https://wagwalking.com/treatment/natural-cough-remedies

Small Door Veterinary. (n.d.-a). *Exercise Needs for Puppies, Adults and Senior Dogs.* Small Door Veterinary. https://www.smalldoorvet.com/learning-center/wellness/exercise-needs-dog-lifestages

Small Door Veterinary. (n.d.-b). *Senior Dogs 101: What changes can I expect in my senior dog?* Small Door Veterinary. https://www.smalldoorvet.com/learning-center/dogs/changes-to-expect-senior-dog

Small Door Veterinary. (n.d.-c). *Senior Dogs 101: Tips to keep your senior dog healthy as they age*. Small Door Veterinary. https://www.smalldoorvet.com/learning-center/seniors/keep-senior-dog-healthy

Smith, A. (2023, January 1). *25 Best Senior Dog Supplements in 2023*. Discover Magazine. https://www.discovermagazine.com/lifestyle/25-best-senior-dog-supplements-in-2022

Stuart, A. (2010, March 17). *How to Figure Out Your Dog's Age*. WebMD. https://pets.webmd.com/dogs/how-to-calculate-your-dogs-age

Tasaki, S. (2022, December 28). *Mental Stimulation for Senior Dogs: Tips to Keep Older Dogs Busy*. The Wildest. https://www.thewildest.com/dog-lifestyle/mental-stimulation-for-senior-dogs

Tracey, A., & Valentini, K. (2022, February 9). *How to Recognize & Treat a Dog UTI*. Daily Paws. https://www.dailypaws.com/dogs-puppies/health-care/dog-conditions/dog-uti

Turner, B. (2021, July 17). *Your Dog Has Diarrhea: What to Do and NOT Do*. Preventive Vet. https://www.preventivevet.com/dogs/your-dog-has-diarrhea-what-to-do

Turner, B. (2022, September 20). *Bad Breath... It's NOT Always Their Teeth*. Preventive Vet. https://www.preventivevet.com/dogs/bad-breath-not-always-teeth

Vecchioni, H. (n.d.). *How to Groom a Dog's Nose*. Daily Puppy. https://dogcare.dailypuppy.com/groom-dogs-nose-3879.html

Ventiera, S. (2021, June 1). *Products and Techniques to Support Your Older Dog*. AARP. https://www.aarp.org/home-family/friends-family/info-2021/products-for-older-dogs.html

Veterinaire Pet Care. (n.d.). *Vet Services for Acute Illnesses*. Veterinaire Pet Care. https://veterinairepetcare.com/acute-illnesses-management.html

Wag! (n.d.). *How to Shave a Small Dog's Face*. WagWalking. https://wagwalking.com/grooming/shave-a-small-dogs-face#:~:text=Hold%20his%20head%20still%20and

Weir, M., & Panning, A. (n.d.). *Instructions for Ear Cleaning in Dogs*. VCA Animal Hospitals. https://vcahospitals.com/know-your-pet/instructions-for-ear-cleaning-in-dogs

Williams, K., & Downing, R. (n.d.). *Feeding Mature and Senior Dogs*. VCA Animal Hospitals. https://vcahospitals.com/know-your-pet/feeding-mature-and-senior-dogs

Williams, K., & Downing, R. (2009). *Obesity in Dogs*. VCA Animal Hospitals. https://vcahospitals.com/know-your-pet/obesity-in-dogs

Williams, K., & Ward, E. (2009). *Hypothyroidism in Dogs*. VCA Animal Hospitals. https://vcahospitals.com/know-your-pet/hypothyroidism-in-dogs

Wilson, W. B. (2019, November 15). *Senior Dog Food: What Is the Best Thing to Feed an Old Dog?* BeChewy. https://be.chewy.com/best-senior-dog-food-choosing-the-best-dog-food-for-older-dogs/

Winter Park Veterinary Hospital. (n.d.). *Canine Chronic Disease Management*. Winter Park Veterinary Hospital. https://wpvet.com/general-care/chronic-disease-management/canine-chronic-disease-management/

Image References: Book 3

Bigandt_Photography. (2015). *Old Staffordshire Bull Terrier* [Image]. iStock. https://www.istockphoto.com/photo/senior-

staffordshire-bull-terrier-gm494571264-
77521367?phrase=old%20dog

freestocks. (2020). *Dog with Intravenous Line* [Image]. Pexels.
https://www.pexels.com/photo/dog-with-intravenous-line-on-
his-leg-4074725/

Glinskaia, E. (2021). *Grooming* [Image]. iStock.
https://www.istockphoto.com/photo/animal-groomer-
shaved-dog-with-electric-shaver-machine-in-cabinet-at-vet-
clinic-gm1317747825-405085360

Liukov. (2020). *Disabled Dog* [Image]. iStock.
https://www.istockphoto.com/photo/the-dog-is-disabled-the-
dog-is-in-a-wheelchair-gm1282821930-380437623

Richards, A. (2017). *Boston Terrier In Car* [Image]. Unsplash.
https://unsplash.com/photos/aYHgchNOsGY

RossHelen. (2021). *Dog Having Teeth Brushed* [Image]. iStock.
https://www.istockphoto.com/photo/dog-ready-for-teeth-
brushing-gm1324673256-409931328

Simpson, J. (2020). *Walking Dog on Lead* [Image]. Unsplash.
https://unsplash.com/photos/8MGPoUWuePA

Wandler, M. (2022). *Dog Collar with Red Rose* [Image]. iStock.
https://www.istockphoto.com/photo/dog-collar-with-a-red-
rose-symbolizing-love-gm1420593110-466522775

Ward, E. (2018). *Retriever Hug* [Image]. Unsplash.
https://unsplash.com/photos/ISg37AI2A-s

Zontica. (2020). *Dog Paws with Healthy Food* [Image]. iStock.
https://www.istockphoto.com/photo/healthy-natural-pet-
food-in-bowl-and-dogs-paws-on-yellow-background-
gm1284996229-381967478?phrase=dog%20healthy